Tell the Children

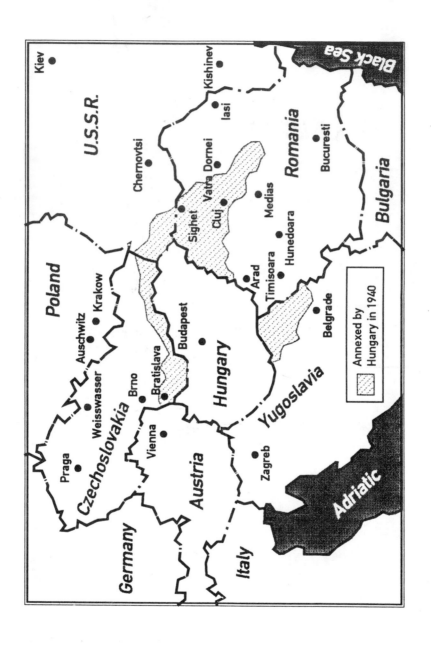

Black Sea

Adriatic

Kiev

Kishinev

Iasi

Chernovtsi

Vatra Dornei

Bucuresti

Sighet

Cluj

Medias

Hunedoara

Arad

Timisoara

Belgrade

U.S.S.R.

Romania

Bulgaria

Poland

Krakow

Auschwitz

Budapest

Bratislava

Brno

Weisswasser

Hungary

Yugoslavia

Praga

Czechoslovakia

Vienna

Zagreb

Austria

Germany

Italy

Annexed by
Hungary in 1940

Tell the Children
Letters to Miriam

Dora Apsan Sorell

Sighet Publishing
San Rafael, California
1998

Book production by Daniel Publication Services
Cover design by Iancu Sorell
Drawing by Patricia J. Wynne

Library of Congress Catalog Card Number: 98-96156
ISBN 0-9663527-0-X

To order additional copies, contact the publisher:

Sighet Publishing
1210 Josephine St.
Berkeley, CA 94703

To my children,

                Silvia
                Yancu
and   Vali

my grandchildren,

                Miriam
                Gabriel
                Rebecca
                Olivia
and   Madeleine

and to the memory of my loved ones who perished in the Holocaust

"Tell the children of it,
and let your children tell their children,
and their children another generation..."

(Joel 1:3)

Acknowledgement

I couldn't have done this alone.

I feel the deepest appreciation for my friend Donald Silver, who with his selfless devotion, understanding and continuous support encouraged me and sometimes impelled me to write all that I would remember.

I could not have wished for a better editor than my daughter Silvia. She spent countless hours reviewing every line of the manuscript, questioning every bit of information. With her compassion, filial love and meticulous work the book took on its present shape. And my son-in-law Dan Kane was of great assistance in overcoming the challenges posed by the computer and in preparing the manuscript for submission. His help in restoring the old, faded pictures was invaluable.

My high school boyfriend and husband of 53 years was always behind me with unwavering faith and confidence. And the rest of my family, children and grandchildren, through their love and concern, desire to learn more and sheer presence were a constant source of inspiration.

Tell the Children

A section of photographs follows page 156

Tell the Children

Preface

When my first grandchild, Miriam, was born, it dawned on me that the new generation of the family, born in America, would grow up without knowing who we are and where we came from, what our life in the old country was like and all that we suffered and lost during the Nazi era. Unless I told them.

I came up with the idea of writing letters to her whenever I had the time and the inspiration. I meant to tell her and the grandchildren still to come everything they may want to know sometime about our past. I allowed memories to flood me whenever events or places reminded me of something that happened a long time ago: a train ride, a child crying, an aria from a familiar opera, a news item, a TV show. They all triggered images from the past, perhaps a more recent one, after emigration, or a distant one from my childhood and school years, when I was still with my family in my hometown. And obviously, I wanted to write about everything that happened during the war years.

I soon realized that the richness of the material was overwhelming. I had to write about the traditions and continuity of life in our part of Romania, about the destruction caused by the Holocaust, about the struggle of building a career and a family under a Communist regime and finally about emigrating to rejoin the rest of the family dispersed over several continents. The letters, written randomly, as suggested by every day's happenings, contained short stories of specific incidents, little vignettes with no literary ambition. Some were sad, others tragic, yet many were funny or sweet, as life and memories usually are. I shared with Miriam not only the facts, but also my thoughts, my pain and my joy. Within a few years the puzzle pieces started to fit together and what emerged was a family chronicle against the backdrop of the main historical events of 20th century Europe.

After I wrote about 100 letters, and thought that I finished the task, my friend Donald, who had prodded me all along to write more and more stories, declared , "Now it is time to start working on them." So I went back to the letters and worked them over, adding more details, deciding what is meaningful and making sure the information is accurate. I also wrote new letters, trying to remember all who were close to me and perished during the Holocaust. By then friends were suggesting that my stories may interest other people too, so I selected about 50 letters and arranged them in chronological order. Miriam had been the catalyst, and soon Gabriel, Rebecca, Olivia and Madeleine, through their presence, their voices and their uninhibited curiosity, stimulated and inspired me to complete the undertaking.

This is how the book "Letters to Miriam" was born.

Part I: Sighet

Childhood

Dear Miriam,

I was finishing some paperwork in my office and the door was open. In the waiting room, I could see a mother sitting with her little girl, waiting to see the pediatrician, and I heard them speaking Yiddish. Down the hall stood the father, a young Chassidic Jew, while a younger child bounced around him. The two little girls looked like any other children, cheerfully dressed, giggling; their parents looked like visitors from another world. The father wore black Chassidic garb: tieless, with a black suit, white shirt and socks, and a black hat just covering part of his long sidelocks. The mother wore a long-sleeve, old-fashioned dress, and her head was covered with a kerchief.

I went over to the little girl sitting by my door and asked her in Yiddish what her name was. She was startled: after all, how many people outside their immediate neighborhood speak Yiddish? Her mother asked me in English if I was a nurse. "No," I said, "I'm a doctor." And how come I speak Yiddish? she wanted to know.

I started to remember how, more than fifty years ago, when I was five or six, my mother also took me to a doctor. I too must have spoken Yiddish at that time, since I didn't learn Romanian until I went to school; and maybe my father came along as this little girl's did.

Now, remembering that visit to the doctor, I can feel the love and anguish of my parents. I was their first-born child. Father had three boys from his first marriage; his first wife died giving birth to my brother Moishi. My mother gave him four more sons, but I was their only daughter. I had some sort of eye trouble -- I don't know what -- but I remember being kept in a dark room, and how blinding the light appeared when someone opened the door. In those times eye problems were considered serious, and I was lucky that mine was cured.

We all spoke Yiddish then, in the midst of a Romanian or Hungarian population. And it seemed to us that things would always stay the same in our little, secluded Jewish world of Sighet, where I was born. Why would it change?

Today, that Sighet of my youth seems so remote as if at the other end of the world or in another universe. Those times appear so far away and isolated not only because of the years that have passed, but because of everything that has happened. It feels sometimes that hundreds of years have passed since my youth. That world has vanished, was swept away.

Our existence was confined to our small town of Sighet between the two rivers, Iza and Tisa, bounded by the Carpathian mountains beyond, and within Sighet, mostly to our own Jewish community. In fact the word *Sighet* means "island" in Hungarian (spelled Sziget).

We did not know another world. Whatever influence came from outside our island, from beyond the mountains and the forests, was looked upon with suspicion and considered strange and alien. We had no radio. Television didn't exist yet. If newspapers brought outside events to our town, not many read them and certainly we children didn't know what was in them. Even public schools were considered dangerous for Jewish children because they might bring outer influences into our world.

It was a world of innocence. Or was it happiness? We didn't talk about whether or not we were happy as so many people do today. Life was a struggle, though we were not poor. Father always worked, providing enough food for the whole family, a decent home and occasionally even a helper for mother. For a time he had a grain store. Later on he was an insurance agent, and when there was no work he stayed in his office and wrote his stories.

We knew who was poor. Poor were the beggars who, by tradition, came on Fridays to every modest Jewish family home to collect Sabbath charity, a small coin or two. Poor were the orphans. Poor were the crippled or the elderly in old-age homes. But those who had a home, a good meal every day, chicken to eat and nice clothes to wear on Sabbath -- they were blessed.

I never had a doll -- at least I don't remember one. I had lots of brothers to play with, but I don't remember them having toys either. Our home never had a bathroom nor running water. Every Friday we went to the communal bath house. Occasionally the lights were turned off because the landlord hadn't paid the electricity bills. Then we used kerosene lamps or even candles to read at night. And did we read! After all, there were few other entertainments. We had lots of friends, all girls, and met every Saturday afternoon to stroll along the river banks, or at someone's house to chat and play games, cracking nuts and pumpkin seeds. On Sundays we would swim in the shallow waters of Tisa and Iza. We sang after dinner on holidays and in the school choir. I had to wait for years to learn about serious music, about theater, and about outings and dancing with boys.

Movies were expensive and my parents rarely took us. I made up for that later when I worked at the only movie house in town. I saw each feature film three or four times -- first alone, then with mother, and then again just listening to the sound track from behind the screen, where I worked on posters and announcements, and popped out front occasionally to see a particular scene again.

Our home had no central heating. In winter only the kitchen was kept warm by a wood-burning stove. At night we put on our warmest nightshirts and went to sleep in cold rooms, covered with thick goose down comforters.

There was only one high school for girls in Sighet; few girls (and even fewer Jewish girls) went beyond elementary school. High school was an eight-year program leading to a baccalaureate diploma. Tuition was fifteen hundred lei a year, nine hundred of it payable in advance. That was a lot of money then. It meant that my family would have to sacrifice much to send me to school. When I passed the high school entrance examination, my father somehow scraped together the advance payment for my first year's tuition. Many months later he found out that children of veterans were exempt from tuition. Since he was a wounded veteran of World War I (I don't remember what kind of wound he suffered), we applied for the exemption, waiting anxiously for a reply. I don't have to tell you how relieved we felt when the nine hundred lei were refunded to us. That made it so much easier for me to continue my education.

Still, even with tuition paid, there were other expenses: we had to wear school uniforms -- a black frock with a white collar and black-and-white polka dot bow tie, black stockings and black low-heeled shoes. Then there were expenses for books, pencils and pens, stationery, drawing and craft materials, a gym suit and more.

Since I was a very good student, I was always tutoring someone, but I didn't start to get paid for it until I was in my teens. First I tutored Bitza Doros, the star of the class, the only daughter of the late mayor. She came from a very wealthy and aristocratic family. The teachers were proud to have her in their classes. Bitza was very diligent, she studied very hard and wrote very neatly, but she never understood math. Still, somehow she always ended up with the top grades in the class and I was always number two.

When I was in fourth grade, Bitza's mother, who was very sick and died soon afterwards, asked me to come to their home every day and help Bitza with her math homework. I was only ten or eleven and I didn't know about earning money, but every afternoon when I left, her mother very discreetly handed me something special "for your four little brothers" -- chocolates, candies, oranges. I was quite proud of my early accomplishments.

It's not that money was not important. It was. I didn't have a good winter coat or many other luxuries. When I was thirteen I started tutoring two other classmates, Itu and Bozsi, and now I began to get paid for it. Every afternoon I would spend two hours with each of them, and I think I received one hundred fifty lei a month from each. I don't know how much that would be today, but that winter my mother had a most beautiful coat made for me, paid for with my own earnings. The fabric was a green wool tweed she bought at Tzali's father's fabric store. I had admired a coat worn by a lawyer's daughter; the fabric and style of my coat were very much like it.

It was one of the few brand-new things I had. Most of my clothes came from the packages sent by my Aunt Fannie in America. Luckily I got a good share of those. The clothes she sent were divided among all of her sisters; all of my aunts had many daughters, but I was the only girl in my family. The clothes she sent were beautiful, although for us in Sighet the fashions seemed odd and recognizably foreign.

Your grandfather Tzali doesn't like me to talk about these things. He feels guilty because he had it easier as a child. They had a private home with a large garden, running water, a bathroom and a radio. But was his family happier because they had more? His father died when Tzali was only twelve, leaving his mother a young widow with four children to support -- Tzali, his older sister Dori, his brother Bela and his younger sister Zsuzsi. For years she had to manage their fabric store by herself; later on, Tzali, Bela and her son-in-law helped her. She wasn't a very good manager and the store never again did as well as it had in her husband's lifetime.

As a girl I loved books, but the few illustrated books and children's books that were available were quite expensive and I don't remember the library carrying much besides the classics. I never had my own books till I was older; on birthdays I received dresses and shoes, not luxuries. But I had a friend, Evi, who was born on the same day as I and lived across the street from me; her father was a dentist and they were quite prosperous.

Evi was an only child, and couldn't attend school because of a heart condition that took her life at eighteen. Her mother often asked me to come and play with her and invited me to spend weeks at a time at their summer home so Evi wouldn't be lonely. Evi was selfish and even mean. Only as an adult did I connect this with her illness. Nevertheless, I loved to be invited to their summer home: it was rustic and beautiful and they had a gramophone. I still recall the music I used to hum when I walked alone in their orchard picking apples from the trees, which I loved to do, and gathering fallen apples in a bag to take home.

Evi had toys and games and lots of books: storybooks, picture books, and comic books. At that time a funny book called *Haplea in Strainatate* -- Haplea Abroad -- was enormously popular. It was a joy to read Haplea's adventures as he traveled abroad, getting in and out of trouble. Evi and I read it together but she never let me take it home, not even for one night. One day when I was eight or nine I went home crying because she wouldn't lend me the book and I didn't have any of my own. At that time we had a maid who couldn't read. I used to tell her stories and read to her from my school books. The two of us decided we would buy Haplea's book together. She gave me some money from her salary and I got my share from my mother. Every evening I read to her from our new book and she would follow the cartoons, and we both enjoyed it so much.

I thought of all this, Miriam, as I saw those little girls in front of my office. I thought of myself and of Silvia at their age. You know now that I never had a doll. When your mother was a child she had only a rag doll. For years she waited for the beautiful doll my brother Yossie in America bought for her. He swears he sent her a doll that could sleep and talk. But it never arrived. It must not have made it past customs.

Maybe this is why I want to buy you a doll for your first birthday. Because I never had any, and Silvia never got the one she dreamed of. You and I, and perhaps Silvia too will play with the doll together.

July 23, 1983

Sapantza

Let me tell you about Sapantza, the place where my mother's family, the Basches, lived for generations. It was a small village in northern Romania, about two miles from the river Tisa, the fourth village along the road between Sighet and the next city, Satu-Mare. Before World War II, the Tisa was the border between Romania and Czechoslovakia.

Sapantza was a village of Romanian peasants. The next village beyond it, Remetz, where my father's family lived, was all Ukrainian. And the village before Sapantza, Campu-Lung, was all Hungarian. All of them were located in a stretch of six miles; this was typical of the whole district of Maramures, where Romanians, Hungarians, Ukrainians and even some Germans lived scattered across the countryside, side by side but in separate villages, the legacy of the Austro-Hungarian Empire.

And in all these villages Jews lived on the main streets, they owned little stores or had little workshops, they were merchants, dressmakers, tailors, shoemakers, millers. For hundreds of years Jews were considered aliens, were not allowed to own farmland and were subjected to many other restrictions. For a very long time they were not even accepted as citizens, and trading was the only thing they were allowed to do. There were perhaps five hundred Jews in Sapantza.

For me, when I was small, Sapantza was the center of the rural world outside Sighet. My grandparents lived on the main street. Theirs was the second house on the right beyond the iron bridge over the little Sapantza stream. The large room facing the street at the front of their house was a liquor store and tavern where the Romanian peasants came to enjoy themselves and celebrate. Jews did not go to taverns to drink.

The tavern had a counter, shelves for bottles and glasses, tables and benches. My grandfather, Alter-Jacov, served the drinks. With his long beard, curly side locks, skullcap or hat and very long pipe -- which he insisted on whenever a picture was taken -- Grandfather looked like a patriarch. At work, serving his customers, he wore knickers, boots, a white shirt, a vest, and always the ritual garment with fringes -- the *tzitzes* -- hanging down at the sides of his waist. After many visits I learned to tell the drinks by their colors. Sometimes Grandfather would give me a little green mint liqueur, strong and delicious.

The family lived behind the store. A huge day room served as living room, dining room and family room. It was furnished with a long table and two long wooden benches, a big grandfather clock and embroidered linen wall hangings depicting Hungarian Hussars with long mustaches. These had all kinds of familiar proverbs embroidered on them. One that seemed to hang in every home had the well known saying, "No matter how dear a houseguest is, three days of stay is plenty enough."

In the day room was also the well-known locked cupboard in which Grandma kept cakes and cookies left over from the Sabbath or holidays. She held the key and opened the cupboard only on special occasions or for special people. Grandmother Frieda-Rifka was a tall, good looking, placid woman who always wore dark clothes -- as all older women did -- and covered her head with a kerchief. She was forever busy with the household, the vegetable garden, marketing, and her other domestic duties, and had little time for her numerous grandchildren.

What impressed me most in the day room was the clock. It seemed so solemn. It chimed loudly on the hour and the minutes passed so slowly when I tried to follow the big hand. One day I said to Grandma, "Five minutes is such a long time! I believe I can go to your sister's house and be back in five minutes."

"You cannot."

"Let's bet," I said.

I checked the clock, ran out of the house, crossed the bridge, took the first street to the left, went down the path near the other bank of the river, arrived at my great-aunt's house and ran back. I lost. It had taken me twenty minutes.

Behind the day room was a porch with a stove and brick oven. Once a week, on Fridays, Grandmother made a log fire in the oven and baked dark wheat bread for the whole week and white challah for the Sabbath. An earthen pot of *cholent*, the traditional bean dish with lots of meat and flour *kugel*, also went into the oven, to stay there overnight and be pulled out still warm for the Sabbath dinner the next day when cooking was forbidden.

On one side of the house were the bedrooms. My grandparents' bedroom, a very plain old-fashioned room with dark old furniture, was toward the front and had a door opening into the tavern. At the back were two more bedrooms. When I was eight or nine only Aunt Goldie, the youngest of my grandparents' eleven children, and the only daughter not yet married, still lived at home. My mother and her sisters Pearl and Esther lived in Sighet. Fannie, the oldest daughter, had gone to America, and the other daughters had married into nearby villages. Goldie had a whole bedroom for herself and shared it with me and the other granddaughters when we visited. There were lots of gay things in that room: painted lampshades, colorful hand-embroidered bedspreads and pillows, mirrors and trinkets on the walls, and all kinds of odd objects that Aunt Goldie received from her sister Fannie in New York.

On the other side of the porch were three rooms where my mother's oldest brother, Favl, lived with his wife, his daughter and her husband, and their child. Favl kept his own household. He owned a small broom factory at the far end of the long back yard, employing several people. The place had such a distinctive smell that even today, whenever I am in a hardware store that has straw brooms, the smell of the straw brings back memories of summers in Sapantza and my uncle Favl's workshop.

Favl was the only son still in Sapantza. Uncle Herman lived in Sighet, Uncle Yeno was in Viseu and Aaron was somewhere on his way to join Aunt Fannie in America.

The outhouse was in the backyard, near the house. There were also coops for chickens, ducks and roosters, a vegetable garden that provided beans, potatoes, squash, corn, cabbage and greens, and the well with its wheel and chained bucket and wooden roof. The backyard, with Favl's workshop, the garden and the firewood shed, stretched along the left bank of the Sapantza river. Along the river bank there were weeping willows, poplars, and large rocks where one could sit and watch the clear, shallow, fast-running water rolling and foaming over the stones, listen to its noisy babble and look across the stream to the house where Grandmother's sister lived, with its fence and tall trees.

At the top of my grandparents' house was an attic full of discarded pictures and antiques. What I liked most was the chest full of fabric samples that Goldie ordered through magazines. There were batches of cottons, silks and satins, brocades and linens, plain and flowered, in all colors and patterns. What a world of dreams those fabrics evoked for me and the friends I showed them to! We would look at these pieces of fabric and imagine the dresses we could make out of them and the festive occasions where we would wear them.

There were other houses on the main street -- all kinds of variety stores, workshops, stalls selling fruit, candy, bagels -- and all of them were owned by Grandfather's friends. The most important building was the Great Synagogue in the center of the village, just across the street from Grandfather's house. The synagogue consisted of the house of prayer, the yeshiva school, and the rabbi's living quarters. Not all of the Jews of Sapantza were Chassidic, but the Rabbi of Sapantza had his own Chassidic dynasty and his own following. Over the years he became quite famous and the large courtyard of the synagogue was always filled with pilgrims. (Today the Chassidim of Sapantza and their present Rabbi live in Brooklyn.) The

Rabbi of Sapantza was related to Grandfather, and his wife, the *rebbetzin*, considered my mother her friend. She would often come to Sighet to shop and Mother would escort her to the best dress makers. She was very elegant, and always wore a long amber necklace.

At either end of the main street were farmers' houses, the school, the post office and the Greek Orthodox church with its wooden steeples. On the side streets Romanian peasants lived at the edges of their farms, in shingle roofed small wooden houses with large carved gates, so typical of the county of Maramures, with their stables, vegetable gardens and pigsties, their cornfields and wheatfields. At one end of the village was the Jewish cemetery, at the other end the Greek Orthodox cemetery.

We grandchildren loved to go to Sapantza in the summers, but there were so many of us that we had to take turns, one at a time. I was sure that my grandparents preferred me to my little brothers. They were mischievous and unruly, but *I* was rather helpful. Instead of causing havoc I sometimes helped with errands, gathering eggs from the coops, feeding the hens and fetching milk from the neighbor's cow. My grandparents called me "Devorele" (little Deborah), never using the modernized Hungarian endearing name "Dorika" as my parents and brothers did, or the shortened Dori, that everyone else used.

I made friends with several village girls and always found something to keep me busy. There was a pine forest on the right bank of the creek, just before it left Romanian soil and flowed into the Tisa. I would go there with other girls to pick berries, stroll, meet friends or just enjoy the woods. Sometimes we would climb the hills on the other side of the village, all the way up to the picturesque Sapantza waterfall. Other times we would go swimming in the village, in the mill pond near a small dam that slowed the stream to power the village mill, where the water was much deeper.

Fridays were devoted to Sabbath preparations: cleaning the house, scrubbing and polishing, cooking and baking, and making everything ready in advance. Since no work could be done on the Sabbath, we even set up the poultry feed. Everyone bathed in wooden tubs in the kitchen, which meant warming up a lot of water and messing up the house. At sundown everyone was clean, dressed up and ready. Grandmother would light the candles, the men would go to the synagogue, and we women would await their return to serve the special Friday night supper.

Saturdays were for quiet and rest in the whole Jewish community. Resting, praying and sleeping were a Sabbath *mitzvah* -- good deed. Grandfather would dress up to go to the synagogue, with a clean white shirt, his shiny black caftan, a twisted sash wrapped several times around his waist, black shoes, white socks, and his Chassid's fur-trimmed hat -- like all the other Chassidim. Grandma would put on her good black dress, her pearls and her white silk shawl and she too would go to synagogue to pray. Everybody was pious and observant. All activity stopped on Saturday, even feeding the poultry or milking the cows. The prayers and the chanting could not be heard outside the synagogue, and everything came to a silent standstill on Sapantza's main street.

After services the mid-day dinner was festive. The table was laid with a white linen tablecloth. On it were set out red wine, challah covered with an embroidered cloth, and the *cholent*, roast and *kugel* taken from the oven where they had been kept warm overnight. Stories from the Bible were told, songs were sung, honey and sponge cakes were served and everybody took time to relax. Then the elders went for their naps, the only afternoon naps in the whole week.

Jewish boys had to stay home in the afternoon for more Bible reading but I would stroll with other girls along the main street where a stream of Jewish girls met rows of peasant girls and boys. The older girls would joke and flirt with the handsome Romanian boys they went to school with; but obviously no real social mixing was allowed on either side.

Sometimes my friends and I would take long walks along the winding roads and across the fields to the next village, Remetz, three miles away, where my father's older brother Avram still lived. Along the way peasants were working in the fields, raking the grass and building haystacks. We would sit down by the roadside and let all our senses be bombarded: the scents of hay, manure, flowers and earth; the sight of the hills and fields, cows and sheep grazing on the mountain slopes, and the stretches of grass and weeds sprinkled with the most colorful wild flowers and beetles; the human and animal sounds; the breeze moving the branches of the trees above; the chirping of birds, the murmur of a far-away stream and the buzzing of bumblebees. Even today, if I close my eyes I can feel again the enchantment and the magic.

Finally, we would arrive in Remetz. Avram was my father's only brother living in the Maramures county. He was much older than Father. His children were grown and had all left home. He didn't know what to do with a modern city girl like me who roamed the countryside, so he would serve me and my friends some honey cake and wine and wish us well.

For us, the non-Jews among whom we lived were simply "them." Sunday was "their" holiday, very different from ours. The tavern was full and more festive than on workdays. During the week the peasants would stop in for a drink still in their working clothes and sheepskin vests, smelling of garlic, and singing and smoking while they drank. Sunday was different. They all wore their best clothes, with beautifully embroidered white linen shirts. There was often a fiddler playing Romanian folk music or gypsy tunes. The tavern was filled with smoke and the smells of garlic sausage, sheepskin, and a plum brandy called *tzuica*. These aromas penetrated to the back room, along with the noise and the music. The main street was filled with the sounds of the church bells and the chants of their women and children.

Jews and Romanians in that region lived together pretty peacefully at that time, all going about their own business during the week -- so peacefully, in fact, that my father wrote a story about it (It is in the book he published before the war). Since most of the Jews recited their prayers at home, occasionally the very religious Jews who went to the synagogue every day had a hard time finding a *minyan*, the quorum of ten men necessary for the daily prayer services. My father's story was about such a situation: there are only nine men in the synagogue and the service cannot begin. One of them leaves the synagogue to look for a tenth man. On the street he sees a slightly stooped old man dressed in black; he calls him in to complete the *minyan* and the services begin. And the stranger, who is in fact the Greek Orthodox priest who has been mistaken for an observant Jew, smiles benevolently as he says his own prayers.

When I was about nine, Aunt Fannie in New York wrote that she was coming back to Romania for a visit. For months nobody talked about anything except her arrival. Aunt Fannie, the eldest of my grandparents' eleven children must have been an unusual woman. She had once been married to the rabbi's nephew, but, for reasons that were never explained to me, the marriage was a disaster. Considering the times, she was quite brave to ask for a divorce, and, surprisingly, the rabbi agreed to grant her the religious *get*. Obviously she could not remain at home. As a divorced woman, she had no chance of remarrying and with six other daughters still waiting to be married, there was no second dowry for her. So she decided on the bold step of leaving the village to seek her fortune elsewhere. Just before World War I she emigrated to the United States and settled in New York.

She worked at various jobs, making a living for herself and sending money and packages to the whole family back in Maramures. Eventually she remarried, rented a large apartment in Manhattan and took in boarders. She had two daughters, Sylvia and Tootsie. In 1930, she decided to bring her girls to Romania for a visit and then take her unmarried nineteen-year-old sister Goldie back to New York with her. Everybody was anticipating her visit and Goldie eagerly prepared to leave.

To us, anybody who could afford to make the long trip from America just for a visit must have been a millionaire. This was confirmed when Aunt Fannie arrived: she brought presents for all the children, clothes for her sisters and all sorts of other trinkets. My younger brother Yossie still remembers and even resents only getting some beautifully wrapped chocolates, while his cousin Izzy received a silver dollar.

In our eyes, our American visitors were so elegant, they had so many suitcases full of clothes; they were so special, so particular and so finicky. Just imagine -- every morning ten-year-old Sylvia and six-year-old Tootsie had to have their oranges or cantaloupes. We only got an orange when we were sick and I had never tasted a cantaloupe before. They were dressed beautifully: I still remember their silk dresses with tiny polka dots, their patent leather shoes and little white patterned socks -- just like in the movies. Every day her mother brushed Tootsie's hair into long curls. Sylvia was just a year older than I and we became good friends. The girls spoke Yiddish so there was no language problem. I think this was when I started to like the name "Sylvia". Over the years I inherited many of her dresses; they made me quite elegant in a foreign, American way.

All summer our glamorous New York relatives commuted between Sapantza and Sighet and all around to see other relatives. My brothers fell in love with little Tootsie and her curls. During a summer festival in the small park near the market place they entered her in a beauty contest for children. Moishi bought up all the tickets and Tootsie from New York became "Miss Little Sighet". She still tells the story of how she was once a child beauty queen.

Aunt Fannie was a sophisticated modern woman by our standards. Married women in our family had to wear a traditional wig and a head scarf; Fannie let her own hair grow. But out of respect for her parents, during her visit she usually covered her hair with a kerchief, and on the Sabbath, like her sisters, she wore a nice blond wig combed and curled by a local hairdresser. One Friday afternoon I was sent to pick it up. It was wrapped in brown paper. I was walking back across the bridge quite absent-mindedly, and as I reached my grandparent's house I realized that the paper wrap was empty. I was so scared about what would happen to me if I had lost Aunt Fannie's beautiful wig that I ran all the way back to the bridge. There, to my great relief, I found the wig, right on the edge. If there had been the slightest breeze, the wig would have blown into the water and been carried away to the Tisa and onward to Czechoslovakia. It would have been a tragedy.

At the end of that summer, Aunt Fannie and her girls left and took Goldie with them. Six years later Goldie came back for a visit. By then she was so changed that she seemed like a stranger. Her hair was short and curled, her nose was fixed, she was quite pretty, and her wardrobe was the envy of any teenager like me. She even dared to wear shorts at home. But at twenty-five she was still single, which continued to worry her parents. Eventually she did marry, but her parents didn't live to see her settled.

Aunt Fannie never returned to Sapantza again. She died at the age of eighty-four, still living in that same building on the corner of Broadway and 79th Street where she and her family had lived for more than fifty years. Whenever I take a visiting relative on a sightseeing tour of New York, I never fail to point out this landmark of ours where the first immigrant from our family lived.

Traveling to Sapantza was not easy, nor was it cheap. There were horse-drawn buggies stationed in the huge courtyard behind the dairy store in Sighet. One went early in the morning to bargain for the price of a seat, then waited for all eight seats to be sold and for the horse to finish its oatmeal feed. It took the carriage four hours to cover the twelve miles from Sighet to Sapantza, stopping at each of the three villages along the way so the coachman could have a drink at the local tavern and rest the horses. I would enjoy the countryside. To the right, the valley of the Tisa and its tributaries stretched away to the distant Czech Carpathians; to the left the road followed the hillside. As the mountains came closer they changed shape and color, then they separated to let us pass and fell behind. I was so fascinated with the landscape that I hardly felt the jolting of the carriage on the unpaved road, shaded by trees that lined it or overhung the hillside.

In winter the carriages were replaced by sleighs. Winter lasts longer in Maramures than elsewhere, since it is the northernmost corner of Romania and gets the most precipitation. Snow fell almost daily; it lay on the ground for months and no one cleared the roads. We would put on sweaters, warm coats, woolen hats, mittens, scarves and boots, and take along thick wool blankets. A sleigh ride was so much fun!

It was not long before progress intruded in Sapantza too. A bus started to run in the 1930's. The trip by bus took only 30 minutes and one could hardly see anything. It was also expensive.

I continued to go to Sapantza during vacations, but as I grew older what had seemed an enchanted world started to lose its magic, and reality took its place. I began to understand how much work and struggle went into this simple living, and how stifling the prejudice was for the Jews in Maramures.

And thus the spell of Sapantza of my childhood slowly dissipated, leaving behind the memories of my grandparents and the beginnings of my family.

June 11, 1985

Traditions

We were invited to a Golden Anniversary for my cousin Sidi, my Aunt Esther's daughter, and her husband Sruli. This surprised me, since I am not close to their family nor am I part of their devoutly Orthodox circle in Brooklyn. But I was very glad to be invited to the celebration because in our family no one else of that generation lived to enjoy a fiftieth anniversary. They emigrated to Palestine with their first son years before it all started, and thus escaped the fate of the rest of the family.

Sidi and Sruli now live in Borough Park amidst very religious and observant Jews who are members of some of the more moderate Chassidic courts -- the court of Sapantza or the court of Vizhnitz, to which my father and most of our family members belonged. Sidi and Sruli have lived there for almost forty years and, while not Chassidic themselves, have raised their children in faith, tradition and orthodox piety. Their sons are named Ebi, Moishi and Yossie, just like three of my brothers, named for the same ancestors.

Moishi, the most religious of the three, became a rabbi. He has side curls and an untrimmed beard longer than his father's, wears a dark suit and teaches in a *yeshiva*. He married about thirteen years ago and since then, as though performing their duties to the Jewish people or fulfilling their covenant with God, their family is constantly growing. Whenever I meet them the wife is either nursing or pregnant. They have nine children already and she is pregnant again.

Ebi became a physician and worked in Maimonides Hospital for many years. He dresses very conservatively, wears a skullcap, keeps a kosher home and now has decided to emigrate to Israel with his wife and four children.

Yossie has adopted modern dress. He married into a wealthy family, became assistant manager in his father-in-law's factory, and moved to a secluded community of religious Jews in Rockland County with his wife and three children.

Cousin Sidi thrives as a grandmother. She and Sruli have lived very modestly in the same rented two-family house for more than twenty years, always helping Moishi and his ever-growing family. Sruli has long been retired from the clothing business he owned. Now, in their seventies, their life is their home, their community and their many grandchildren.

The party was in a hired hall in Borough Park. The atmosphere was convivial but sober. Most of the men wore Chassidic dress -- black suits, black hats and white shirts -- while the women wore elegant long-sleeved, high-cut dresses and beautifully coifed wigs. The food was not merely kosher, but "*glatt kosher*", under even stricter rabbinical supervision. The waiters, all men, wore skullcaps, black suits, white shirts, fringes hanging down at the waist, and had long beards. There were lots of children -- little girls in ruffled dresses and ribbons, little boys with curls, older ones with *yarmulkes* and side locks.

My brothers Alter and Yossie, who live in New York, were there. Aunt Goldie came in from Washington, where she and her husband and son live now. She is the same age as Sidi and they are close friends. When the toasts began I rose. "I am grateful and happy to be here," I said. "I guess I know why I was invited: I was at the wedding in Sighet fifty years ago. My brother Yossie was there too, which makes us the only eyewitnesses from that important event to be here tonight. I still remember Aunt Esther's home at the end of the long courtyard on Avram Yancu Street where they were married. There was a little porch, and the *chupa* was held in front of it, and we children watched and admired our cousin getting married.

"And now, fifty years later, I watch and admire this large and close-knit family. I am impressed by Ebi's plans to leave a thriving medical practice and settle in Israel so he can wait there for the Messiah. I am impressed by Moishi, so dedicated to teaching the Jewish traditions to youngsters, and adding another beautiful baby to the Jewish people almost every year. This is what I call to have *naches*. And Sidi and Sruli, presiding over this large and devoted family, do have *naches,* they are blessed." I was applauded.

Afterwards I thought a great deal about what I had seen at the party. Sidi and I come from the same town, from the same family, the same upbringing and the same traditions. I asked myself, how did we end up so far apart in our beliefs, our way of life, our goals and everything else? I reflected on the meaning of the life they chose in Borough Park -- God-fearing and righteous people, who continue the traditional life of the old country, in spite of thousands of miles, decades of time, and a whole history that separates them from those times, insulated from those outside their community.

Once again my thoughts take me back to Sighet, where we had our beginnings and where our parents lived peacefully. What a traditional life it was for all of us! Mother and her two older sisters, Pearl and Esther, were very close. There was little difference in our upbringing, Sidi's and mine: we all observed the laws of Judaism. Though some of us were Chassidic, most were not; but everybody kept kosher homes, observed the holidays, went to the synagogue; those who fell short were disowned by the community.

There were over ten thousand Jews in Sighet, with many sects and many Chassidic courts, each with its own synagogue or houses of prayers, *shuls,* so there were varying degrees of observance. My father was a little different from most. He was one of the so-called "progressives" who permitted some degree of modernism to intrude in their lives. He had a short, trimmed beard and no sidelocks. He wore less conspicuous clothes than many others, and didn't even own a fur-trimmed hat, although his head was always covered, a skullcap at home or a hat when outside. He was more enlightened: he read the great Yiddish writers of the time and all the Jewish and Hungarian newspapers he could get.

He was also versed in worldly matters: business, the wheat export, even the stock market. During the First World War he had been a sergeant in the Hungarian army and was decorated with three stars, of which he was very proud. Like others of his generation who grew up when this region was still part of the Austro-Hungarian empire, he was fluent in Hungarian. At the end of the war, when Transylvania became part of Romania, he browsed avidly through my history and geography schoolbooks, but he never really mastered Romanian. When the Hungarians returned during the Second World War, he helped me with the difficult Hungarian spelling for the work I was doing at the movie house. He would stay up with me till midnight, with the dictionary in his hands, overseeing my work. Was this just an excuse to keep me company?

Father sent his children to public schools, not to *yeshivas*, and he was ready to make any sacrifice so I could stay in high school. This presented a dilemma for him, since public schools held classes on Saturdays and going to school on the Sabbath was widely discouraged. In my case Father decided, "Yes, attend if you must, but you should not take notes." And I complied. It is thanks to my father's convictions that I am what I am and where I am, a physician living in Westchester County. I appreciate this today even more than I did before.

Of course there was never any question about our basic religious beliefs and observances. From our earliest childhood our lives were geared toward compliance with the precepts of Judaism. We celebrated the Holy Days, observed traditional customs and rituals, followed hair and dress code, and took part in the activities of the community.

The dresses had to be modest and of subdued colors, and even the length of the sleeves had meaning: grown women had to wear long-sleeved dresses, and girls had to keep their elbows covered. Married women had to shave their heads, and wore a kerchief or a wig. But I was not required to wear elbow-length sleeves, and my mother had her own hair under her kerchief.

Little boys could keep their hair untrimmed and uncovered until the age of three; then they were taken to the barber to have it cut. What was left in front of the ears identified the particular religious views of the parents: it might be long sidelocks, short ones, a little puff -- or nothing. I remember when my little brother Yancu, the baby of the family and my favorite, was taken to the barber and his beautiful blond locks were shaved off. He cried, and so did I. What an ordeal! He was left with nothing, not even a puff -- such was the progressive attitude of my parents! But a cap he had to wear.

After the age of three, having become clearly recognizable as Jews by their haircuts, little boys were sent to Hebrew school -- *cheder* -- to begin their studies. That was our equivalent of day care and the teacher, called a *melamed*, was the caretaker. It just seemed that the *melamed* was always a bearded old man with a whip or a stick in his hand. He taught the children Hebrew and the Torah. He also taught them obedience and discipline.

All my brothers attended *cheder* at one time or another. Somehow, I was also sent there -- although girls usually did not have to learn religious matters. Alter, my oldest brother, who remembers those times better than I do, claims that I was the best student in the class and that I progressed very quickly to advanced studies. Our *cheder* was a shabby, dark room with a low ceiling in the teacher's home. The children sat on two benches at a large table and memorized the Hebrew letters and syllables. One of the lullabies my mother sang to us went like this,

>"In the fireplace, a small fire burns and the room is hot.
>And the rabbi teaches the little children
>the Aleph and Beith,
>And the rabbi teaches the little children
>The Aleph and Beith,
>Repeat it again and again:
>The Aleph and Beith.
>Repeat it again, dear little children,
>The Aleph and the Beith."

Every child knew this song, and, obviously, the Aleph and the Beith.

One of my earliest memories is of the dark classroom, the old teacher and a long narrow courtyard facing the door. The teacher kept pigeons in a woodshed at the end of the courtyard. One day, when I was perhaps four years old, I opened the door of the woodshed to see what was there, and the pigeons flew away. The old teacher must have punished me with the stick or a slap, because I came home very distraught. When I got there I found that we had company: Aunt Czili had arrived from Sapantza to introduce her fiancee, Ignatz, to the family. I always liked Aunt Czili with her striking long red hair, but that day I was so upset about the pigeons or the punishment that I refused to look at them, I just stared at the floor.

As I grew up I went to the regular public kindergarten and afterwards to the elementary school, which was across the street. At the end of my first grade we moved to the Jewish Street in the center of town. We moved many times but this was the only time I had to change schools. I was so worried I wouldn't be accepted at the new school that I went to talk to my teacher, Miss Dunca, by myself; she reassured me. I was also sorry to leave behind my friend Suri, but she remained one of my best friends even though we lived far from each other and never more went to school together. I recently met a woman from Sighet who surprised me with one of her recollections. She was a second grader in that new school and she remembers when my father brought me to her class holding me by the hand, and the teacher introduced me and assured the children that I was a good student.

Our new home was closer to Mother's sisters. On Saturday afternoons, after the mid-day meal, mother would take my little brothers and me to visit Aunt Pearl and Aunt Esther. They would talk and argue about their parents in Sapantza; about their brother Yeno, "the rich one", who lived in Viseu, had a stationery store and a house, and would only lend his sisters money against a pawn; about Fannie in America, whose packages were never enough; about household problems, children and privations.

While they talked, we would play games with our cousins and munch on cookies. I don't recall any toys or puzzles, but we had pebbles, carob seeds and playing cards and that was enough to amuse us. We could play hopscotch only if it was drawn on the sidewalk from before.

Pearl and Esther envied my mother, Zissel (or Zali, as she was called in Hungarian), even though she had married a widower with three children and had to work so hard. But my father Herzl (or Herman, to use his Hungarian name) was the nicest, most considerate person, gentle and calm, well read and handsome. And he had such a gift for telling stories that he kept the whole family entertained.

Aunt Pearl had many children. I remember five daughters and one or two sons at home; other sons, perhaps three of them, must have been away at *yeshivas*; they were deeply observant and would not attend public school. Aunt Pearl's husband was a rabbi. He had been to America once and made enough money there to buy a large home in Sighet where he opened a prayer house. He also returned with a gold pocket watch with a very long gold chain that brought him respect and envy in his congregation.

But his *shul* did not go as well as he had expected -- there were too many other synagogues in Sighet. According to the family legend, when he needed money to support his family, he went to the jeweler, had a link of his gold chain cut off, and sold it. Eventually the whole chain was gone and even the watch had to be sold.

Behind their house was a large garden with apple, pear and walnut trees where we would play with our cousins on Saturday afternoons. If I saw ripe fruit on a tree and wanted to pick it, they would shout in outrage, "But it's Saturday -- how could you!" If I had already picked it, I had no choice but to throw it away. If nobody reminded me, I sometimes reminded myself. Once I found a green walnut under a tree. I automatically picked it up, broke the shell and started to eat the pulp when I suddenly realized that it was Yom Kippur and I was breaking the fast. I spit it out, but I had already sinned and the guilt stayed with me.

I remember all this with great sadness, for none of Aunt Pearl's family survived the war.

Aunt Esther, Sidi's mother, had a rounded figure and a very outgoing personality. She was the oldest, the wisest of the three, and an expert in everything, always consulted and always dispensing advice. She was also the best cook. Her two daughters and three sons were already grown up when I was a child. Some were already married and all had moved away. The daughters had left to join a *Hachshara,* an agricultural commune in the countryside that prepared them for emigration to Palestine. So Aunt Esther had taken in a boarder, rich Uncle Yeno's son Feri, who was attending high school in Sighet. Uncle Yeno paid her quite well and the other sisters envied her for the extra income and because their brother favored her.

Because Esther's older children were fortunate enough to have left Sighet before the war, they all survived. Today they live in America and Israel.

But in middle age, Aunt Esther unexpectedly had another child, a son named Eber. When the war came and we were all forced into the ghetto, they lived two streets away from us. And when the houses on that street were returned to their gentile owners and the Jews were evicted and had to move out to other assigned lodgings, I helped Esther and her husband carry their belongings. I was the only young and able-bodied member of the family around. We worked a whole day on the move.

Not one of them survived.

Yes, religion was an integral part of our life. Nobody questioned those values. I myself did not doubt them. I believed with all my heart, I trusted, I prayed and I hoped. Then calamity fell on our part of the world. What happened to the beliefs of all our people? They were forfeited by many who experienced the death camps. Yet many others emerged trusting more than ever, their faith unshaken and their devotion reaching new heights. Just look at Borough Park and Williamsburg!

I admire those who preserve values they have inherited, who cling to a way of life that has vanished long ago. It gives such a comforting sense of continuity. For thousands of years, keeping up Jewish tradition has assured the survival of our people. Yet today it seems like a reminder of bygone days.

Or is there a future for a resurrection of the past?

January 15, 1984

Faigi

Ellie is getting married next week in Israel. Who is Ellie? you may ask. He is Faigi's son. And who is Faigi? She is my cousin, one of the three cousins who survived the deportations. I have to tell you about her and her family.

Before the war Faigi lived with her parents in Borsa, a large mountain village in Maramures, about thirty-seven miles from Sighet in the opposite direction from Sapantza. Faigi's mother, my Aunt Mantzi (Miriam in Yiddish), one of my mother's younger sisters, was very pretty, tall and slender. She and her husband Lazar settled in this village. Faigi was the oldest of their four daughters. Borsa was a beautiful place in the foothills of the Northern Carpathian mountains but it was far from Mantzi's family, and hard to reach in those days of horse-drawn carriages and little money.

Almost all the people living on the main street of Borsa were Jews, most of them observant and God-fearing. Faigi remembers Borsa as a busy place, bustling with intense Jewish life, culture and identity, with Zionist and Chassidic movements, a Hebrew school and even literary activity. Borsa had only one movie house, one doctor and one pharmacy, but it had many houses of prayer.

Most of the Jews there were poor, as were the Romanian peasants who built their cottages in the foothills next to their small farms. There were a few well-to-do Jews, who owned sawmills in the nearby forests, lumber being the only industry at that time. As in any other village, there were also a few craftsmen and merchants. The rest, who had no special trade, tried to scrape together a living as peddlers. According to Faigi, her father Lazar, the youngest of eleven children, was not considered poor; he had inherited some land from his father and grandfather. But like me she remembers very trying times when there was not enough for the children. Whenever anyone suggested to Lazar that he sell a piece of land so he could improve his lot in life, he would say that he had four daughters and would only sell his land to provide them with dowries.

Meanwhile he tried one thing and another to earn a living -- trading, bartering, selling whatever was needed. Sometimes the house was full with goods he was dealing in at the moment: baskets of vegetables, sacks of grain, fattened geese tied together. He rented orchards, picking the fruit and sending it to nearby markets. His own land was up in the mountains and was leased for pasture. In the spring, the peasants would come to their house with their sheep and cattle. Lazar would mark the animals and send them up to the grasslands; the peasants would pay for the grazing and return for their animals in the fall. Hired shepherds took the livestock up to the mountain pastures and stayed there all summer. Faigi's mother dreaded the times when the house was full of smelly peasants and the backyard full of animals; but for the children the comings and goings, the people, and the whole commotion were most entertaining.

From time to time Lazar would go up to the fields to check on the herdsmen and Faigi remembers that he would always return with something for the children -- a special goat cheese or a few blossoms of edelweiss (called "the queen's flower" in Romanian). These were rare and precious, hard to find because they grew only at alpine heights, hidden among the steep rocks. When she returned from the camp after the war and searched her parents' house for any remnant of her family's life, she found one of her father's notebooks. Between the pages were a few pressed edelweiss for the children. She still has them.

While the region was under Romanian rule, Borsa and the surrounding countryside remained wild and undeveloped. Romania was full of picturesque mountains. Tourist facilities were built in the South, closer to Bucharest, and few people cared to travel to the far-off Northern Carpathians. But much of Hungary is flat, and when the Hungarians took over the region in 1940 they were struck by the beauty of these mountains, with hills and dark forests, green meadows and snow-covered peaks, and dark precipitous ravines, so like the Austrian Alps. They started to develop fancy winter resorts, ski slopes, exclusive hotels, chalets, roads and supporting industries in the village. For a time Borsa became an important tourist attraction and ski resort.

Borsa was probably the largest Jewish village in Maramures and it suffered from the great anti-Semitic outbreak in Romania in the late 1920's. I was still very young when I heard that radicals of a very chauvinistic and anti-Semitic party organized a pogrom and set fire to Jewish homes in Borsa. Almost all of the main street was engulfed in the blaze and destroyed. The Jews from Borsa took refuge in Sighet and appealed for help to the Jews there and overseas. As help arrived, the village was rebuilt, but some houses did not get finished before the war. After the infamous fire, Faigi's father, then newly married, built a small house on the main street but he couldn't afford to complete it. Whenever I visited I had to squeeze in with the other children in one room because the back rooms had a roof but no walls. Chickens and ducks and geese roosted there, turning it into a barn.

During summer vacations I loved to visit mother's sisters or brothers in the country villages. Borsa was cooler than Sighet, the air was fresh, the mountains close and inviting, and the shady, dense forests were full of mystery. There were streams and footpaths, and on the main street an impressive steel bridge crossed a shallow creek. A little mountain train would take me and Faigi on a most exciting ride to the top of a nearby peak, where a military cemetery overlooked the winding valley. Faigi was my playmate; she looked up to me because I was older, because I came from a big town and I even attended high school.

Two of my schoolmates lived in Borsa. My high school had a boarding school where rich girls from nearby villages lived. Maria Anderco was one of them. Her father, a famous landowner, owned practically half of Borsa and had a huge farm on the outskirts of the village. One summer I took Faigi along to visit Maria, who served us bread hot from the oven, with butter spread as thick as the slice itself, and eggplant salad with ripe tomatoes. That was quite a novelty, even for a city girl like me, because tomatoes and eggplants didn't grow in our part of the country and were very expensive.

Maria's house was a manor set far back from the road, hidden in the shade of huge chestnut trees. The kitchen where the bread was baking was larger than Faigi's whole house and at least half a dozen servants were kept busy. It was fascinating to see the luxurious way of life of the rich Romanian landowners, so different from anything we knew, and having such friends only added to my distinction in the eyes of my little cousin.

The other schoolmate was the daughter of Borsa's doctor. She was two years behind me in high school and did not live at the boarding school: she was Jewish, and Jewish girls stayed with Jewish families. She was pretty and she was spoiled. When I saw her in Borsa, she showed off her elegant house and fine manners and her family's prominent friends in the village. She took me to the school principal's home, where his daughter served us a torte with wild strawberry icing and real coffee in elegant porcelain cups. It was all so special, and I still remember how wonderful it tasted.

Life was simple in Borsa: walking along the main street, going to the river and up the stream, hiking in the mountains, stopping in the forests to gather wild flowers, reading in the shade of tall trees, watching sheep and cattle graze. I would help in the house, go to the market, feed the poultry, gather the eggs or attend to the children. Friday was the most exciting day. The big brick oven was prepared for baking challah for the Sabbath and other bread for the whole week. When we children got up in the morning, Aunt Mantzi had already prepared the *langosh*, little flat breads that were quick-baked on top of the oven, rather like pizza crust. She served them to us with sour cream and garlic and they were delicious.

In May 1944 this world came to an end for all of us. I found myself in Birkenau, dizzy and bewildered, not really knowing or understanding what was happening around me, separated from my whole family. There were thousands of girls around me, all recent arrivals from the Hungarian transports. Some were from Sighet, others from nearby villages, all looking alike with shaven heads, gray sack dresses and scared looks, all speaking Hungarian or Yiddish. I had been *There* for just a few days when a young girl approached me; she had been looking for me for some time.

It was Faigi! I hardly recognized her. She had grown since I saw her, but she was still small and frail, no more than fourteen years old, probably one of the youngest girls, and the only one of her family to have entered the camp. She was so happy to find me and I felt so fortunate to have a cousin there. She lived in the barrack next to mine. We met every day after roll call and hoped to stay together. But very soon I lost her. This happened all the time: one would wake up in the morning and run to a certain barrack to meet a friend or a relative only to realize they were gone. New people had come overnight, and no one knew for certain where the others had gone. At that time I did not know enough to worry about her fate, but it broke my heart that she could not be with me so I could help her and protect her as a little sister.

When I came home to Sighet in 1945 I found out that Faigi had returned to Borsa and was living with some relatives of her father's. I wrote to her immediately and asked her to come and stay with me in Sighet. She wouldn't; she was busy disposing of the property. I asked her to come to my wedding. She couldn't; she didn't have money to buy proper shoes.

The new Communist government was pressing land owners to sell their plots to make way for large collective farms. In Faigi's family only a few cousins returned from the camps, and they were ready to sell and move away. So they sold. They all received huge amounts of money, perhaps hundreds of thousands of lei, but inflation was rampant and paper money was losing value daily. They deposited the money in the bank. One week later, a "stabilization" of the currency was decreed and all such fortunes became worthless overnight. All Faigi could buy for her new money was a nice leather bag and some clothes. Maybe she even got a pair of shoes.

She finally came to Sighet after Tzali and I were married, and she stayed with us for a few weeks. Since we were preparing to go away to the university, Faigi decided to go to Medias and live with Aunt Czili, Uncle Ignatz and their three daughters. Medias, located in southern Transylvania, remained Romanian during the war and the Jews were not deported. Aunt Czili's son had already left for Palestine and the whole family planned to join him as soon as possible. Meanwhile they offered Faigi their home, their family and their love. Faigi was there when we visited Aunt Czili with our first child, Silvia. She loved the baby, pampered her, fed her, played with her and yearned for a daughter of her own.

Faigi became part of Aunt Czili's family, but she was ambitious and determined, always striving for acceptance and recognition. She wanted to become independent and soon got a job with a dentist and was trained as a dental technician. After they all emigrated to Israel, she continued to work hard as a dental technician. She still does, saying that she will always remember what it was like to be poor. She and her husband Geza have good jobs, steady incomes, and a beautiful home in a good neighborhood in Tel Aviv. After all these years they are still happily married. She did not have a daughter after all; instead, they have two sons, Ellie and Shimshon.

Ellie is getting married next week, which is where this letter began. There will probably be hundreds of people at the wedding: the whole company or the whole village or the whole kibbutz. This is how they do it in Israel, they share their joy and pleasure with the whole community of friends and relatives.

So now you understand, Miriam, why I care for Faigi. She means much more to me than just a cousin. She is part of my past, one of the few people left from the large family that I once had.

August 9, 1984

Tango Bolero

For some time I have been obsessed with writing these letters. Some of the memories I shared with you have been gay, others sad, but I wanted to capture them all as I remembered them, for I was afraid they would dissipate or fall into oblivion. But now the holiday season is here, and you will be arriving with your parents in a couple of days -- a happy event. Snow is predicted. You haven't seen snow before, you'll have so much fun. There are signs of holiday spirit everywhere. At work there are parties and chocolates and colorful, wrapped gift boxes on every desk.

So what should I tell you about in this cheerful season? I wanted to write about some happier times, happier events, but nothing special came to mind. I began to wonder if it was time to stop writing for a while and take a rest.

But this morning something happened. Overnight it had snowed. Not too much, just enough. Tzali left for work before I did, insisting as usual that I leave later and drive very carefully. I went to the garage and there, in the driveway, written in the snow, was the word *szeretlek*, Hungarian for "I love you". As the thin film of snow began to melt, the letters became larger and deeper as if to tell the whole world.

I was so moved. I knew I had to write about this while the emotion was still fresh. No, not about how your grandfather still loves me after all these years, but about these foolish things he continues to do just as he did when he was a teenager in love.

Tzali and I... My nostalgic thoughts take me back to the summer of 1939, the summer before my senior year in high school, when it all started. As always during vacations, there were so many outings and hiking trips. My friend Rita had a crush on Tzali and for some time she had been telling me how much she liked him. I was getting tired of hearing her talk about him. He was handsome, just over eighteen -- a little older than I was -- but to me he was just another boy in my crowd. I had a crush on Rita's brother Otto, who wasn't interested in me at all.

One Sunday in August, our crowd decided to go to Sugatag, a well-known resort twelve miles or so from Sighet, about a four-hour hike across the mountains. Sugatag, thanks to nearby salt mines, was famous for its salt-water swimming pool. For some reason Rita couldn't come along, so she told me to keep an eye on Tzali (who was very fond of girls) and report back to her everything he did.

We started before dawn, walked until sunrise, rested in the shade of

a big tree on a mountaintop, ate from our knapsacks, talked, laughed and
sang. By the time we arrived at Sugatag we were ready to enjoy the pool
and have a beer at the pool-side restaurant. We sat down at a little table and
listened to the band that usually played on Sundays. Tzali had a little camera
and was taking lots of snapshots (as he always did and as he still does
today). It took me a while to realize that he had me in all his pictures: the
swimming pool and me; his friends and me; a landscape with sheep in the
background and me in the foreground (one day I will show you this picture
in our album and tell you how it survived). At first I thought he was paying
extra attention to me because I was Rita's friend, but when the band started
playing tangos and waltzes, Tzali danced only with me. One particular
melody comes to my mind, a waltz inspired by the overture of *La Traviata*.
Very romantic. The day went by fast.

It got late and we decided to return on the little mountain train. The
cars were crowded, but the train moved along very slowly so we stood on
the car steps. Tzali wanted to hold my hand. I was flustered. What was I
going to tell Rita?

From that day on, every time I went out with the crowd it became
clearer that Tzali was pursuing me. My eighteenth birthday came a few
weeks later. At our house my birthday was the only one that was celebrated
(which is why my brothers still remember the date). I invited all my
girlfriends to a party -- boys were never invited -- and afterwards we went
for a stroll on "the Corso," the promenade on the main street. Rita and I
were strolling along together when who should join us but Tzali. Rita was
flushed, Tzali kept his eyes on me and I was embarrassed.

In December the local Zionist organization prepared a Chanukah
celebration to be held on the stage of the movie house. There would be a
candle-lighting ceremony, songs, dances and sketches. Every member was
involved in planning, selling raffle tickets, organizing the program, or
performing. My talented brother Moishi made the sets, with skyscrapers
painted in the background like some he had seen in a magazine article about
a Broadway show. A song named *Tango Bolero* with music by Llossas was
very popular, and Rita and I were chosen to dance to it. We wore Spanish
gypsy costumes, Rita a velvet bolero and black pants and I a gathered skirt,
embroidered white blouse with strings of colorful beads and a huge floral
shawl. (There is also a tiny snapshot of me in this costume in our photo
album, taken after the performance). We were backed by four couples,
children who just moved to the rhythm of the music.

For Sighet, it was a big event and very successful. So was our
number. Afterwards there was a dinner dance at a nearby restaurant.
Because I was one of the stars of the show, lots of boys asked me to dance.

But the two who would not leave me alone were Tzali and Otto, who by now had noticed me. They were fighting for me, cutting in on the dance floor. It was a glorious party and I made my choice: Tzali got to take me home that night and he gave me a goodnight kiss, on the cheek. And *Tango Bolero* became our favorite dance music. As for Rita, I don't remember how I told her, and how she accepted it, but we remained friends.

That Chanukah party remained memorable for yet another reason. It was the last one before the war and the Hungarian occupation. We often ask our friends from Sighet, "Do you remember that Chanukah party in 1939? That's when Tzali and I first danced together, to the tune of Tango Bolero!"

December 22, 1983

High School

Tzali called me at the hospital today to tell me something important and exciting: a letter had just arrived from Romania with a page of pictures of my high school graduating class. One of my former classmates who still lives there learned of my whereabouts and sent it to me.

Any picture from my past, and more so from the faraway past is like a treasure from another world. We have so few reminders of those times. We have tried hard to recover a few family pictures from people who lived abroad during the war. We even went to a Hungarian photographer still in Sighet after the war and rummaged through his old negatives, looking for old family pictures. Surprisingly, and to our delight, we found a few.

I'm anxious to get home. I haven't seen the class graduation picture since before the war and I can hardly remember what it looks like. I don't think I even remember most of the girls in my class. We graduated more than forty-four years ago, and very soon afterwards the war started, and our small stable universe disintegrated. Nothing was the same any more, people scattered: the Romanian students left during the Hungarian occupation, and when the Romanians returned after the war, many Hungarians left. Meanwhile the Jews had vanished into the camps and few of the survivors returned. There was no one from my graduating class in Sighet after the war.

I'm trying hard to remember my classmates. I know our class was very small; it wasn't fashionable for girls to attend high school. Most girls only completed eight years of compulsory and tuition-free elementary school. If one wanted to attend high school one had to take an entrance examination after the fourth grade of elementary school. Work in high school was hard, the rules were rigid, tuition was expensive and not everybody made it through to the end. One might fail a subject or two and have to make them up during the summer, or even repeat an entire year. Others might be content to finish the first four years of high school. On the other hand a high school diploma was a prestigious accomplishment that opened many doors, almost the equivalent of a college degree today.

I remember Etta Tessler, who sent me the picture. I often see her sister, who lives in New York, and we talk about her, recalling the times when I would go to their house. Etta was a big girl, a little plump. She stuttered and had difficulty with many subjects, and I tutored her on and off. Her father was a cabinet-maker, and had a workshop at the end of their backyard where he made fancy custom furniture. Etta was deported with her family, and when she returned she got married and settled with her husband in the city of Oradea. Her two sons live in Israel, but she is too ill to follow them there.

Then there was Olga Odoviciuc, a tall girl of Ukrainian origin who lived on the quiet and shady alley leading to our famous Mill Garden, a most romantic park visited by young couples in the evenings or by families on Saturdays. Olga also needed my help. I keep wondering why so many youngsters needed tutoring, or rather what drove them on when they had to struggle so hard.

I remember Bitza Doros best. She was a well bred, delicate girl from an old and prominent family. She was tall, slender, had fine dark features and very dark hair. Her late father had been mayor of the town. In an earlier letter I told you how her mother used to give me oranges and chocolate for helping Bitza. After her mother died, she lived with her uncle, who was the only public health physician in the city. He would come regularly to our school to inspect our nails for dirt, our scalps for lice and our eyes for infections. Bitza was not exceptionally bright, but she was industrious and orderly in her work and her habits. Although she was poor in math and average in other scholastic subjects, she made up for it with high marks in gymnastics, arts and crafts (knitting, crocheting, needle point), music and other non-academic subjects like homemaking. This was a most important subject in the girls' high school; cooking and baking were part of their education. Every two or three weeks, a girl from each class was assigned for a whole day to the large, well-equipped school kitchen. With the teacher's help, we would put together a fancy French menu with three to four courses. We learned to whisk egg whites by hand and make mayonnaise from scratch. At the end of the day, we would write up all the recipes in our notebooks, then sit down at a nicely-set table, eat the food we had prepared (I didn't eat the meat) and send some dessert -- perhaps some pastry or torte -- to our teachers. The Romanian girls excelled in cookery; what they learned there became a valuable asset to marry into high society. Whether or not Bitza was the most skillful cook or pastry maker, the highest grade, a ten, was assured for her anyway.

After the war I met Bitza again. She lived for some time in Timisoara where Tzali and I were going to the university. She had married early, had two children already and had become a simple, hardworking housewife. She seemed embarrassed; was it because she was living so very modestly? Or because I was a medical student and she never went on to higher education? She had changed a great deal from the fine, aristocratic, sheltered girl she had been.

Who else was in our class? I am not sure about the others. But I do remember some of the events surrounding graduation. It was June of 1940.

Tell the Children

To get the baccalaureate diploma at the end of high school one had to take a written and oral exam that was given only in the larger cities; for our area the exam was in Satu-Mare, about sixty miles from Sighet. The fees and the cost of travel and lodging made it expensive. It was also a very strenuous exam; not everybody took it.

There was as much work as anxiety involved in that grueling test. Almost everything we had studied in the past four years was included: languages -- Romanian, French and Latin (which was the most important), mathematics, philosophy, science. How well did I memorize the Latin names of trees and flowers, insects and mammals, the entire textbook of zoology and botany! I have never felt so smart, so knowledgeable, so erudite as at the time of that examination. High school had given me a solid, well-rounded education.

In Satu-Mare the girls stayed at a convent. The nuns took care of us and even catered to my diet requirements -- I still kept kosher. On the morning of my oral examination I was preparing to leave for school when I heard the "Toreador Song" from *Carmen* whistled under my window -- the signal tune in our crowd. I knew it had to be Tzali, who was in the city to take his driver's test. We hadn't talked for several days after an argument and I was rather unhappy about it (we had a lot of arguments during our courtship; we still do). But he had turned up anyway. He walked me to the examination center. We talked, and we made up. I was almost late but in a much better mood.

I did very well on the exam; I was satisfied. It didn't even bother me that Bitza got a higher grade, as always. Nobody really expected a Jewish girl to come in first. I returned to Sighet exhausted, relieved, content and back with Tzali.

I'm home now, Miriam. In front of me is the page with pictures of each of us, and I'm amazed. A whole new vista opens up, as if I was eighteen again. I look at my classmates and at my teachers through a teenager's eyes. I start remembering so many faces, places, events. How could I have forgotten the other girls in my class? Is it that so much time has passed, carrying with it all my memories? Or did the traumas of the following years blot them out? Or was it just the absence of something -- a person, a letter, a picture -- to take me back to that time and place? I have always searched for that something that could help me recover my memories, for I was afraid that my past might be erased along with them. These pictures lift the lid, releasing memories that were not, after all, buried so deep.

This page is a copy of the large panel of pictures of my graduating class that used to hang in the principal's office next to many similar panels from other years. It is labeled "The Graduating Class of the Princess Ileana Girls' Lyceum, Sighet 1939-1940." There are photographs of ten students and seven teachers, arranged in three rows. As I look at it, I can remember other teachers; I don't know why their pictures aren't there. I see mention of a class reunion planned for 1950. Obviously it was not held. No one was around then.

The students are all in uniform -- not our daily black frock with the white collar and polka dot bow, but the formal uniform: a white blouse and tie, with a navy blue V-neck pullover and navy pleated wool skirt. The yellow patch on the left sleeve was the royal emblem, embroidered in golden thread with our own student numbers stitched in by hand. At the bottom of the picture is a pretentious motto by the Romanian writer Lucian Braga: "One prayer I have, oh God: don't ever let me be satisfied with myself."

The school was an imposing building in the center of the town. Our classrooms had rows of two-student benches; the last I remember, I was sharing a bench with Bitza. From the three large windows we could look down to a narrow alley that led from the town square to a small park called "the strolling garden," where there were large chestnut trees and wooden benches. It was a very quiet and relaxing place except when, on occasion, it was turned into an amusement park or a fairground.

Behind the school, facing the park, was the boarding school and its gardens surrounded by a wrought-iron fence. On the opposite side of the park was a club with tennis courts that were converted into an open-air ice skating rink in winter. I never played tennis but I often skated there. If it was too cold or windy, or it was snowing, I would warm up with my friends in the club's parlor with a glass of warm, spiced wine. Sitting there, sipping wine, talking to friends, and making new acquaintances was as much fun as skating in the cold.

Beyond the park, a street continued several blocks to the Catholic cemetery. The corner house on the second block belonged to Tzali's family. When I was a senior Tzali had already graduated from the business high school and was working in his family's textile store on the main street. On his way home for lunch, he passed between the school and pharmacy and crossed the park. All the girls in my class knew about us and would look out the window at recess until one of them spotted him and yelled, "He's coming, he's coming!" Then they would watch him and tease me. I don't think he ever knew the excitement his passing created in the whole class.

I look again at the photographs.

The top row is all teachers, the bottom row is all students, and the middle shows two teachers and four students. I'm in the middle row on the right, next to a teacher. I can't help but appreciate how young and lovely I look with my wavy hair combed back: the school code forbade bangs or long hair unless it was braided.

Under the picture is my name, family name first: Apsan Dora. I liked my name, which was very Romanian: the cedilla -- the little comma under the "s" in Apsan -- is read "sh", giving the name a Romanian ethnic flavor. There was another Apsan family in the city, a Romanian policeman whose son attended the boys' high school. I wonder whether my ancestors took the name from one of the villages on the Czech side of the Tisa River called the Upper Apsa and the Middle Apsa. I still don't know why they changed a Jewish name to a Romanian one.

I enjoyed it when I was taken for a "real" Romanian. People would say "you don't look Jewish" as a compliment. I had a Greek profile like my father, and spoke Romanian with no trace of a Hungarian or Yiddish accent, though I spoke both at home. This proved very useful many years later in medical school. I simply relished being judged on my abilities, and was relieved that prejudice, which continued during Communism, did not play a role in my grades.

Looking at my other classmates, I am most disturbed that I seem to have forgotten Rozalia Abordan. How could I? She was a few years older than the rest of us. She had had polio, which kept her out of school for a couple of years. On one leg she wore a heavy metal brace with a leather corset and she had a severe limp. Rozalia was a very good student, but she was the only Hungarian in our class and the teachers were not always fair to her. The Hungarian language was officially outlawed and using it in school was punishable by a fine of a few pennies for every word spoken.

On September 1, 1940, just a couple of months after graduation, the Hungarian army marched into the whole region of northern Transylvania. For the rest of us it was the beginning of all the tragedies to come. For Rozalia, however, it was a godsend. She went on to a Hungarian medical school in Debrecen. I also applied to the university there, but to no avail: anti-Semitism had become official and the prewar Jewish quota of 5% (*numerus clausus*) was eliminated, and no Jews at all were accepted at universities any more (*numerus nullus*). But I continued to see Rozalia during her vacations. She told me everything about the school, the classes, the exams. How I envied her! But I liked her very much, and I still wonder why I forgot about her, as she was the only non-Jew to stay on in Sighet after 1940.

And here is Irina Matesan. I hadn't quite remembered whether or not she stayed on through the last year of school. Irina was a newcomer to our city. She and her mother, who worked as a cleaning woman, lived very modestly near the railroad station, as if they were in transition. Sighet was a frontier town on the border of Czechoslovakia and many officials and customs agents were sent here to work for a year or two. Working people also came from southern Romania, perhaps because jobs were more easily available.

There was something mysterious about Irina. She must have been two or three years older than the rest of us and to me that seemed like a generation apart. She was very pretty and had a very definite individual style. She wore her dresses longer and her heels higher than the current fashion and her hairdo was unusual: two braids twisted over her ears and a white head band. I never really understood what was so provocative or intriguing about her. I remember there were rumors about a man or men. Once she told me some exciting stories about her sister being a parachutist. As for her father, I wasn't sure she had one. She is still the prettiest girl in the picture. I wonder what happened to her.

Looking at Litza Pascariu's picture brings back bitter-sweet memories of an evening in her home. She was another well-to-do Romanian girl, the daughter of the railway station master. Her family lived on the second floor of the station building. Like other Romanian girls, her ideal future seemed to be a match with one of the junior officers stationed in Sighet, so in our senior year Litza gave a party at her home and invited the entire class and what seemed like a battalion of handsome young officers. It was a fancy party and I wore my newest, most elegant outfit, a grayish-green tweed skirt and matching sweater. My brother Miki had sent me the fabric from Italy and I had the skirt sewn by the best dressmaker in town.

I didn't belong at the party and I knew it even as I accepted the invitation. I always felt like an outsider at such parties. But we arranged for Tzali to visit his friend Sanyi, whose parents owned a little hotel across from the station. When dinner was over and the company broke up into small groups, I slipped out and walked over to the hotel. Tzali and I went for a long stroll along the railroad tracks. I returned as quietly as I left, but nobody at the party had noticed my absence. The girls were so involved with the officers, drinking, chatting and flirting, that nothing could have distracted them.

The other girls in the picture were related to the teachers and had come with them from around Bucharest. I don't remember much about them. They probably stayed in Sighet only during their school years.

Among the teachers, the picture of Miss Ciolan, our class mistress and philosophy teacher, really speaks to me, reminding me of so many times when our teachers inspired, provoked and intrigued us. Miss Ciolan was an exciting, articulate woman who came from Bucharest with many new ideas. For three years she taught us psychology, logic and philosophy. It was fascinating to learn about philosophical trends and the great thinkers of all times.

She used to test us, but she didn't tell us in advance the purpose of the tests. One day she burst into the classroom, went to the blackboard and wrote the words "mountain", "water" and "sky". "Now," she said, "write whatever comes to your mind in relation to these words." It turned out that she was testing our imagination. Not having guessed that, I had labored to write a scientific paper, so her verdict was that I had no imagination whatsoever.

But her greatest contribution was to introduce us to the revolutionary idea of the I.Q. We had never heard about intelligence being tested. We were in our junior year when she applied I.Q. testing to the seniors. One of my cousins, Etu Felberbaum, was found to be the most intelligent girl in the senior class and Miss Ciolan made a big fuss over that. Then at the end of the school year she tested our class too. I soon figured out all the tricks of the test and scored best in the class, best in the school. She was very excited about it and made an even bigger fuss. But I never found out what my score was, so to this day I don't know how smart I really am.

I worked hard for my grades though, and in my last year of high school I did better than ever before. There was an award ceremony every year, held in the large courtyard. The report cards were handed out and prizes were given to the best students, usually a couple of books, a nice prize because books were very expensive. As always, Bitza got first prize with the score of 9.72, and I got second with 9.71. Oh, well, I was used to that. Afterwards I walked down the long corridor to the school exit. Bitza was in front of me. Miss Ciolan came toward us. When she saw Bitza, she stretched out her arms and exclaimed happily, "You made it! You made it!" and hugged and kissed her. She didn't see me coming behind Bitza.

We liked Miss Boldisor, our knowledgeable science teacher, who made beautiful anatomical drawings on the blackboard. Her biology lectures gave us our first scientific explanations about sex and reproduction, dissipating some of the mysteries that surrounded it for adolescents then.

The music teacher, Mrs. Jurca, was a sweet old lady. She taught us music theory and led the school chorus, which performed at all the school events. She was also the principal of the boarding school.

And there is Mrs. Juga, the history teacher. Her picture is set prominently in the middle of the page, probably because she was a political celebrity. She had a doctorate, and was attractive, always elegantly dressed; and she was known as a famous speaker, a Romanian nationalist and chauvinist -- her anti-Hungarian views were well publicized. When the Hungarians arrived, she was one of those who fled.

The Latin and math teachers, the French and gym teachers left no strong impression on me. I never heard about any of them after I graduated. I suppose they must have returned to Bucharest or to some other part of old Romania.

I am so grateful for the pictures. For days to come I will look at my classmates, and through the eyes of my memory I will return to those happy times when I was a carefree teenager, as one should be.

October 3, 1984

Tosca

We just bought a piano for Gabriel and we're waiting for your mother to be ready for a piano for you. You are both still too young to play it, but we want our grandchildren to grow up with music, and a piano is our present for the firstborn of each of our children.

There has never been a piano in our family. When your mother Silvia was growing up she really wanted to play the piano, but the most we could afford was a violin.

When I was young a piano was a dream that few could afford, and classical music was unknown in my family. As I told you before, music for us meant singing, at home on holidays, with friends at outings, and in the school choir. This is why I remember the first radio concert I listened to, at my friend Hedi's house, when I was in my teens. It was Beethoven's *Pastorale* symphony and Hedi interpreted the music for me, explaining the wind blowing, the birds singing, the love songs, the storm and the resolution. It was such a new and wonderful feeling! After that I went with friends whenever local concerts were played.

But I longed to play piano. When I was nineteen, out of school and earning my own money, I decided to indulge in the luxury of piano lessons, even though I didn't have a piano. What free time I had, I spent practicing on friends' pianos, rushing through two books of the Karl Czerny piano method in a few months. Tzali's little sister Zsuzsi, who had been playing for several years, was very impressed with my zeal and progress. But it all ended ten months later because of the worsening political situation and the approaching war.

In later years I tried piano again a few times but I never could really stick with it. There was always something that interfered and I had to give it up for long stretches. I still enjoy it when my boys play, especially Vali. He started piano after we arrived in this country and were finally able to afford an old upright, but his teacher wasn't very good and after a while he began to rebel and say he hated the piano. So we let him stop. Then a few years later we came home from a vacation and to our surprise we found him playing ragtime music. He had gotten interested in rags and taught himself to play them.

Your Uncle Yancu, on the other hand, wanted lessons and was always interested in the classics. He played on and off for many years, and to this day, whenever he comes home he goes straight to the piano and tries Beethoven's *Bagatelles*.

So I dream of one day being able to play Scott Joplin's rags,

Beethoven's *Bagatelles*, and perhaps even some old favorites. Maybe when I retire and have more time. I still haven't given up. It's a shame to have a piano in the house that just catches dust.

I remember the first opera I attended. It was in the heat of the war, while I was visiting Tzali in Cluj where he was in jail for his political activities.

The anti-Semitism and discrimination we faced under the Romanians before the war became even more oppressive after the Hungarians occupied Transylvania under the Vienna agreement with the Nazis. The youth of Sighet reacted by joining various organizations. Some of my friends were Zionists who dreamed of a homeland for the Jews dispersed all over the world. My brother Ezu joined the *HaShomer Hatzair*, a very militant Zionist movement. Others, who were very religious, believed that God and the Messiah would solve all the problems of mankind; oblivious to what was going on around us, they just went on praying. But most of us aspired to more revolutionary ideals: we dreamed of a society in which all people had equal opportunity if they worked hard, in which schools were free and open for everyone without prejudice, pure socialist goals. Who could argue with such youthful idealism?

I was just out of high school and had joined a group of friends in so-called "subversive" political activities: reading banned literature, meeting to discuss philosophy -- materialism and idealism, dialectics and metaphysics --, and interpreting the writings of Hegel, Marx and Engels. Some of us joined cells of the outlawed Young Communist Organization. We collected money for jailed comrades.

Soon the crack-downs came. There were searches. A few dozen young people were arrested and tortured to reveal more names and tell where prohibited books, leaflets and other materials were hidden (mine were under the firewood in the woodshed). Tzali was among them. They were held in an old castle in Sighet. Families brought food parcels to their loved ones, and gathered outside the building hoping to get some news. But only when a few prisoners were released did we learn about the beatings and torture. One man who could not bear it jumped from the top floor of the castle and died of his injuries. A package of Tzali's clothes was returned to his family. When they opened it, they found torn clothing and a bloodstained shirt; Zsuzsi still cries when she remembers her mother's suffering.

At the time I was working as a secretary at the only local newspaper, "The Life of the Maramaros." It was a Fascist journal, but ironically, most of the employees were Jews. Two of my brothers, Ezu and Ebi, were printers and were involved in setting type, printing, and folding and distributing the newspapers. Some nights, when they were too tired, I helped out in the print shop, stacking the blank sheets of paper in the printing press. I would ask my brothers to insert a few extra words into some of the articles: "Tzali we are with you, Tzali we love you, Tzali be strong." They ran off a few copies of the doctored articles. Then we wrapped food for the prisoners in these newspapers, knowing too well that Tzali and the others would read every line to find out what was happening outside. And so they did. Tzali read all those messages printed only for him.

Shortly afterwards all the prisoners were sent to Garany, a political detention camp in Hungary. A year later they were brought back to Sighet for trial. The courthouse was close to our home. From our porch, looking across the large orchard of our neighbor, the Greek-Orthodox priest, one could see the tall windows of the courthouse corridor.

I hadn't seen Tzali since his arrest. The chief editor, who was also Jewish, covered the trials. He knew about my commitment to Tzali, and was able to take me with him into the courtroom. There were a few Hungarians and Romanians on trial, but most of the prisoners were Jewish young men. How absurd to have a Jewish editor write for a Fascist newspaper about poor Jewish boys who were supposed to be "a threat to the regime!"

In the courtroom I listened to the trumped up charges and heard Tzali being sentenced to five years. When I saw the guards taking the prisoners out, I rushed to Tzali and kissed him. Then I ran to an open window in the corridor from which I could see my father sitting on our second floor porch, reading. I waved and waved until he noticed me, then I held up five fingers to let him know Tzali's sentence.

As I recall this scene, my heart sinks and my eyes fill with tears for my father. Poor Father! He had only one daughter, he loved her dearly and wanted only the best for her, and here she was involved with a young man who was not religious enough, not rich enough, had no profession yet, and on top of everything, had been sentenced to five years in jail as a communist. Father's hopes, hurts, disappointments... did I understand him then? Probably not.

Tzali was taken to a military prison in Cluj, the capital of Transylvania. He wrote letters to his family and love letters to me. They have all been lost. In fact, all family possessions were lost or destroyed during the war, including the family albums. Only a small pocket album, which Tzali carried all those years was preserved. In it were pictures he took of me when we first met. One snapshot shows me in skiing gear, smiling at him. On the back I wrote: "Will it ever be, again?" These pictures and a few others we were able to find later are the only mementos we have of that period.

I decided to visit Tzali in Cluj despite my parents' objections. By then I was quite independent and they did not try very hard to dissuade me. Tzali's mother sent with me all the delicacies a Jewish mother could make for her son.

Luckily, prisoners sent to military jails were better off than those in political prisons. During the day they worked as gardeners at the public nurseries on the outskirts of the city. The guards could be bribed to look away when visitors sneaked in, so Tzali and I could spend almost the entire day together, gardening and dreaming about freedom, yearning for the end of war and of hardship. I stayed about a week. In the evenings I visited some of his relatives, who were very nice to me.

One day they surprised me with a ticket to the opera, Puccini's *Tosca*. It was not just beautiful, it was overwhelming. When, in the second act, I saw Cavaradossi as a prisoner being beaten and tortured to disclose the whereabouts of his friend, I burst into tears and cried the whole evening: I felt I was Tosca.

And this is how I learned about opera and music. And also about love that can endure and gives strength and courage under great adversity.

Of course, that was more than forty years ago. So far away. And Tzali... well, just two days ago when I was trying to organize these letters to you, Miriam, I found that he had made some notes on each of them. I have to tell you about the note he made on this one; "This was in 1943, I still love you in 1984 and for ever."

I wish you, Miriam, this much luck in love and in marriage.

March 20, 1984

Hungarian Occupation

It is strange Miriam, that certain events, images of the past, stick in my mind, as if engraved forever, vivid and sometimes removed from their reality, while the general atmosphere of those periods, the day to day life, escapes me. As my mind returns to the war years, 1940 to 1944, I keep asking myself: How did we live? Where were my brothers? How did we make a living? How did mother take all the privations? What did father do during the Hungarian occupation years when there was no work or business possibilities? What happened to the Jewish population?

I can see father's deep frustration being unable to support his large family. He had published his book just before the war. To sell it he traveled from town to town and from village to village all over Transylvania, reading from it in many synagogues. He made a decent living, and enjoyed traveling and meeting people.

During the war, however, there was harassment, there were rumors of bearded Jews being beaten by fascist thugs and thrown out of trains. Travel became too hazardous. Although the Hungarian villages with large Jewish population remained largely untapped and he still had books to sell, father gave up trying to sell his work. Nor could he sell insurance any more, for who trusted that life could be insured, anyway?

The new Hungarian Administration was a boon for draftsmen and in particular for Moishi; every sign in a business or office, every advertisement, all displays and billboards had to be changed to Hungarian. We were flooded with Hungarian names for streets and schools, with monuments for Hungarian heroes; Sighet became Sziget (or Maramarossziget), and the county, Maramures, became Maramaros. Suddenly there was so much work that I had to help. And we earned enough money to support our family. But this intense activity lasted only a few months.

Soon other kinds of work came my way. The anti-Semitic laws came into effect just before the schools opened. A quota system was decreed for Jewish children: they would be allowed in very small numbers *(numerus clausus)* in high schools and middle schools, like teachers' preparatory, business school or the four year Catholic high school for girls. The few admitted were children of doctors, veterans or other prominent people; the rest were shut out of school beyond the elementary grades. Jewish parents had to come up with some alternative plan for educating their youngsters. There were a few private Jewish high schools in the larger cities like Oradea or Cluj, but they were far from their homes, and boarding schools were expensive. Nevertheless, a few went away to finish high school, mostly the richer pupils and those who were only one or two years away from graduation. As to the others, an arrangement was made to register them for end-of-semester exams at those schools, and to have them study at home with private tutors. Since I had just graduated from high school, I was supposed to know math, sciences and languages, including Latin, French, German, etc. Together with a few other girls I was in great demand. Parents with lesser means had their children come daily to my house in groups of three to five to study for those exams. For some, even that was a sacrifice. I had many "classes" of students: I taught all day long, from early morning to late afternoon.

I remember how the first student arrived at 6 in the morning. He was a very observant and bright Jewish boy from Slatina, a village across the river Tisa, about 2 miles away. As mother heard his steps at the entrance near the gate, she would wake me up, help me dress in a hurry, and by the time he arrived at our door on the second floor I was already seated at the kitchen table. While I taught, mother would comb my hair and bring me breakfast. Oh, Mother, did I ever tell you how much that meant to me, and how much I loved you?

Those who could afford more had me go to their homes and tutor their children individually. I recall some of them: Baba, who prepared to go to Cluj, and who impressed me with her intelligence, her eagerness and her modern attire -- she would wait for me in pants, and she smoked. Another one was Abe Maged, who needed to master physics and calculus. I had to learn these along with him because they had not been taught at my high school. He was forever grateful for my help.

All my students had a keen desire to learn and in the absence of classrooms, maps, blackboard, or any other teaching material, they all studied hard just from textbooks and memorized a great deal. I don't recall any who failed the exams.

The greatest problem for me was the Hungarian language and culture. I spoke Hungarian fairly well but had never read much, nor studied its grammar, which was quite difficult. I also had to learn Hungarian history, geography, and literature. When I had to help one of my students to write an essay on Ady Endre, the famous Hungarian poet, it was a great effort. Sure, essays had to be written only by those few who still attended school. But they too needed tutors. One was the daughter of the chief of surgery, Berko; the other one was Yunger, the only daughter of the ear, nose, and throat specialist. I spent a lot of time in their homes because of their daily assignments. (I mention them because of their tragic end -- Berko Bori never returned from the camps; the Yunger family committed suicide in the ghetto, and the girl was saved only to be taken to Auschwitz and vanish there.)

By late 1941 Moishi had landed a good job as the draftsman of the movie house, making posters, placards, announcements and all kinds of graphics and slides. The films changed three times a week and occasionally when there was urgent work he needed my help. The job paid well and was quite prestigious. Moishi thrived in it; he loved the work and the environment, and he created spectacular posters that everyone admired. Moishi was also very social, he was good looking, had friends and girlfriends, dressed well and went out a great deal.

Moishi must have picked up this trade from his older brother Miki, who in 1932 had gone to Padua to study medicine, although as talented as he was he would have learned it on his own. In 1934 Miki had to return to Romania because of his military obligations. He was not drafted, but he had to remain in the country. While here he made a living drawing caricatures and cartoons and exhibiting his work in many cities. The exhibit in Timisoara, where he had graduated from high school, was very favorably reviewed in the newspapers, where they referred to him as "the young artist from Italy, who has studied in our city." He was very skillful, a virtuoso at capturing the likeness and peculiarities of any person in just a few strokes. He would set up a stall at clubs, fairs, and amusement parks. His advertisement said, "Have your caricature done in two minutes, it will cost you five leis only", and people stood in line not only to have their caricatures drawn, but also to enjoy watching how fast he drew them and how well he could make fun of people's little physical imperfections, a longer or shorter nose, a small or long chin, bald or bushy hair. One day, as he was working at the famous Cismigiu park in Bucharest during a summer fair, one onlooker said to him, "You have competition. There is another fellow, at the other end of the park, who does the same sort of thing". Miki was astonished. When he finished his work, he went over to see who the other artist was. And whom does he find but his younger brother Moishi, not even twenty and already so skillful. The two brothers worked together while the fair lasted. Then, in 1935 Miki was permitted to return to Italy to complete his studies, and they never saw each other again.

And then came the drafts. In 1942, with the war raging and the Hungarian army having joined the German in advancing toward USSR, scores of young Jewish men were drafted into the Forced Labor Battalions. Soon almost every able-bodied man was sent away to the front in the Ukraine. These young men were not armed and had no uniforms; they only wore a recognizable cap and an arm band over their civilian clothes. They performed hard labor like digging trenches on dangerous battle fronts and sweeping mines, and usually advanced ahead of the Hungarian soldiers, thus being the first ones to be shot at by the "enemy" or injured by the exploding mines. They were heckled, abused, even beaten by the soldiers; they were fed poorly, and had to sleep in barns, haystacks, or outdoors, under an unfriendly sky. Conditions were harsh, and accidents happened often; and when taken prisoners by the Soviet army, they were treated as enemies, just like the Hungarian soldiers, their previous tormentors. There was always some family in Sighet mourning a loved one killed on the Ukrainian front.

Moishi was drafted too. For us it was devastating, not only because of the dangers he might encounter, but also because he was the principal breadwinner. That good and safe job at the movie house to be given up! Moishi had an idea though. He went to Vidovici, the manager of the theater, and told him that his sister was also a very talented draftsman and that she could do the job in his absence. He agreed to take me, and the job was saved for now. But I was very worried because I had never worked independently. Although I had helped Moishi all along, he was the artist, the one with the ideas. What was I going to do? But then Moishi was able to get the schedule of the next few months and he made me sketches for every movie to come. That made me feel safe for a while, but I remained apprehensive: what was I going to do when I ran out of his ideas?

By then, of course, I had learned some of the tricks -- how to make an outline, how to change the shape and character of the letters to suit the type of movie, and how to use the material that came from the distributors. I finally relaxed and was able to handle posters, flyers, announcements, slides, etc. I enjoyed the work. I remember how much fun I had drawing the Disney characters from "Pinocchio" and "Snow White and the Seven Dwarfs" when these movies came to our town. But most often what we got was cheap Hungarian movies -- their well developed film industry just celebrated its 200th movie, all mass produced. On Sundays I would help out at the cashier and I was able to get tickets for my friends to the more popular movies so they would not have to fight the lines. Brother Ebi was a great help, he was able to mix the paints, fill in the letters, paint the background. He was very meticulous and most conscientious. Yancu, the youngest brother, was not asked to help, he had to study.

It is funny to think that I earned a living doing so many different things, but I never became what Mother hoped I would be, a successful dressmaker, like my cousin Serena. I want to write you about her, because she was so dear to me. She was warm and understanding, always ready to listen, like an older sister.

Serena was my only cousin in Sighet from my father's side. Her father, my uncle, owned a modest room and board undertaking on the main floor of our building, frequented by the very observant Jews who came from the villages for business or to see a rabbi. He had died long time before, and Aunt Henya, a hard-working, fat woman, continued the business with her second husband. There was a large kitchen where she did the cooking with a helper, a large dining room, and a few small, separate entrance bedrooms. One of these was turned into a workshop for Serena. Serena was a few years older than I, and very skinny, even sickly, although I don't know what the problem was. I still remember seeing, on the kitchen stove, among the huge pots with food for the guests, a small frying pan with some special delicacy like goose liver, that her mother prepared for Serena because she was so "fragile."

Serena was a good dressmaker and always had two or three girl apprentices. During my pupils' school vacation, when I had less work, my mother would send me to her workshop to learn sewing, still considered one of the most befitting careers for a girl. There was one dressmaker on almost every street. Some were fancier than others, more expensive, had Parisian fashion magazines and even advised on fashion trends and on fabrics for a certain event. "And they all make a living", Mother would say. I liked to go to her workshop. I learned some sewing, and Serena used my skills well. I could copy patterns from ready-made clothes -- this is how she made a trench coat for my mother, much cheaper -- I could match striped or checked material in a most symmetrical way for collars, pockets or seams, and I made the most perfect shoulder pads. I have always liked sewing since. Once, several years ago, I attended a sewing course at Sears and as I went with a friend, she told the group that I was a doctor. "A doctor?" they all marveled, "what are you doing at a sewing course?" "Well," I told them the truth, "my mother always wanted me to be a dressmaker." And she didn't live to see that I became a doctor instead.

Serena was very active and committed politically. She and many friends, all working people, joined underground organizations and when the crack-down came she was arrested together with them. But after a few days she was released. Was it because of her sickness or because nothing was proved against her? I don't really know but this is how we found out what was going on behind the walls of that old castle where the prisoners were kept.

And now she was back at her dress shop, but work was scarce, people did not care for new dresses any more, and I did not have time to learn that trade.

It felt odd to have such good work and enjoy financial rewards while most of the community suffered from increased harassment. Jobs were lost, Jews could not hold public office anymore, property was confiscated, Jewish institutions were closed, businesses had to hire Hungarian managers to stay open. Children were out of school. Travel was restricted. Most of the Jewish young men were gone, Tzali was in jail, Bela, his brother, had been drafted. The fate of the whole Jewish community was unknown, but enough rumors came from Poland to make my parents worry about the future. But the news from the Ukrainian front, about accidents and deaths, caused the greatest anguish. At least we got letters from Moishi and knew that he was alive.

After the war I had nothing left of his work. I only remembered his drawings, his posters, and his exhibits in Sighet with cartoons and caricatures of the town notables or the political celebrities of the time -- Hitler, Mussolini, Ghandi, -- always admired. How I wished I could find some of his artwork!

I want to mention some of the letters Father and Moishi wrote to Miki at that time, letters that I found at Miki's house after his death. No matter how heart-breaking it is to sort through a loved one's belongings, the voices coming from Sighet during those difficult years were a precious find for me. In the early 40's Father writes to him about hardship, he asks Miki to send a package with clothes for the boys, he has heard that one can get good second hand clothes at flea markets, and the boys could use them. In one letter he says, "Dorika has applied to Medical school in Cluj, I know she does not have a chance, nor could I help her with the tuition, but there is no harm in trying." He also laments that he has not heard from Yossie and he just hopes that he got safely on the other side of the mountains on his escape to USSR. In another letter he expresses his relief that Miki finally graduated from medical school and he advises him to go for surgery and not dentistry, "all the dentists I know are poor people." He talks about sending Miki the proper documents so he could come to visit. This apprehension is echoed in many letters, the need to prove to the Hungarian authorities that the family has lived there for generations, so they are entitled to Hungarian citizenship. How fortunate that he could not come.

Ezu writes, "We are all happy that you will come home. I would ask a small favor from you, when you come, please, bring me Italian cigarettes, many, but don't tell father. Please, bring as many as you can, I will print you calling cards and whatever you need for your office, just bring me cigarettes because the Hungarian ones are very bad". This sixteen year old boy was already an expert in cigarettes. Ebi asks for stamps for his collection. Yancu would like Miki to send him 10 liras.

There is a letter from Moishi written in 1939, the day after that famous Chanukah festival in Sighet. I never knew his handwriting, and it is beautiful. He writes, "Dear Miki, last night was the Chanukah celebration, the local Zionist association organized a show followed by a banquet, and I designed excellent sets (they were a great surprise for the audience) and I earned 900 leis on the work. Dorika also danced with great success. So, as you see, the Apsan family showed strong participation. I am leaving for Bucharest, I would like to find employment there. I will write you from Bucharest".

Unfortunately, he did not go to Bucharest. And this sealed his fate.

April 20, 1993

Part II: A-7603

A Pair of Shoes

Dear Miriam,

  April is approaching fast, time to prepare income tax returns. Your grandfather Tzali is getting together all the information he needs for our accountant.

  Last year, two days before the deadline, the accountant called to say he urgently needed another document. Tzali was away, so I drove to Queens to deliver it, although I don't like to drive alone at night, in the rain, on unfamiliar streets.

  The accountant wasn't home yet. I waited in the living room, where his ten-year-old daughter Sharon was bouncing around noisily in front of a television turned up very loud. Her mother yelled at her to turn it off. They argued, they screamed, and the little brat defiantly turned on the record player, too. I sat down on the couch amid this bedlam.

  On the coffee table I saw a booklet entitled *The Holocaust*. To make conversation, I asked the mother about it. She said it was Holocaust Week and Sharon had been given the booklet at her Hebrew school; she had to study it and write something about the Holocaust.

  The racket was too much for me. I beckoned the girl over.

  "Sharon, would you do me a favor? Turn off the T.V. and the record player and I'll show you something. You won't be sorry."

  Reluctantly, she turned everything off and came to me. I rolled up the sleeve on my left arm and showed her the number tattooed in my skin.

  "Do you know what this is?"

  "It's a number from the concentration camp, isn't it? Wow!" Her eyes opened wide. "Are you a survivor?"

  "Yes, I am."

  "Really? I can't believe it!" She couldn't contain her wonder. "Would you give me an interview?"

  "Sure I would."

  "Wow! I'll be the only one in my class to talk to a real survivor. Will you answer all my questions?"

  "I will try."

  Flushed with excitement, she ran upstairs and came back with her notebook and her list of questions. "How did you feel about being taken away?" she asked. "What were your feelings about being in a camp? When did you realize what happened to your parents?" Her questions were impossible to answer, almost trivial compared to the reality of Auschwitz.

  "You know what, Sharon," I said. "I don't think I could answer your questions, even if I had enough time, which I don't. Suppose I tell you a story about something that happened to me in the camp and then you write the answers to your questions the way you want."

She sat down all absorbed.

"Well," I began, "it was in the fall of 1944. I had been in Auschwitz for several months and my only shoes were coming apart, worn out from marching in the sun and rain and standing in the mud.

"The way to get another pair of shoes was to ask the supervisor. She agreed that I needed shoes, so she told me we would go to the "shoe place" the following day. In the morning she took us, about four or five girls, to the other end of the camp, where she showed us this mountain of shoes. Some of these shoes had been brought by the new arrivals on their feet and in their baggage. Here, too, were the shoes of those who died in the gas chambers and of those who were sent away, to wherever...

"The shoes were gathered into one pile. There were also piles of dresses, of eyeglasses, of suitcases, of anything that could still be used. Prisoners were assigned to sort through everything. Those sorting the shoes were lucky, because they could choose the best for themselves.

"The shoes were paired only by size. Neither the style, nor the color or the height of the heels mattered. When the sorters found a right shoe and a left shoe of the same size, they tied the shoes together to form a pair.

"So there, from that big heap, I picked a pair of shoes in my size, one brown and the other black. They fit me, they seemed sturdy enough and I was quite satisfied. We had become used to wearing unmatched pairs of shoes. Few prisoners had a real pair.

"The following morning, as usual, we marched for hours to get to work, five girls in a row, hundreds before me and hundreds behind. I was looking down at the marching legs -- and what did I see, far ahead of me, but the shoe matching my brown shoe. I got so excited, I could hardly wait for the end of the march. When we broke up after roll call, I went to find the owner of my other brown shoe. At first I lost her; it was not easy to find one certain shoe among thousands of feet -- but eventually I did find it. I asked the girl to give me her brown shoe in exchange for my black one. But she also wanted a matched pair of brown shoes and said that I should give her mine.

"Every morning after the roll call we argued -- "You give me the brown shoe." "No, *you* give it to *me*" -- to no avail. This went on for some time. Then I didn't see her for a while and didn't know what had happened to her.

"A week or so later, another girl brought me the brown shoe. The owner of the shoe, sick in the hospital, believing she might never get out of there alive, decided to send me the shoe, so at least I could have a real pair."

I looked at Sharon. She had stopped writing and had tears in her eyes. Then she asked, "Can you tell me another story?"

But her father had come home and there was no more time for stories.

March 17, 1984

Yortzo

A few years ago I had an accident. I was working at Metropolitan Hospital in New York at the time, and on my lunch hour I drove over to Flower Fifth Avenue Hospital where I once worked to pick up some material for a paper I was writing on profoundly retarded children.

I parked across from the hospital and went in. When I came out a few minutes later and started back across the street to my car, I was hit by a speeding bicycle coming the wrong way. I don't know what happened next. I opened my eyes. I was in a daze. I saw a policeman bent over me and a few people standing around. I was bleeding from my mouth, my face and my hands hurt. I looked around and saw my papers scattered on the pavement. I heard the siren of an approaching ambulance. I wound up back in Metropolitan Hospital for two days with a concussion and facial lacerations. I spent hours in X-ray and surgery. I had a headache, I felt nauseous, I was restless, I moaned and groaned and couldn't get comfortable. I felt I was suffocating, I couldn't breathe. I had the urge to jump out the window to escape the air-conditioning and get some fresh air. I was sure I had something more serious than a concussion. Tzali and your uncle Yancu were with me all the time, worried. Finally, I came home and went straight to bed, still shaken.

Our wedding anniversary was two days away. To celebrate, we had bought tickets to the opera for the whole family. Your uncle Vali and his wife Debbie were coming from Massachusetts. I knew that no one would go without me so I said I felt well, and off we went to see *Boris Godunov*.

Actually, I felt pretty lousy, weak, tired, forlorn, ready to weep for any reason or for no reason at all. We went straight to our balcony seats. I glanced around at all the people seated in the rows in front of me. Suddenly, a striking red blouse caught my eye. Further ahead I saw yet another red blouse. Two red blouses! I was overcome. I started crying. I couldn't contain myself and covered my face with my hands. The family was alarmed. They couldn't understand what had happened. By now I was sobbing. How could they know that I was weeping for little Yortzo, the only baby in Tzali's family back in Sighet?

Yortzo, the son of Tzali's older sister Dori, was born in 1940. Dori had a disease in one eye causing her eyeball to bulge and her cornea to become opaque. Her father took her to well-known professors in Vienna, Budapest and Paris but no one could diagnose the problem or help her, so she had to wear thick glasses. Otherwise, she was quite pretty and very intelligent, and she loved to read and spent hours with books. No one could make better pastries or tortes than Dori, but she disdained mundane and routine work like cleaning the house or everyday cooking. She was moody and often restless.

She had been in love with Izzy, a bright, handsome young man, but after several years of courtship he left her and married someone else. Though Dori was devastated, her mother was pleased, because she thought Izzy's family was too poor for her daughter. A matchmaker was sought to find her a suitable husband. He arranged for Dori to marry Usher, who came from the nearby city of Satu-Mare. He was smart and he was good-looking, though he had a severe limp. Dori's dowry was a partnership in her mother's textile store, so after the wedding Usher went to work in the shop. It turned out later that he was unreliable and inefficient in running the business. Nor was he an affectionate or devoted husband. This contributed to Dori's frustration.

A year later Yortzo was born. Actually, "Yortzo" was a nickname. His real name was Samutzi -- "little Sam" -- after his late grandfather Samuel, but he was called Yortzo, no one remembers why.

When I was going out with Tzali I often heard about his charming little nephew and eventually I met him. Yortzo was a smiling, cute, talkative child. He was always very elegantly dressed. Dori liked nice clothes and the fabric store enabled her to dress Yortzo as she pleased. I particularly remember a snapshot in their family album, showing him in a dark velvet suit, playing in the park next to his mother.

As Tzali and I got more serious I visited his family more often. Little by little Yortzo and I got to know each other. One spring evening I was having dinner with them. I was wearing a short-sleeved embroidered blouse of a red-orange color. Yortzo, sitting next to me on a high chair, looked at my blouse and said, "Why aren't you wearing the red blouse?"

"But this is a red blouse, Yortzo," I answered.

"Not this one, the big red one!"

He was thinking of a wool blouse I had worn in winter. It was brighter red, with long gathered sleeves and a big collar.

"The big red one," Yortzo repeated.

Not long after that evening, part of the town was turned into a ghetto and all the Jews of Sighet were herded there by the Hungarian police. Tzali's family was assigned to the same street as my family, so now we were together even more. By then most of the men had long since been sent away to the forced labor units behind the front lines in the Ukraine. Tzali was still in jail. Dori's husband Usher had remained at home for a while because he was considered disabled, but by now he had been drafted too. Dori was more irritable and impatient with Yortzo than usual. Zsuzsi and I tried to help. We played with him, told him stories and took him for walks. He must have been four by then, and more charming than ever.

A few weeks later the ghetto was evacuated and we were all sent to Auschwitz on the same train -- in the same wagon, in fact. It was a cattle train. Sixty or seventy people were crammed into the car and the doors were sealed. We sat close to one another. In the corner was Dori's grandmother, old and sick, lying on suitcases. Close to her were Dori, her mother, and Yortzo, all huddled on the floor. Next to them, near the wall, was my family: my parents, my brothers Yancu and Moishi, and I. Near the middle, among so many others, were Tzali's sister Zsuzsi and her boyfriend Laichi, two teenagers desperately in love, holding on to each other for what they did not know would be their last few days together.

We were so crowded that not all of us could sit at the same time. There was no food and no water. No lights, no seats and no toilets, just a slop barrel. When the train arrived at a station, the German guards would unlock the door, and order some Jewish men to take out the full barrel and give us an empty one. Inhibitions had to yield to necessity.

The heat was stifling. The train was noisy, filled with the muffled sounds of human suffering. It smelled. Occasionally a breeze would come in through a latticed window so high up that we could not see outside nor could we even guess where we were. We just heard the clatter of the wheels on the tracks and the silence of the stops. I remember that we crossed a bridge and I thought, how good it would be if the train would turn over, and we could tumble in the cold water. What a relief this would be!

After two days of travel, some people still had some food left -- dry bread, rice, beans or potatoes -- but most had long since finished their reserves. I don't remember if I was hungry or thirsty because I was overwhelmed with other feelings, fear, sorrow, pain, sleeplessness. At night I watched people lie on the bare floor, rest their heads on someone's chest or legs and try to get some sleep despite the human noises: children crying, sick people suffering and moaning, and elders praying and wailing. My mother cried and grieved. She had a premonition. "They will kill us," she would say. Father tried to soothe her; he suffered in silence, holding her hands and occasionally stroking my forehead.

Yortzo was crying. He was hungry and thirsty but there was no water. At one stop we raised him to the little window and taught him to say in German, "*Bitte schon, ein bischen Wasser!*" -- "Please, give me a little water!" No one heard him. Who would have?

And yet, in retrospect, that almost seems a happy time, those last few days when we were all alive and could suffer together.

So I cried for Yortzo. How could I explain this to my children, that night of celebration at the glamorous Metropolitan Opera House in New York City? How could I tell them why just then a long-lost image from the past had crept into my heart and overwhelmed me. My children had rarely seen me cry before.

The opera was impressive. Mussorgsky's music had its majestic moments and its melodious folk songs and choruses. Boris Godunov cried out in terror, haunted by guilt, grieved by the poverty of his people. The young monk's lamentation was the most beautiful music I had heard in a long time.

We got home late that night. I was very tired and slept late. The next morning my department chairman woke me with a worried call.

"Dora, are you all right? Where were you last night?"

"At the opera."

"Are you crazy? I called the entire evening. I was so worried that I even called the hospital to see if you had been readmitted."

No, I was not readmitted to the hospital. I was with my family last night. And with little Yortzo.

November 16, 1984

Beatings

Every now and then I am asked, "Did you witness any beatings in Auschwitz? Were you ever beaten?"

Yes, I was hit and I was beaten, probably more times than I can remember, but only a few occasions have stuck in my mind, because of their special meaning or their unique circumstances. Why did I forget all the others? Perhaps because beatings were as common as any other torment inflicted upon us, so why remember them in particular?

The most cruel one occurred when we first arrived there. We were ordered out of our cattle car amid shouts and threats, *"Alle heraus! Alle heraus! Schneller!"* -- "All out! Faster!" The command came for women to form a separate column from the men. As we saw what was happening, we all embraced and wept while a mass of thousands of people swept us along in one direction. That was the last time I saw my father and my brothers Moishi and Yancu. Mother almost stumbled; she seemed to sense what was to happen and she was crying bitterly. With tears in my eyes, I held her up, I hugged her and kissed her and promised her, "Mother, we're still together -- we'll take care of each other."

Hundreds of women were coming from behind us, pushing us ahead with the moving crowd. Holding my mother's right arm with my left, I kept talking to her, caressing her. It was night. Lights were glaring in front of us. Somewhere I could see smoke and flames. SS officers were shouting and hitting. Their aides were screaming and pushing the crowd ahead. Dogs were barking and women and children were crying. Distant shots were heard.

We advanced swiftly towards a well-lit platform where a few officers seemed to be sorting out the women. As we got closer and closer to the officers, I realized that older women, mothers with little children and some of the young girls were all being sent to the left and only a few girls to the right. Instinctively, I felt I must look older if I was to remain with my mother. I pulled my kerchief over my forehead. I walked stooped and tried to limp. Could I fool them?

We arrived at the front of the crowd. I looked at the German officer who seemed to be in charge. I didn't know it then but later on I found out that he was the infamous Dr. Joseph Mengele. He made some sign, his fingers pointing toward Mother and toward the left. I went with her to the left, holding tight to her arm. Suddenly I felt a blow to my left wrist; an officer had hit me hard with his club. The pain was so intense that I let go of my mother's hand. She was grabbed by uniformed men and pulled to the left. I ran after her, but I was pushed back and dragged to the right. I looked back at my mother, who was standing there, bewildered and transfixed.

This is how she has appeared ever since in my dreams: this image became engraved in my memory -- a marble statue of anguish and despair.

Other girls were also sent to the right. We were pushed ahead into a path that ran between two rows of trees. I kept trying to see my mother, but I didn't see her again. Then I saw Zsuzsi coming towards me with tears in her eyes. She had just been separated from her mother, her grandmother, her sister Dori and little Yortzo. And behind her other girls were coming and still others. Lights were blinding us, officers were shouting orders, women, chased from behind, were running, falling and crying. And we were forced to march ahead.

I must have been in shock, because at that moment I no longer felt the pain in my wrist. But for days and days afterwards that pain reminded me of my attempt to stay with Mother and it felt good. I relived the scene in my mind again and again, I cherished that image in my heart and I was overcome with love for my dear mother. I would have taken so much more beating if I could have just stayed with her.

Another night *There*, another beating. As happened so often, we were awakened in the middle of the night for no apparent reason. Whistles were blowing. Floodlights were glaring. *Kapos* were screaming, "To the baths, to the baths!" *"Heraus, heraus!"* All of the girls in my barracks -- almost a thousand of us -- were driven out, herded together and marched toward the baths. Outside we saw women from other barracks being chased as well. Pandemonium seemed to have broken out. Blows were falling from every direction and we ran to escape them. Were we really going to the showers this time or were we being taken to the "shower room" of the crematorium? Because of the tortuous erratic paths along which the mob was driven at different times we couldn't even guess what direction we were going in, less so at night. And at that hour, did any of us really care? We were being hit and chased to go faster. As I ran, I suddenly felt a sharp pain on my shoulder. I had been struck with a club or a gas pipe and I almost collapsed under its weight. I put my hand on my right shoulder and felt a large, painful bump.

That night we indeed went to the showers. The hot water, followed one minute later by icy cold water, made my pain excruciating.

I remember a different kind of beating. It happened at the end of summer when we were working outside the camp, building a military hospital for SS officers. By then I had been separated from Zsuzsi, Hedi and my other friends. I don't know why, but I was put in charge of supervising a work crew of about ten girls. I must have been the oldest. On that particular day we were raking grass, leveling the ground in front of the building site, clearing a path. I knew that my job was to make my girls work hard and fast but when nobody was around I would tell them, "You can rest." Then, when I saw someone coming, I would shout, "You! Work now, faster, faster!" *"Schneller, schneller!"*

This went on for some time, until an officer unexpectedly came out of a nearby building. He must have been watching us from his window, for he was furious. He came straight to me and shouted that I didn't make my girls work, that this girl had been resting and that one had been sitting. He demanded that I teach them a lesson by hitting them. He screamed for me to slap the girl next to me and I became terrified. I raised my hand to slap her face, but it came down like a soft, gentle caress. The officer went mad, shouting, "What is that? Should I show you how to do it?" He took off his gloves, put them between his knees and started slapping me, first with one hand, then with the other, again and again. I staggered under the weight of the blows. "Now that you know how to do it, go ahead!" he ordered.

By then I didn't care what happened to me. I was no longer scared of him or of anything he could do to me, although he could have decided my fate with the simplest gesture. I didn't make a move. And for some reason he stopped and left. Perhaps he thought he had taught me a lesson. But I could not beat the girls.

There were many prisoners in Birkenau who quickly mastered this type of behavior for survival, who learned to administer the beatings for the Nazis and to impress their supervisors with their new-found cruelty. These prisoners were usually promoted to *Stubenalteste* (room leader) or to *Blockalteste* (barrack leader); and those with special penchant for brutality might even become *Kapos*. I have this recollection of two sisters who were starved and beaten like the rest of us when they first entered the camp. A few months later, as more Jewish transports were arriving from Hungary, I saw the older sister commanding a squad of prisoners. She was well fed and well dressed. Her younger sister was now in the first row of the formation and their mother was with them, too.

Can I accuse anyone, even now? I have thought about this a great deal and I still do. What makes a person break down? How does someone react under such extreme conditions? What would I have done if I had a younger sister or mother whose survival depended on me? But I was alone there; I had to care for no one but myself.

Months passed. It was late autumn, and very cold. We were dressed

Tell the Children

in layers of old, ragged clothes. To keep warm we had to obtain warm underwear or a jacket from those working at the crematoriums, and pay for them with our meager bread rations. Every one of us was infested with lice and had to be disinfected. When the time came we were taken to the delousing barracks and were told to make a bundle out of our clothes, throw the bundle into the disinfection chamber and then go to the shower room. We came out wet from the shower -- there were never any towels -- and waited. Finally, when the delousing was over, we were ordered to form a line. We waited for hours in the steam and heat to get back some clothes. There were hundreds of us. Each was given a bundle of clothes from the disinfection chamber. No one got her own clothes back. We just took whatever bundle we were handed.

I don't know how the incident started. I think I got the bundle belonging to a girl who was still waiting at the end of the line. Anyway, she recognized her clothes; she wanted them and snatched them. I shouted at her to stand in line and get another bundle, and then we would exchange them. She wouldn't wait. I tried to grab the bundle back. We started fighting. I don't remember who hit first, who won the fight, or who got the clothes. It really didn't matter. All I remember is that we fought fiercely, hitting each other in desperation, as if we were fighting for our lives.

And all for a bundle of lousy rags.

October 23, 1984

May 17th

Some days will stick with me forever. Every year when they approach I start remembering what happened and I become irritable and gloomy. After so many years they should not touch me so deeply any more. But they do.

May 17 is the most infamous of those days. It is my memorial day. Every year I light a candle for all those who perished that day. I call my two brothers in Brooklyn to remind them. They were not *There*, so they easily forget the exact date. All day long I am cranky, I don't know what to do with myself. I can't work, I am in a daze. Then at night I relive in my mind what happened *There* and *Then*.

Somehow in the past few years it's been different. I have greater difficulty recalling the events as they happened.

I remember May 17 one year ago. My mind reacted to the day, but not my heart. Yet when I went to bed I couldn't fall asleep. Instead I found myself thinking about the sequence of events: the journey in the freight car, arrival, quarantine, the different camps in Auschwitz. I wondered why all these memories left me cool, did not seem to move or affect me any more. Oh, well, I told myself, thirty-eight years have passed and it's time for wounds to heal. My mind drifted to the summer *There*, and the fall, and I thought of that younger girl who was my friend after Zsuzsi, Livi and Hedi were gone.

What was her name?

She was pretty and sweet and her hair had grown into beautiful, dark curls. She was so dependent on me...

What was her name?

I liked her so much. She came from the Hungarian city of Beregszaz and was completely alone. We slept together, we ate together, she would steal food ("organize") for both of us. She would have done anything just to stay close to me. She needed my support, my strength. I was like an older sister to her.

What was her name?

She stayed with me for weeks. Then she became ill with some kind of underarm infection and one day at a "selection" her gait was a little hesitant and she staggered slightly so they pulled her out. She cried, she ran back to me, but she was beaten and dragged away. She then disappeared into the crowd and I was devastated.

What was her name?

By now it was late at night. I tried so hard to remember her name. I was so upset, so frustrated, that I started crying bitterly because I couldn't remember her name.

Her name was Violet.

This was last year. This year the day was filled with trivial chores. As I drove back from work I was reviewing in my mind the patients I had seen that day, the papers I was working on and the students I had taught. I was aware that I was driving a beautiful new car. Around me I saw spring in full bloom, red and white azaleas, lilacs and dogwood trees scattered through the lush greenery of the woods. I turned on some music and tried to identify the piece -- I think it was one of Schumann's *Arabesques* played by the great Rudolf Serkin. I met Tzali at the shopping center to select a fabric for our new living room couch. When we got home, I didn't have time to cook so we had cold chicken, salad and fruit. My piano teacher came at eight -- I'm still trying.

In short, it was a nice, ordinary spring day in picturesque Westchester county.

But before going to bed I went again into the kitchen and saw the candle I had lit that morning, the seventeenth of May. I looked at it. I stared at it. Was the person who lit that memorial candle and spent the day at the hospital and buying upholstery, driving a car and enjoying the amenities of modern living, the same person who was *There* on May 17, 1944? Do these two entirely different worlds have anything in common? Do they connect? Did I live in both of them? Which one is real?

I went to bed disheartened yet I was able to sleep through the night. Driving to work this morning I thought about myself, about the way I was forty years ago on the morning of May 18, when I entered the camp -- after the grueling journey, after being separated from my family, after the night at the showers, after all the events I have not written about yet. I saw myself as I was *Then* -- all hair shaved off, dressed in a gray short-sleeved dress, men's boxer shorts and a man's sleeveless undershirt. From all that I had brought from home I was left only with the pair of sandals I had been wearing.

Let me tell you about these sandals, Miriam. While we were in the ghetto in Sighet my parents decided that I should keep some jewelry on me so that in an emergency I would have something valuable to trade. As a girl I was more vulnerable, and they felt this would help protect me in case of danger. So my parents bought me a pair of shoes with wide wooden heels and took them to the shoemaker. The shoemaker removed the heels and hid some of mother's chains, rings and earrings in the hollow centers before reattaching them.

Over the next three weeks the Hungarian gendarmes raided our home many times, each time taking more and more of our possessions. I became very self-conscious about wearing the shoes that contained all that was left of our modest "fortune". Finally we were herded into the freight cars for the journey to an unknown destination. During the three days of this journey, without food and water, lying on the floor or on the baggage, everybody tried to make themselves as comfortable as possible. I removed the heavy shoes and put on my younger brother Yancu's light, open sandals. When the train pulled into the Auschwitz station there was panic and confusion in the car and I forgot all about my precious shoes. They stayed behind in the car with the rest of our belongings. I was left wearing Yancu's sandals.

After I was separated from my mother, I was standing in line in the large hall to go to the showers, naked except for the sandals. An old-timer, a Polish prisoner working at the showers, passed me, saw the sandals and made a sign that she would like to exchange her good shoes for my sandals. At the time I didn't understand why she did it, but over the next few months I was so grateful to her for those sturdy, comfortable shoes she gave me.

When I left the showers early that morning and entered the camp it was very cold. I shivered, covered with goose bumps. Everyone around me had shaved heads. As I marched past a window I saw my reflection and thought I looked like Yancu, how funny! It started to drizzle and the drops of rain on my barren head felt so strange that I had to touch my head and feel the scalp.

I realized that only a few of the girls from our transport were there. I had no relatives among them, but Zsuzsi was with me. Her three cousins were also with us -- little Ilu, and two sisters, Hedi and Livi. Hedi had been a good friend of mine in Sighet. We decided to stick together. We were among the last ones to leave the shower building. Lined up five in a row, I heard the SS officer count our group and say, *"Vierhunderteinundzwanzig"* (four hundred and twenty-one). Only later on did I realize that this number was all that was left of the women in our transport of 3000 people, that the rest were already dead or dying, sent directly to the gas chambers, without ever entering the camp. (Later yet someone told me that of the men only about two hundred entered the camp that morning.)

I can still see it clearly: we start marching, five abreast, as ordered. A huge iron gate is opening for us. Above it is a corrugated inscription, *Arbeit Macht Frei* -- Work Makes You Free. We enter the camp. A band is playing marching music for us. We pass thousands of women, all of them dressed in layers of rags, jackets, shawls, some with kerchiefs on their heads. They are crying as they see us march by. Why are they crying? So far everything is so ridiculous, so eerie. Around us everything is gray: the sky, the air, the ground and the people. We see barracks and more barracks, hundreds of them. We see girls and more girls, by the thousands. Few are in sack-like gray uniforms like us. Fences and barbed wire surround the camp. I think, if this is the women's camp there must be a men's camp somewhere beyond those fences, and for that matter, an elders' camp where parents are and perhaps, some place out of sight, a camp for mothers and their children where conditions are a bit better. We are told this is Birkenau.

Occasionally I see female SS officers, stocky and beaming in their immaculate uniforms. Some have dogs. There are lots of supervisors in striped uniforms. They all scream at the prisoners. Some hit them, push them around. Not one tree can be seen, not one patch of green grass. And far in the distance there are some large brick buildings with high smoke stacks. Are they factories?

We are led to our barrack. This is Block 12, where we are going to live. Inside, all around, there are bunk beds like cages. Ten of us are assigned to one bunk bed, ten to the tier above. Each bunk is about the size of one large bed and has two blankets. We put our muddy shoes on the cement floor, under the bunks. We look around at one another and we smile, embarrassed. What is this? Are we going to live here? We don't understand anything.

As my mind returns *There*, I feel the shock of recognition. Yes, it was me. Yes, I feel the raindrops on my shaved head; I shiver in the cold morning wind; I feel the touch of the large wet shoes against my feet. The shoes have no laces. I have no stockings. I am aware that I am part of a huge crowd at the mercy of a few armed SS men. I wait for that bowl of warm soup to be passed around and watch with the others to make sure no one drinks more than her share. I breathe in the air, I smell strange odors. The sight of the gloomy surroundings adds to the fear, the panic, the impotence, the confinement.

The more I think about it, the more real it becomes and the more it causes me pain. Yes, it was me *There* and *Then*; and as I become that person again, my heart bleeds. I cannot contain my tears. How did I think that I could ever forget, that those wounds would ever heal?

May 18, 1984

A-7603

Sometimes when I have to fill out a form and write down my identifying features, I feel that I am absolutely average: not too short, not too tall; hair no longer auburn, but not yet gray, just average for my age; eyes green-gray; weight, not slim, not fat; even my skills and my talents seem average. Often, though, there is a question on the form, "Any identifying signs? Scars? Tattoos? Handicaps?"

Yes, I respond. I have something very unusual and highly personal -- a number tattooed on my left arm. A very special tattoo that some might find interesting or even intriguing; but those who know what it means find it disturbing and very upsetting.

I often think about the significance of having a number tattooed on my arm and why it was done *There* and *Then*. Not everybody had a number. Actually very few of the millions who arrived in Auschwitz were tattooed. Most of the people who survived the journey to Auschwitz never made it to the gates of the camp; they were taken from the trains straight to the gas chambers. As far as the Germans were concerned, they never existed, although the total number of the new arrivals was probably recorded on daily logs. Some were only kept in the camp until being sent to Germany to work in factories -- a few days or weeks, sometimes months. These prisoners were also not tattooed. Most of the thousands who vanished from the camp through "selections" also had no numbers.

Had any of these been killed by gassing, by disease and starvation, or by an Allied bombing, there would have been no documentation as to who they were or where they came from. The Germans could have said (and have sometimes said) that they never existed at all. But those who, like me, were tattooed, were at the same time registered alphabetically by name, city and country of origin. Perhaps some day I will be able to track down these logs and see for myself what they contain.

The numbers tattooed on our arms were checked daily during a long *Zahlappel* -- roll call. If any number was not found, the sirens went off and searches by guards were begun. But how could someone escape? Suppose a miracle happened and the gate opened or the barbed wire fence was cut or a board was placed over the ditch separating one part of the camp from the other. Suppose we could get out. Wearing our uniforms, with our heads shaved and with numbers tattooed on us, we would have been so easy to spot in no time. And who would have hidden us? Or fed us? Even imagining such an escape is utterly impossible. And yet the Nazis were afraid that someone would get out and tell the world.

So, rain or shine, wind or snow, the roll calls went on for hours and hours, until all the inmates were accounted for. And if someone with a tattoo was killed, a record was made of the death. In this way the Germans could say, "Just a few thousand Jews were sent to the concentration camps and all of them received a tattoo as proof that they were there. Many of them died of natural causes. Others were victims of the Allied bombings. But we never killed millions of Jews. Check our careful records, it's all there." Thousands were accounted for. Millions were not.

No one else in my family has a number. Very few of my friends have. But all those who were with me in the second camp, Weisswasser, had a number because, like me, they had been kept in Auschwitz until December 1944 when they were sent to the labor camp.

Naturally I knew my number by heart, in German: *A - sechsundsiebzignuldrei* -- A-7603. (A- was a new series the Nazis had started with the arrival of Jews in the Hungarian transports.) This is how I heard it day after day and this is how it entered my dreams, or rather my nightmares.

No one had a name *There*. You might as well not have had a face nor a body, just an arm with a number on it to show. Even today, if someone shows me a number close to mine I get excited and ask, "Were we *There* together? Did we arrive on the same night? Was our tattooing done by the same person, who wrote these ugly and uneven numbers?"

Sometimes I forget about my number. When I am with the family, colleagues, or friends I might not think about it. In Israel I am completely unaware of its existence. There I know no one would stare or comment or get excited about it; people might quietly and sympathetically acknowledge it as a part of their heritage, of their history, and this makes me feel much at home.

But if I am on a bus or subway in New York wearing a short-sleeved dress I may suddenly realize that people are staring at me, whispering to each other and pointing at my number in what they imagine is a discreet way. I become uncomfortable as I try to read in their reactions whether they know anything about the extermination camps, if the number means anything to them and if they are disturbed by it. I would never wear a short-sleeved dress in Germany. I would probably never go to Germany at all.

I remember my first few weeks in New York in 1964, when I was working as an intern at Jewish Memorial Hospital. There was another intern, a young Polish girl. Our summer uniforms had white jackets with short sleeves, and whenever she saw my number she got upset and said, "I hate seeing it." To please her, I put a Band-Aid over it; but since the two of us could never agree on anything else -- schedules, sharing the call room, covering patients -- we ended up not talking at all anyhow.

Even now, every morning I ask myself what kind of dress to wear. In warm weather I may be about to choose a light summer dress but then I remember that I will be lecturing to medical students and add a jacket. What if the students see the tattoo and stare at it? What if they whisper to each other and comment on it? What if they know something about the camps? I would rather avoid any of this: I want the students to pay attention to my lecture, not to my number. A few weeks ago I arrived at one of our hospitals to deliver a lecture, and suddenly remembered the tattoo. I became panicky when I couldn't find a lab coat to cover my arms. I promised myself to be more careful the next time. Why didn't I remember the Band-Aid?

Sometimes when a young child asks me what is on my arm, I say, "It's my telephone number, so I don't forget it." Your little cousin Gabriel points to the numbers and starts singing the alphabet song, "A-B-C-D-E-F-G" to "Twinkle, twinkle, little star." He even tries to wash it off with a wet finger. But if an older child asks, I venture to explain, "This is a number that was tattooed on me in a concentration camp during the war." Often such a child looks at me as if I had just come in from another planet and says, "Really? Are you kidding?"

Occasionally I feel like deliberately showing my number, explaining it, even lecturing about its history and mine. I did that when I met the accountant's little girl because I thought it would be special for her. She was so excited at meeting a "real survivor" that she wanted to tell her whole class about it. Why not? Another time I was visiting the Yad Vashem museum in Jerusalem when I saw a group of Dutch tourists surrounding a memorial obelisk in the garden that displayed hundreds of pictures of tattoos. I went over and showed them my number, I wanted them to see a "real one". I felt how much they appreciated it.

Miriam, do you see what I mean? The further and further I get from the time and place where it happened, the more "special" and "interesting" the tattoo seems to become. Suppose I reach a ripe old age of eighty or ninety or more; very few people with such tattoos will be left. Will anyone around remember what happened in the death camps during the years 1940-1945? Will anybody believe me? Or will they say I have become confused? But I will still carry on my left arm the proof of the shame of the century.

I was coming home from San Francisco after a short visit to see you. Tzali had taken an earlier flight so I was alone, concentrating on a book, quite oblivious to my surroundings. On my left, the aisle seat was empty. Once in a while I put my book down on that seat and did some writing on one of these letters to you, then returned to my book, the first volume of Proust's *Remembrance of Things Past*.

Across the aisle a young man seemed to be doing much the same thing, with a book in his hand and paper and pencil on his folding table. He must have been watching me for some time because when I looked up, he caught my eye, smiled and said, "I see you're reading Proust." We talked a bit about the book. "And you also write?" he asked. "What are you writing?"

"Well, I have to think about how to classify it," I told him, "but I write letters. I see you are also writing. What do you write?"

"I'm writing a journal and some poetry."

"That's very exciting! What do you write in the journal?"

"Everything that happens" he answered.

"Is everything interesting?"

"I don't know; it might be one day."

"What were you just writing?" I asked.

"A poem."

He showed it to me but I had a hard time understanding it. It had no rhyme, no cadence, no content, just a few disparate thoughts. I apologized, saying that I don't read much poetry in English. He returned to my writing and asked,

"And who do you write letters to?"

"To my granddaughter."

"How old is she?"

"Two."

He looked surprised but asked,

"Would you show me some?"

I said yes, but realized that I only had a draft of the one I was working on -- the one about little Yortzo. Even so, I felt like talking about it. I was pleased to find a sympathetic listener on a plane. I knew I wouldn't regret revealing my feelings. Confiding in strangers is usually safe because you will probably never meet them again. I didn't even know his name; he didn't know mine.

"First I have to explain what I'm writing about," I said. "I have to give you a little background information." He moved to the empty seat on my left. In five minutes I told him a little about my family, my experiences during the war, the camps, the meaning of *There* and *Then*, my tattoo, my coming to America, my children and of course you, Miriam. I explained that through my letters I would tell you and my other grandchildren what I wanted them to know about my family and my life. He seemed even more interested in the letter.

"You carry your letters with you?" he asked, concerned. "Suppose you lose your luggage. Suppose there is a fire or something happens to you. You should carry only copies," he said with authority. This was intriguing, because Silvia had said something very similar that very morning. The thought that my letters had become more important than me struck me as most flattering.

I started to read the letter about Yortzo, all the while explaining who everybody was and what ultimately happened to each person. He was very touched. He told me that he was so anxious to know about these things because, though his father was Irish, his mother was Jewish -- but they never talked about her family in Poland.

He looked up from the letter and said, "Can I ask you a favor?" I wondered what he wanted. "Could you show me your number. I've never seen one."

"Sure." I pulled up my sleeve. I showed him the tattoo. He looked at it in awe. He then took my hand and kissed it. He thanked me tenderly. He was so moved that his eyes were misting. Then he returned to his seat, watched the movie and listened to music. But later he came back to ask,

"Could you tell me what happened to gay people in the death camp?"

I couldn't, for I really didn't know. The Germans sent many people to the camps for reasons of so-called "immoral" or "criminal" behavior. Many of these people suffered the same fate as the other inmates. Some became instruments of the SS to beat and torture other prisoners. Indeed, most of the Kapos were not Jewish.

"And what if they were gay and Jewish?" he asked.

"I don't think the Nazis cared. To have been Jewish was deadly enough. They didn't need any other reason to kill them."

After landing, as we stood in line waiting for the door to open, he slipped me a piece of paper. It read, "I wish you the strength to tell your story of '*There* and *Then*' and also of 'Here and Now'".

Now that really sounded like poetry.

April 15, 1984

Tattooed

I recall vividly the day I was tattooed. I had been *There* for six weeks and everything still seemed unreal. I remember well the bleakness of those weeks; the dullness of our gray uniforms, of our shaved heads; the desolate landscape formed by the muddy earth and rows of gray barracks against the gray sky.

The five of us were still together. At twenty-two, I was the oldest. The four cousins, Hedi, Livi, Zsuzsi and Ilu, were all teenagers. Ilu, the youngest, was probably no more than thirteen or fourteen. We were still confused and disoriented, not really understanding where we were. None of us reacted very strongly to anything. We were numbed. Was it purely psychological? There was talk about the food containing a sedative; this might explain why so few women screamed or went mad.

We were still awakened in the middle of the night, long before the crack of dawn, by shrieks, sirens and barking dogs. We were still chased outside into the cold to line up in front of the barracks. Hungry, sleepy and dirty, we moved as if in a daze. It was very cold in those wee hours. Standing in formation for the *Zahlappel,* the roll call, we stood as close to each other as possible for as long as we could in order to keep warm. Hedi stood in front because she tolerated the cold best. Close behind her were her sister Livi, Ilu, and Zsuzsi. I covered the rear because I could take cold on my back better. We shivered. But when we caught sight of the *Kapo* we had to jump back quickly to maintain the proper distance between us.

The sky was still dark, the stars had not yet started to fade. Standing five in a row, we were counted and recounted time and again to make sure no one was missing. The count was then reported to the officers who made their rounds from one barrack to the other.

Roll call would last for hours. As we stood we could follow the changes in the sky as the stars slowly dimmed. The sky would become brighter in the East, gleaming rays spreading to give us light as the sun rose on the horizon -- such beautiful sunrises on this flat land with no hills or trees to obscure it. The sunlight would move closer to us until it finally would warm us. To this day I hate the dawn. I fear it and try to avoid it. If it catches me somewhere, in a train, in a plane, the memories and feelings of those endless roll calls creep slowly into my consciousness until I am overcome by pain.

When roll call was over and daylight had made the atmosphere less eerie, our lines could break up and we all rushed to the latrines and washrooms. No matter what, we could not use them earlier. While waiting our turn for one of the hundred or so latrine holes, we got a chance to meet and talk to girls from the other barracks. I found two cousins and some other friends from Sighet who had come to the camp in one of the other transports and lived in an adjoining barracks.

Then we had breakfast: some tepid, black fluid that they called coffee and our daily ration of dark bread, one square piece, an eighth of a brick-shaped loaf of bread, well-dried and sometimes moldy, enough for a few bites but not enough to relieve the hunger; occasionally a little margarine or fermented cheese.

Birkenau was organized into many sub-camps but there was no communication between us and prisoners in adjacent camps. We were in *lager* (camp) A, *Block* 12. Camp A was separated from the rest of the camps by ditches and a high-intensity electrified barbed-wire fence. The *haftlings* (prisoners) in Camp A were from all over Europe, speaking all kinds of languages. Only a few of the barracks housed girls from the new Hungarian transports.

We were still together with the other girls from the first transport from Sighet who made it into this camp. At first, none of us could figure out where other friends from Sighet could be. Where was Gitta? Where was Renee? Where were Aunt Pearl's five daughters, my cousins, who were between sixteen and twenty-four? Why didn't they get in with us?

We stayed in Camp A for six weeks. This was a transition camp for the new arrivals, so we didn't work. Day after day we waited for something to happen, for some decision to be made. We thought that eventually we had to move on to work in Camp B, Camp C or in a factory, if for no other reason than to make room for the other women arriving by the hundreds every day, mostly from Hungary. Though we were aware of the chimneys, the smoke and the flames, their meaning had not yet penetrated our consciousness. Nevertheless, "selection" was the word most feared by everyone. It always spelled doom.

The five of us, along with five other girls, lived, sat and slept in one *koya*, the bunk bed made of a wooden plank surrounded by brick walls on the sides and at the back. Lying down I could just reach the opposite wall with my toes. And when I sat up my head touched the plank above, where ten other girls slept. I remember one day Hedi and I were lying on our backs -- a luxury we could enjoy only because the other girls were all sitting up -- and we tried to touch the plank above with our feet. We joked about our legs being muscular and strong compared with the younger girls' skinny legs, though hardly shapely.

Since Hedi and I were older, stronger and more mature, we tried to support the others as best we could. Livi and Zsuzsi, who were both slender and immature, clung to us. Ilu, the youngest, was skinny, frail, frightened and forlorn. Since being separated from her family she felt completely lost. We feared most for her: she might not be able to tolerate the harsh conditions. Perhaps this was the purpose of those weeks in quarantine -- to see who could survive and who could not.

Our barrack housed almost a thousand girls. With such overcrowding if someone developed a contagious disease it would spread immediately from one girl to the others in her koya and from one koya to the next, until all girls in the barrack were ill. It might even spread to the guards. Fear of disease and lice so obsessed the guards that they had prisoners cleaning all day long, mopping the floor and spreading disinfectant. The smell of chlorine was stronger than that of the unwashed bodies or even the latrines. This dread of disease was also one reason why our hair was shaved on arrival.

There were about thirty such barracks in Camp A, quite close to one another. If a disease spread -- and scabies often did -- the guards did not hesitate to isolate the infested girls in a "scabies *block*" and to send the girls from that barrack and the adjoining ones to the gas chambers. Rumors went, they would then set those barracks on fire.

We soon learned that "selections" would take place to weed out those girls who could not endure on the starvation diet, could or would not eat the horrible, tasteless food or became sickly. Many formerly healthy, even fat girls, soon became emaciated, walking skeletons with wasted bodies, hollow cheeks and frightened, dazed looks. They were called *mussulmen*, a camp slang we learned from the Polish and Slovak girls, the old-timers. Just seeing one of these girls one already knew what their fate would be.

When a "selection" was announced, usually at the showers, we had to march naked in front of a few SS officers, who easily picked out those girls whose bones stuck out through their skin, those with sores and those who were utterly pale. Some girls tried pinching their cheeks but this didn't make them look healthier. Most of us were quiet, resigned to whatever would happen; but when sisters were separated during a "selection", it was heartbreaking to hear their cries of desperation, to see the beatings that followed to forcibly separate them from one another.

Toward the end of six weeks our time came. We were chased out of the block amid shouts of an upcoming "selection". There, behind the barrack, we had to march, this time dressed, in rows of five before a group of SS officers. We kept straight and tall, but they seemed to be looking at our legs. Were they looking for the strongest? There was always something so arbitrary in these "selections", except when they singled out someone who was obviously sick or emaciated.

A gloved hand pointed to me and to Hedi. It was the same hand that had separated me from my mother: Mengele's hand. We were pulled aside to the right while Zsuzsi, Livi and Ilu continued marching, too scared to react. Girls were pulled out of almost every row, separated from each other just as we had been separated from our friends or family. Some were relatives or sisters. Most on both sides were crying or screaming. Hedi was devastated. I don't know how Zsuzsi, Livi and Ilu felt; they just marched ahead and disappeared into the crowd.

And it was over. Our group was gathered and taken to the baths, which were in the Brzezinka building -- the same building as the crematorium. We thought we were doomed. But, no, not this time, for when we entered the large hall there were people waiting for us at tables. The guards called us out in alphabetical order and to our amazement we were registered for the first time since we arrived -- by name, age and country of origin.

Then we were tattooed.

I was among the first ones because my name began with the letter A. I got a number on my arm: A-7603. Did it hurt? Well, it was a pretty bloody procedure, but that did not matter, for what was a little physical pain compared with the anguish, fear and horror? Hedi's turn had not come yet: she was letter S. After a short while, those of us who had been tattooed were led to the shower, got back our same gray uniforms, and were sent back to Camp A -- but this time to Block 31.

It was already night when I entered an almost empty wing of the barrack. I could take any *koya* I wanted, so I took an upper one -- they were always better, with more space overhead and near the windows. From the window I could see the crematorium. I waited and waited for Hedi to come; she was now the only friend left with me. Another group returned from the showers and yet another, until the *koyas* were filled; but Hedi was nowhere in sight. I cried in my loneliness until I fell asleep, exhausted. My sleep was brief: sirens and shouts woke me up soon. Again we were chased out into the dark and lined up for roll call. Now I had become a number to be checked and rechecked. Hedi was not there and I could not understand why.

When our lines broke up a few hours later, we rushed to the lavatories and latrines. As usual, thousands of girls were there. I was now desperate to find Hedi, but instead I saw Zsuzsi and Livi in the crowd. They had been given other clothes, some civilian rags, and had been moved to another barrack. Suddenly, behind them, I saw Hedi. Only when I saw her civilian clothes, did I realize that she was back with Zsuzsi and Livi.

She told me what had happened. As she waited for her turn to be tattooed, our ration of food was sent over from Barrack 12. Several girl prisoners carried the food barrels under the supervision of an SS guard. One of the girls was in tears because she had been separated from her sister, who was waiting in line to be tattooed. She and Hedi were able to exchange places, which was relatively easy to do since neither of them had a number to identify them. Hedi returned with the empty barrels to the other girls.

Hedi was greatly relieved to be back with her sister and Zsuzsi and hoped to remain with them. But what had happened to Ilu? Where was she? No one knew. They just told me that there had been a second "selection" that same evening and Ilu had been taken away.

So now I was alone. It is strange how lonesome one can be in spite of sleeping with ten girls in the same *koya* and sharing a barrack with hundreds of others. Most did not speak my language, they were from other transports and from other countries. And there was no one there I cared for, no relatives, no friends, no one I had grown so close to during those six weeks. If only I had a sister or a cousin with me -- I needed someone so much.

I was happy for Hedi though. We continued to look for each other in the washroom every morning after roll call. Neither of us broached the subject of who would go where from here or who was the luckier. Who could know that anyway?

Then one morning about two weeks later the girls did not show up at the lavatory. Their barrack was empty. My heart sank. I didn't know what had happened. All of them just disappeared, and my loneliness was nothing compared to my conviction that they had been taken to the gas chambers.

I still thought so when I returned to Sighet a year later. Gently I tried to tell Tzali and his brother Bela that their sister Zsuzsi and her cousins had been selected for death. But I was wrong. They had been sent to another camp in Germany. In fact, while I was being liberated on the East by the advancing Red Army, hundreds of other concentration camps were being liberated on the West by the American and English armies; but it took many months for the first survivor from those camps to reach Sighet and tell us that Zsuzsi, Hedi and Livi were all alive. They had been in Bergen-Belsen and after liberation the Red Cross had sent them to Sweden to recuperate.

As I write this letter, the fortieth anniversary of the liberation of Bergen-Belsen is being remembered and celebrated. Harrowing pictures and documentaries are being shown all over. At the end of the war, as Russian forces advanced into Eastern Europe, the Nazis herded together hundreds of thousands of prisoners from the camps in the occupied territories -- those they didn't have time to murder -- and forced them to march West to camps on German territory, like Bergen-Belsen. During these "death marches" more than half of the prisoners dropped dead from hunger, cold and exhaustion. Many were shot because they couldn't keep up.

Those who reached Bergen-Belsen found little food or water. Everywhere in the camp people were dying of starvation. The additional crowding caused infectious diseases to spread rapidly. Corpses piled up, decaying, with no one to bury them. When the British Army, and later the Americans entered the camp they were stunned and appalled. The stories they recounted and the pictures they sent home were horrifying. In one week twenty thousand corpses had to be buried in mass graves; the Allies forced the former SS guards to do the disagreeable, dirty work of burying the already disintegrating bodies. Zsuzsi still will not talk about those days.

And now, forty years later, those British and Americans still remember. One journalist wrote that on the first day of liberation the surviving prisoners were dying of joy, but on the second day they were dying from extreme weakness. When the Americans gave them chocolates or canned food many died of diarrhea. Those with typhus were so weakened they could barely crawl. Many went mad. With every day of liberation, the death toll climbed.

From Birkenau Zsuzsi and the other girls were taken to Hamburg, where they worked in the shipyard. Quite a few girls from Sighet were sent there. The port was a strategic target. It was bombed often and many prisoners were killed because no one would let them into the shelters. Toward the end of the war they were among those marched to Bergen-Belsen. There Zsuzsi and Hedi contracted typhus, and it was Livi who cared for them and managed to bring them some food. One of their good friends, Magdush, died of typhus a few days after liberation. The Red Cross came to their aid and Sweden offered to take a few thousand survivors to help them recover.

Yesterday on the telephone Zsuzsi, who now lives in Hawaii, told us that Hedi called from Sweden to congratulate her on the fortieth anniversary of their liberation. She tried to remind Zsuzsi of the events that happened there, but Zsuzsi insists that she remembers nothing about Bergen-Belsen. I know how difficult it is for her and that she does not want to remember.

Out of the five of us who entered camp on the morning of May 18 and tried to stay together, only I remained in Auschwitz so long. After the other girls disappeared, I found out that Ilu had been put in a special scabies barrack together with other very young, fragile girls and older girls infested with scabies. I managed to see her a few times. She was so wretched, so helpless, so miserable. I don't think I ever saw her smile. Then one night all the girls in the scabies barrack vanished. The barrack was not burned down, as some old-timers had suggested; but there was no question as to where the girls had been taken. Today I realize that Ilu's continued presence in camp, as sickly as she was, should have indicated to me that Zsuzsi and the others had not been sent to death. But who could draw such rational conclusions *Then*, in July 1944?

I remained in Auschwitz. Hundreds of other groups of girls left camp, but all of us who had tattoos were condemned to remain *There* to work almost as long as the camp itself lasted -- through that summer and autumn and into the final winter of the war.

April 20, 1985

Hedi

Tzali's cousin Hedi is visiting us from Sweden. I'm busy at my office so Tzali is taking her sightseeing in Manhattan. He's also trying to get her interested in helping him paint the house, fix the floor and buy a new car.

Hedi wants to see more of me. She wants to talk. So in the evenings we go for long walks just as we used to do in Sighet before the war. We were very good friends, part of the same crowd, and went hiking and skiing together. We were also together *There* and *Then* for the first six weeks and we talk about that time, too. She's writing a book about her experiences and she wants to refresh her memory.

I like talking to Hedi. We seem to have similar emotions and reactions to past events, even if we each remember them in slightly different ways. I am still amazed by the range of feelings that memories of those times can evoke in the survivors: from denial and rejection to pain, sadness, grief and resignation; to resentment, bitterness and anger. I know people who have refused to face the past, others who have grieved for a lifetime, and still others whose deep-seated anger and resentment embittered their present lives.

Sunday afternoon we sat in the den and talked for a long time. Hedi had many questions; so did I. I was pretty sure that no one could have smuggled anything into camp at Birkenau. After all, the night we arrived we entered the showers naked and were given uniforms to wear before entering the camp. Yet Hedi told me her sister Livi smuggled in a toothbrush.

"How was that possible?" I asked. "Nobody had a toothbrush *There* and nobody brought in anything. Didn't we all have to turn over whatever we still had left of our possessions to the SS?"

"Watches, chains and earrings, yes," said Hedi. "I even had to turn over the metal ring I received from my boyfriend Puiu; and it was as dear to me as a diamond engagement ring. But Livi was able to keep her toothbrush by holding it tightly in her hand so nobody noticed it."

Hedi wonders whether we were given two pieces of clothes to wear or three. I think there were three: a dress, an undershirt and underpants. Hedi remembers only two.

"Did the dress they gave us have a pocket?" I asked.

"I don't think so."

"Then where did we keep the piece of soap we got once in a while? We had to save it for several showers. Or where did I keep the handkerchief my cousin Serena sent me from Brzezinka that had so many uses?"

We must have had pockets.

I told Hedi that there were 421 girls in our group as we entered camp. She couldn't understand how I knew the exact number until I reminded her that we were in the last row of girls leaving the baths and I saw the SS officer counting the girls and heard him say, "*Vierhunderteinundzwanzig.*"

Hedi thinks we each ate off separate plates. I remember differently -- one bowl for the five of us.

"Don't you remember, Hedi, that we had no spoons, and as we passed the bowl we counted the gulps each girl took. One bowl had enough for five or six mouthfuls for each girl and if any was left we had to figure out a way to divide it."

While we sat and talked in the den, Tzali was painting the living room. The heavy odor of the fresh paint crept into the den until Hedi cried out, "Open the door, I can't take the smell. I'm suffocating." We opened the door, and she went upstairs to take a nap.

I continued to browse through the Sunday *New York Times*. In the Book Review section I read a review of an amusing detective story. The reviewer described part of the plot: someone has been kidnaped and the ransom note lists instructions for making the payment: "Go to the supermarket, take a cart, buy a steak and some vegetables, put the money under the steak and leave it in the cart at a certain spot in the parking lot". The lot is now surrounded by policemen disguised as shoppers who watch the cart and wait impatiently for the kidnapper to approach it. Suddenly a dog appears from nowhere, jumps into the cart, picks up the steak, and the money flies all over the place in full view of the startled policemen. And where was the kidnapper? I laughed out loud.

In the Travel section a familiar name caught my attention. Elie Wiesel, the famous Jewish writer from Sighet, had written an article about our hometown, "Pilgrimage to Sighet, a Haunted City". It was beautifully written. He describes the city, its picturesque mountain setting, and the peasants whose way of life has not changed for centuries. He contrasts the Sighet of today with the town he remembers from before the war, when thousands of Jews lived there. When he goes back to visit, he is haunted by their ghosts: every street corner reminds him of friends, family, neighbors. I enjoyed the article, but the last paragraph disturbed me deeply. He writes that some Jews could have escaped, that "the ghetto was not very well guarded", and we could have "fled, hidden in the mountains or in the villages". Wiesel concludes that what hurt him most was that this tragedy "could have been prevented".

Later that day I had an intense discussion about this with Hedi and

Tzali. Could over ten thousand people have escaped, could they have run away? Where? Who would have hidden them? How could the tragedy have been prevented? Hedi, who got married after the war (but not to Puiu; he never returned), told us how her late husband, who was 30 in 1944, had run away to the mountains with a few friends. The peasants, rather than give them refuge, turned them in to the police, who brought them back to the ghetto. He felt that being sent back to the ghetto instead of being jailed was a bad omen: if the ghetto was punishment enough, it must mean that all of the Jews in the ghetto were destined to suffer a terrible fate. He was right.

That night I had a strange dream. I was with Hedi. We arrived *There* and were stepping down from the train, many, many of us. We were told to leave everything in the cattle cars and just walk into the long, dark corridor. Hedi stopped to buy a steak, had it wrapped in plastic and tied with a string, and she held it very tight, close to her body, so no one would see it and take it away. Slowly we walked toward the long and dark corridor. I was near the rear of the crowd. Hedi was still outside.

In the corridor there was fog coming towards me. Was it gas? It was engulfing me. I became dizzy, I was suffocating. I knew I was going to die, but I wanted at least to be with Hedi, to cling to her and to hold her hand. I called out to her but no sound came out of my throat. I sat down on the floor, leaning against the wall. I became more and more sleepy and drowsy but quite resigned.

I woke up in a sweat. I hadn't had a nightmare for a very long time.

October 14, 1984

The Weberei

I am on my way to visit you. I wish I could be with you more often, but it isn't so easy to make these trips from one coast to the other. Fortunately you're too young to know that I am a few days late for your first birthday. I'm bringing you that special doll I've been searching for, to make up for all the dolls neither Silvia nor I ever had.

Let me tell you about something I was reminded of yesterday. I was making my weekly rounds at a nursing home near the hospital. The home has a large activity room where the elderly people work on crafts -- weaving, knitting, crocheting, carpentry. The room is cheerful and bright. The window sills are lined with toys they've made and large balls of the twisted and braided yarns that they use.

When I saw those large balls on the window sills, I couldn't help remembering a time when I was a inmate in Auschwitz and I was working in the *Weberei* -- the weaving workshop. It was early fall, and I was still in Camp B. This work seemed easier than some other I had done, and I was glad to be working with a roof over my head. We, too, sat at workbenches, but it was far from cheerful, in a dimly-lit, cold, wooden barrack. We had to cut dirty, ragged old clothes that were left in bundles on the tables into narrow strips and tie the strips end to end like a kite tail. When there were piles of rag strips on the floor, we had to braid them, adding one strip of cellophane or plastic to two strips of rag. Then we wound the cords into a ball, larger and larger. By the end of the work day the ball was as big as a giant pumpkin. Each ball was placed on a table and the tattoo number of the prisoner who rolled it was written on a piece of paper and pinned to it. To this day I have no idea what the chords were used for. At the time we thought that they might serve as fuses for explosives. Who knows?

This cutting, shredding and braiding left so much dust, lint and scraps on the floor that the prisoner assigned to supervise had a difficult time cleaning it all up. One day she told me to help her sweep and clean. In return she promised to give me larger rags that could more easily be cut into long strips. That way I could make a big ball in an hour or two, and still reach my daily work quota.

And so we did. I would help her clean up the Weberei and in the afternoon she would give me a blanket or towels; in no time I would have it cut, braided and wound. In my fervor, though, I began to forget to make each ball as large as possible.

One day some SS officers came to our workshop. They went straight to the table with the balls, picked up the smallest ones, read the numbers and called for the prisoners with those numbers. I was one of five girls who evidently couldn't do the required amount of work. We were judged to be lazy or weak and we were pulled out.

We had to wait near the entrance of the Weberei while the SS officers gathered enough girls from the other workshops to fill a truck. We knew of only one destination we could be sent to.

But I am still here, as you see. I ran away. I know you, children, like to hear that. Don't you always ask me, "Why didn't you run away?" It was not that simple. I'll tell you some other time how a Polish girl helped me and how the SS officers returning to the barrack simply forgot about me. When I think of how my life hung by a thread!

August 17, 1983

Mother's Day

Yesterday was Mother's Day, the day when children and grandchildren are supposed to call, send flowers, buy presents, or select the perfect card to delight their mothers and grandmothers. For weeks, ads on radio, TV and in magazines suggest Mother's Day gifts guaranteed to convey all those intended precious sentiments.

This year as usual I told myself that I don't care for this commercialism. I have my birthday, which is always remembered by everyone I love, and that should be enough. But although I didn't expect much to happen, I ended up having quite a busy Mother's Day, and a surprising one after all.

At noon Tzali and I drove to Manhattan. Tomorrow is my friend Donald's birthday -- he is the one who helped me and encouraged me to write -- and I had a small gift for him that our mutual friend Patricia would take over. It was a pleasant spring day. Patricia came downstairs from her apartment and we stood outside, near Central Park, and chatted. Patricia is an illustrator and she made an exquisite drawing for me on the fortieth anniversary of my liberation last week. I keep it on my desk at the hospital. Everyone admires it and tries to interpret it. In fact, it is based on a recurrent dream I had when I was in the camp: in my dream I arrive back in Sighet, go straight to our home, walk into the narrow arcade and look up towards the entrance to our apartment. I see signs of life there; and I realize that at least someone in my large family is alive and waiting for me. I am extremely relieved.

The picture, in black and white, shows a two story building behind a massive arcade at the end of a cobblestone courtyard. On the second floor, one window stands out: it is open, and radiant, yellow light pours out. This is the only color in the picture, the "sign of life" in my recurrent dream.

When we came home the telephone rang. It was Zsuzsi, calling from Hawaii. She is very thoughtful, she never fails to remember special occasions.

Zsuzsi always had a difficult time dealing with the past. For a long time she refused to talk about any part of it -- not only about her camp experience but about anything related to Sighet, her mother, her sister Dori or little Yortzo. Anyone who reminded her or asked questions evoked a very painful reaction. Nevertheless, after the *Holocaust* series was shown on television, and someone realized that she was a survivor -- the only one in Honolulu -- Zsuzsi was interviewed, and an article with her picture appeared in the local newspaper. Afterwards Zsuzsi was invited to join a panel discussion on a radio talk show. She attempted to respond to all the questions until a German accented voice asked, "Would Mrs. T. tell me what is the difference between the German concentration camps and the American detention camps for the Japanese." This upset her so much that for days she would not even answer the telephone. Since then Pista, her husband, has tried to shield her from any reference to the war years.

But Zsuzsi is coming around. She has unexpectedly started to show interest in her past. Yesterday, when she called to wish me a happy Mother's Day, she began asking me some questions.

"Dori," she asked, "when did we arrive at Auschwitz? On May 18th?"

"No, on May 17th."

"How is that possible? Did we travel only one day?"

"No, we traveled three days. We left Sighet on May 15th."

"Please, tell me about the journey, about my family, about your family. Do you remember anything?"

"Zsuzsi, I have written nearly all I remember in a letter about Yortzo. Do you want me to read a few paragraphs to you?"

"Yes."

I started reading about Yortzo and the red blouse. Zsuzsi interrupted. "Dori, I remember your red blouse."

Then I read to her about Laichi.

"Oh, Laichi! We were in the same cattle car. I remember how we held onto each other tightly during the whole journey. I can't forgive myself for spending so much of those last few days with him and not with my mother."

"Aren't all children this way?" I said. "You were young and in love. Did you or anyone have the slightest idea where we were going or what would really befall us when we got there?"

I read to her about passing the bridge.

"Yes, the bridge... it all comes back to me... and little Yortzo begging for water. Did you know that I kept a piece of chocolate hidden for him, for when we got off the train? During those days on the train I squeezed him so hard so he wouldn't cry. Now, please, what happened when the train stopped?"

"It was late in the evening. First the train stopped at a station. Some people climbing on suitcases could read a name -- "Auschwitz." We'd never heard that name before. Then the train moved again, very slowly, changed tracks, and came to a halt again after a few minutes. There was no station where we stopped, but there were noises and lights in the distance. This must have been Birkenau."

"What happened then? Who were the men in striped uniforms? Who was screaming? Where did the glaring lights come from? How did we get down?"

"The people in the uniforms were probably old-timers -- Polish or Slovak prisoners. Some spoke to us in German, others in Yiddish. They opened the doors wide and shouted at us to get down from the cattle car. Then they pulled us down to the platform."

"Was Mengele there? Was he that young officer who made signs with his hand?"

"Yes, that was Mengele!"

"Dori, do you think he was always there?"

"No, he wasn't. I learned later that when the second transport from our town arrived, Mengele wasn't there and the selection was much less severe. Many of the younger mothers got into the camp with their daughters. Very few of ours did. Ours was one of the most brutal selections among the transports from Hungary. So many healthy and young people who came on our train didn't even get into the camp."

"On the platform, Dori, did you kiss your mother goodbye?"

"Yes, I kissed her, but I didn't know it was goodbye. When the men were separated from us we hugged and kissed and cried."

"I didn't kiss my mother and I still feel guilty about it. I missed her so much. I remember her always dressed in black. I don't think she ever smiled or laughed. For a long time I thought she was angry at me but now I know how overwhelmed she was when she became a widow, how she suffered. What happened after you were separated from your mother?"

"I was pushed ahead by the others coming behind me."

"Did you see your mother after you left her?"

"I saw her for an instant. She looked petrified, as if she was turned into stone. Then you and the other girls came."

"Was I crying?"

"Yes, Zsuzsi, you had tears in your eyes, I saw them."

"And then, please... "

"We were gathered into a large hall that led to the showers. The few hundred of us were all that was left of the women and children."

"What was the hall like?"

"It was brightly lit. We stood in a long line along the walls and had to take off all our clothes and put them in a big pile in the middle of the room. We spent the entire night naked, waiting to take a shower."

"And then?"

"We were shaved all over before they let us take a short shower. With our shoes on we had to step in some disinfectant, then each of us was given a gray dress and some underwear. As soon as we put them on our wet skins, we were chased out through another exit into the cold morning air."

"Was there a gate into the camp?"

"Yes. We marched a little until we reached a gate on top of which were wrought-iron letters spelling "*Arbeit Macht Frei.*" The gate opened. We went in. Thousands of women were standing on the sides of the road, in formation for roll call. We passed between them. There was a band playing some music. Some women were looking at us and weeping. They were dressed in rags. It was so cold. We had on only thin, short-sleeved dresses; nothing covered our shaven heads."

"And... ?"

"We were taken toward some barrack. I think ours was number twelve. Inside it looked like there were cages on three levels. We were shown to a cage on the middle level -- it was to be our bunk bed, our *koya.*"

"How many girls slept in one *koya*?"

"Then, I think about ten. But whenever more girls arrived we had to squeeze together to fit in two to four others.

"Yes, I remember. At night we had to lie in two opposite rows like sardines. How did we ever manage to sleep? Do you remember, Dori, how we all had to turn at the same time? Only Hedi wouldn't turn with us."

"She wanted to sleep on her back. Can you blame her?"

"And how was it in the mornings?" Zsuzsi asked.

"We had to line up, five in a row. All of us stayed together."

"You, me, Hedi, Livi... and who was the fifth, Dori? Was it my friend Magdush?"

"No, Zsuzsi, it was Ilu."

"Who was Ilu?"

"Your cousin. Don't you remember your Aunt Fridush's daughter?"

"Oh, my, I completely forgot about her. How could I?"

"Everyone forgets, Zsuzsi. It was so long ago, more than forty years. Maybe you didn't want to remember those times so they retreated deep into your memory to where your mind couldn't reach them."

"Now that you speak of Ilu, my memories of her are returning. She was so young and frail. What happened to her?"

"The same thing that happened to all the frail, young girls."

"You stayed in Birkenau for such a long time. How did you resist, Dori? I never asked you what happened to you after we were separated and I was sent away from there to Germany. I'm so ashamed."

"Don't be, Zsuzsi. I never asked you what happened to you either. My own experience was enough. For such a very long time I couldn't take knowing more. Probably none of us wanted to know more. We could hardly cope with what we knew."

"I heard there was a program on TV about Bergen-Belsen. I'm so sorry I missed it. It might have helped me remember what happened to me while I was there."

"It wasn't for you. The scenes were too gruesome."

"But I want to see it. Someone I know taped it and will show it to me. Livi called me from Stockholm on the anniversary of our liberation from Bergen-Belsen. I recall so little of the last days before our liberation."

"But you were sick with typhus. How could you remember?"

"I'd like to visit Livi and talk about those days. And I also want to make a visit to Sighet. I think I could take it now."

It was good to see her so interested. Zsuzsi is part of our inner family, as close to us as our children, and even more interested in everything that happens to us. I have known her since she was 12, much before Tzali and I started going together. Naturally she was most excited about this turn of events. For me she still is my little sister, as she was in the camp. Tzali is her "wise brother" whom she calls whenever in need.

Later in the afternoon, Miriam, you and your mother called to wish me a happy Mother's Day. I asked Silvia how she was and how was the baby she is carrying. I knew that she had found out what the baby was but did not want to tell us.

"The baby is talking to me," she joked.

"What is he or she saying?" I asked.

"*She* is saying," Silvia said slowly, "that... "

"Bravo, so it is a girl! We thought so."

"Why?" Silvia asked.

"Because you seemed upset when you found out. You probably wanted a boy."

"No, Mama, I wasn't upset about that. It was the whole idea of knowing ahead of time, of taking away the mystery, that bothered me. This is why I did not want to know the sex of the baby when I carried Miriam. But I am really happy of having two girls."

"Silvia," I said, "girls are better for mothers. They will call you for sure on Mother's Day."

But I spoke too hastily, for very soon Yancu called. He always calls, even if it is midnight when he remembers. He is so busy with his computer work these days, and on top of this he had to move out of his painting studio because the landlord quadrupled the rent. I wonder how he will fit all his stuff into his small new apartment. I worry especially about when he will ever find time to paint again.

In the evening we spoke to Vali's wife Debbie, who was in high spirits. For Mother's Day Vali and Gabriel brought her flowers, took her to the beach and then out to dinner. It is good to talk to Debbie. She's like a breeze of fresh air, always cheerful and talkative, and everything around her seems wonderful. I should have sent her a special card like the one they sent me, but I never send cards on Mother's Day, so I called.

Well, I'm not sure if I care for all this Mother's day commotion, but I am beginning to think that it is not such a bad thing. Perhaps I should tell myself, "Come on, Dora, you are in America now, forget about how things used to be in the old country. In Romania we never had the time, the energy, the patience or the money for celebrations like Mother's Day. Go to the stores, buy nice gifts and wrap them in a fantastic array of papers. Find a real card store and choose the most perfect card. There are more cards than you can imagine and they all voice the thoughts and feelings that should be expressed on such a day. And they say it more wonderfully than you could ever say it."

Maybe if my mother had lived, I would have taken her out, bought her a wonderful gift and felt what it is like to love and express that love to your mother.

May 13, 1985

Lodz

Last night I was watching the late news on TV. Tzali was napping on the couch. A news item was announced about a new production of *Fiddler on the Roof*. Ah, this I had to watch. Years ago, *Fiddler* was a hugely successful musical on Broadway. It impressed me so much that I saw it two or three times; later I also went to see the movie several times. Everybody enjoyed it. And everybody understood the Jewish milkman Tevye and his problems with his wife and daughters, his arguments with God and his sufferings in Russia at the turn of the century. The play had such universal appeal that it was performed all over the world and in many languages, even Japanese.

The music in *Fiddler* had a familiar sound and the atmosphere it created reminded me of old times in Sighet. But what moved me most was the ending, when Tevye and his family, along with the other Jewish families, were forced to leave their village of Anatevka in Czarist Russia; as the curtain came down, they plodded off, loaded with their bundles and carts and singing sadly, "Soon I'll be a stranger in a strange new place, searching for an old familiar face." This image of leaving one's home with bundles, never to return, reminded me so much of...

To my surprise, the news report was not about a revival of the musical here in New York, but in Poland -- in, of all places, Lodz, a city where 200,000 Jews lived before the war. The announcer stated that the few Jews still living in Lodz after the war had all emigrated in the late 1960's because of widespread Polish anti-Semitism. Now, in this city where the Jews had been persecuted for centuries, from where they were deported under the Nazis, and finally driven out, an American musical about them is so successful, the demand for tickets is so great, that three productions are running simultaneously and the Poles are standing in long lines to get tickets. They come by the thousands to see how it was to be a Jew in Czarist times and they apparently find the musical appealing.

During the war, what happened to the Jews of Lodz was infamous.

The Jewish community in Lodz was second in size only to that of Warsaw. The Lodz ghetto was allowed to exist until almost the end of the war, long after all the other Polish ghettos had been emptied and the population deported. Recently a diary kept by the ghetto's Jewish Council officials was published in English. It had been preserved by someone in Poland, and was discovered only a few years ago. The facts it reveals are quite troubling.

The diary details the daily activities and problems of the ghetto, and contains a log of births, deaths and deportations. By 1941, when the diary was begun, about 230,000 people were jammed into the ghetto. Chaim Rumkovski was the Chairman of this Council, *Der Alteste der Juden,* who had to carry out the demands of the German authorities. He was a controversial figure. He believed that so long as his people worked and made themselves indispensable to the German war industry, they would be kept alive. Over the years he managed to establish all kinds of workshops which employed tens of thousands of men, women, and children, and which provided for the German army. Rumkovski ran the ghetto as a Jewish kingdom: he ruled with an iron hand and had hundreds of Jewish policemen, and even ministries. He was nicknamed "king Chaim." He is credited with the survival of the Lodz ghetto until almost the end of the war.

A few weeks ago we watched a television program based on the Lodz diary. The pictures showed the Jews of the ghetto suffering horribly, devastated by starvation, diseases, random killings by the SS, executions for crimes such as stealing bread and periodic deportations to death camps. It was heartbreaking.

But those who were left kept working, struggling and hoping. We heard one of Rumkovski's speeches in which he asked the healthy Jews in the ghetto to "turn over to him their sick, their old, and their children so he could meet the SS deportation demands", telling them that "he knew how painful it would be but that to save the body it might sometimes be necessary to cut off a hand". He ended by saying, in justification, "We're still alive, aren't we?"

They listened to him and they bled. Years passed. By 1944 all the other ghettos in Poland had been liquidated, but the Lodz ghetto continued to survive, although its population had dropped by half. Then in late 1944 nearly all its remaining inhabitants were deported to Auschwitz, including Rumkovski himself. Rumors circulated that he was killed in the camp by one of the prisoners, but most likely he perished in the gas chambers with the rest of his people. Only seven hundred were left behind to clean up the ghetto. These were all that was left of Lodz's Jewish population when the Soviet army liberated the town in January 1945.

I was in Auschwitz when the Lodz Jews arrived. We had heard that a very large transport was arriving from Litzmanstadt, the German name for Lodz. We could not figure out, though, whether the transport carried Jews. Were there Jews still left alive in Poland? The Polish Jews in camp were veterans; they were among the first to arrive, they had built the barracks, installed the plumbing. Some had been in camp for years and they were considered the most hardened inmates.

They had suffered a great deal, had lost most of their family and friends, and many of those who survived had become Kapos. When we arrived, and they told us bluntly what those brick smokestacks meant, we were angry at them, and could not excuse their outright meanness; but we should have. I know now that they resented us for having lived a few more years at home and for having ignored the fate of the Polish Jews. In a way they were right. Should one be blamed for one's ignorance?

I saw the Jews from Lodz arrive. It was late summer or early fall, only months before Auschwitz was liberated by the Russians. They came by the tens of thousands in the long trains of cattle cars. The chimneys worked full blast, day and night, spitting smoke and blaze, flooding the atmosphere, turning the sky and clouds a menacing red and pink. The activity around the crematoriums was more intense than at any other time.

At the time I was in Camp B, close to the train station and to the crematorium. I saw people being chased out of the box cars, their packages and bundles thrown on the platform in piles while some men from the *Sonderkommando* feverishly sorted out the belongings and others herded all the people in one direction. Then they climbed into the emptied cars, lifted out the many corpses and threw them onto waiting trucks, one on top of the other. Occasionally a sick person who had been left in the car was thrown into a truck, too. I saw one of them try to jump up, but more bodies were hurled on top of him until the truck was full and driven away.

I was stunned. At last I had seen the truth with my own eyes. Did I really have to see it to believe it?

And lines kept forming under the supervision of these prisoners in striped uniforms. People were crying, screaming, holding onto or carrying children. They were all herded to those buildings on the left. Hardly had one group entered when another train pulled into the station.

They just went in. We never saw anyone come out. I don't know if anyone made it into the camp alive.

And today the Poles in Lodz stand in line to buy tickets to see an impressive American musical about a Jewish milkman who had to leave his home in Anatevka. They enjoy it tremendously. They find it beautiful.

Are they moved by it? Do they shed any tears for the fate of the Jews? Are they tears of sorrow, compassion, or of shame and remorse?

I cry for them, for those who inflicted the suffering on our people, for those who collaborated, for those who simply stood by. They are tears of shame for humankind. I hope that the young generation that appreciates this musical will learn something from it. Or from history.

October 27, 1984

Chimneys

For the past five years, I've been working at the county hospital. The area has woods and broad green lawns and was called Grassland before the college moved in and the hospital was built. Today as I was driving home from work, the hospital and the college campus were all behind me; ahead of me were the road and the green fields. Then I saw the two tall chimneys. I must have seen them hundreds of times before. I often thought they looked queer, but never before had I reacted to them in such a strange way and with such keen emotion as today.

Today was one of those very clear, almost autumnal days, when the air is transparent and crisp, the sky is intensely blue, and the foliage, swaying in the gentle wind, displays patches of yellow and rust. Against the clear, radiant sky and scattered trees the two chimneys, one of them pouring out dark smoke, suddenly appeared menacingly tall and foreboding.

I was stunned. The chimneys looked just like the ones in the camp, the chimneys of the crematoriums, the incarnation of all the horrible things that happened *There* and *Then*.

Those chimneys spewed smoke and flames day and night. During our first few weeks in camp, when we were so scared, so bewildered, and so confused, we thought that the smokestacks were part of a factory, a bakery or even a laundry. We were certainly not able to accept any other explanation, least of all what they really were. And when, in answer to our anguished inquiries about our families, Polish or Slovak girls, who had been there for quite a while, would point to the chimneys and say, "Look, that is your parents going up in smoke," we were shocked by their answers and thought they were being malicious, cruel, even downright vengeful.

Thousands of images from those months in Auschwitz crowd my memory. They flood me in a confusion of places, people, and times. I walk through the different barracks in the many camps, the brick buildings with built-in *koyas* from camps A and B, the wooden shacks with shaky three-tiered bunk beds from C. Memories of the girls I was with and the various work teams come back in bits and pieces. I see the peak activity of the crematoriums in early fall, when many thousands arrived and died every day, and I see the eventual slowdowns after entire sections of the camps had been "liquidated."

In my nightmares I see a frozen landscape, hundreds of barracks, mountains of barbed wire interrupted by watchtowers. I hear sirens in the middle of the night, screams and piercing shrieks in the predawn hours. I watch the sky made colorful by the blazing flames spewing forth from the tall chimneys. I feel the craving for food, the shivering, the fear, the resignation, the listlessness, the desolation...

And, hovering over everything, is the grim presence of the crematoriums, forewarning of doom and destruction, the visible evidence of the evil that ruled us, of the madness that the Nazis have unleashed.

I try to recreate the succession of events, I want to understand when and how I reacted to the reality around me. When did I become aware of the meaning of the chimneys? When did I finally believe it? There was no sudden revelation. Slowly, gradually, I had to accept the fact that the smoke and flames of the chimneys came from the burning of the gassed bodies of the victims.

I try to recall our daily life, which became a routine as if we had been born to it, as if no other life had ever existed.

I am in my koya, I am awakened by harsh sirens, yells, screams and blows by the Stubenalteste. It is still dark. I am groggy, everything hurts. It is the end of another sleepless night, with so many of us huddled together in one koya, body against body, pushing each other, trying to get a more comfortable position on the hard plank. My shoulder aches, during the night a girl climbing to the upper bunk stepped on it, she was coming back from relieving herself outside, she must have been sick with diarrhea, I can smell it. The Stubenalteste is shouting and hitting the girls who get in her way, slapping some, kicking others to make them move faster. I hear cries, sobs, hysterical screams. This will be another day of abuse, hunger, and misery.

We line up for the morning roll call in front of our barrack. I help to drag a girl who can hardly get up, and try to hold her up straight without being noticed. If the sick girl stays behind, we will not find her there on our return. In another row a girl collapses from exhaustion. It is very cold, I stay close to the girl in front of me but my back is freezing. It has been hours, the count is still going on, is someone missing from one of the barracks? The darkness recedes in the East. Smoke obscures the sunrise, a few flames like long tongues leap from the chimneys toward the sky. My legs hurt, my stomach craves something to eat and drink.

I rush to the latrine, I cannot wait any more, but there are girls in front of me already waiting for that same hole. Many fight, cry, some cannot hold it. The smell is nauseating in spite of the pungent chlorine. There is no toilet paper.

I wait for my portion of food with burning impatience. There are dozens of girls before me, elbowing each other. I am so hungry, I hear and feel the growling of my empty stomach. Today I get only six mouthfuls of the tasteless soup, it is more watery and less filling than yesterday, not one piece of vegetable in it. I look jealously to those who are still drinking it, I am as hungry after the meal as before, I am so distressed, I don't even have a spoon to try to scrape the remnants from the cauldron.

We sit outside, the girls from my town crouched together against a wall. We talk about events from before, we dwell on the past, it is beautiful, while the present is intolerable and we dread the future. We reminisce about real food, about delicacies, about recipes and ingredients, about parties. We dream of a loaf of warm, fresh bread, with thick and appetizing crust, and we munch on our daily ration of moldy bread. Just talking about such things gives us headaches and stomach cramps. We don't yet look weak and wasted like the girls in other barracks, but we too are getting thinner and weaker by the day. The painful grip of hunger is relentless. I am always hungry, when I get up, when I go to bed, when I eat, food is constantly on my mind, it is an obsession.

I am dirty, my clothes, that I am wearing day in day out for weeks, are filthy, I smell, I itch and scratch myself all the time, I am infested with lice. I remove my dress and find some in the seams but I don't bother to smash them, it is useless. My companion has wounds that are infected from scratching and from beatings. We don't let her go to the hospital, it is too dangerous. We heard that patients are routinely selected, even if all they have is an infected wound or a fracture. The doctors work in simple barracks with bunk beds like ours, they have no instruments, no bandages, no drugs. They may open an abscess, but even they advise against staying in the hospital overnight and recommend going back to work.

We look up and see the chimneys. The sky has changed color, the few clouds reflect the blaze, the wind blows the smoke toward us, and we smell that peculiar and by now familiar odor!

I work from dawn to dusk, I carry heavy rocks, supervisors shout and hit me and order me to work faster. Men work nearby, they want to help but are not allowed. Their eyes express compassion, we exchange glances of understanding and empathy.

We are beaten by SS woman guards, they look at us with hate, contempt, and disgust, we are less than dirt in their eyes, we don't deserve to live, we have long been reduced to subhuman status.

I am always part of a crowd of thousands, standing in line for food, going to the showers or to the disinfection chamber, running to the latrine, fighting for a hole, always fighting for something.

We march from the camp to the workshop. The road, between two camps, is bordered by rows of electrified fences. We pass a column of haggard inmates going in another direction, dragging themselves sluggishly, some crying. A truck with sick and wasted people is following them, we don't even wonder where they are being taken. Is that a body there, hanging on the wires of the fence? The image of the woman I saw there a few days earlier follows me everywhere. Did she do it on purpose? Did she go insane? Or was it an accident? Perhaps she rushed toward a sister on the other side of the electrified fence. I hear music, cheerful tunes, an orchestra somewhere out of sight is playing the familiar, sweet melody of the *Tango Notturno*. And we march on.

And far away, the sight of smoking chimneys continues to instill in us fear and terror.

I try to sort out how I felt. Did I ever really understand? For a while I still had thoughts and feelings, fear and anxiety, hope and trust in the future, I still felt human. But there came a time when the harshness of the surroundings overwhelmed me, I had no more thoughts, no hopes, no feelings, not even pain, when all around me was a blurring greyness, and nothing mattered anymore.

I remember the panic and terror when a selection was announced, more so in the first few months, when we had to strip naked in the showers, a thousand exposed bodies, all pale, some skin and bones, some injured, some covered with sores, ankles swollen. We waited for hours for that life-or-death verdict inflicted by the pointing of a finger, we pinched our cheeks to give them some color, we heard the desperate screams of those separated, we watched exhausted *mussulmen* drag their tired, emaciated bodies with quiet resignation. For them, at least, it was over. Shock and despair filled the air, relief when it was over and we were spared, for now. How long could we hold on? The more we stayed, the more we looked like those victims. I would hardly recognize myself when I saw my reflection in a window. But I didn't need a mirror to know what I looked like, I needed only to see the others, wretched human shadows they had become.

Outside again, we look up at the sky, we mourn for those selected, we know that tomorrow our friends and comrades will feed the voracious chambers and the ovens, their incinerated ashes will blow into our faces!

With time we became scared to go to the showers. We were taken there every two or three weeks; occasionally we were even given a piece of soap. Later we heard rumors that the letters R.J.F. on the soap meant *Reine Juden Fat* -- pure Jewish fat. The shower room was large, with numerous showerheads. A few of us stood under each one, the water started running warm, we soaped, and it felt so good. Then, suddenly, the water turned icy cold or it stopped altogether. Still soapy, we were pushed out into the chilly outdoors where we put our dirty dresses on our wet skin.

When we knew more, we somehow thought that similar showers were used in the gas chambers, except that instead of water, gas would come out of the shower heads. How could we know what it looked like in there? Nobody had returned from a gas chamber! But we heard people whispering horror stories. And our suspicions were enough to instill in us fear and panic every time we were taken to the showers.

Yes, sometimes emotions overwhelmed me, I was able to feel and cry for those condemned. One evening stands out in my memory. We were returning from work tired and exhausted, marching toward our barrack in formation, as always. It was dark. As we approached the crematorium building I glanced toward the fence and it seemed to me that people were standing there, that heads were moving between and above the slats. I was horrified. Never before had I seen people behind that fence. Were they waiting to be gassed? This part of the crematorium grounds facing the camp was always so neat and quiet. During the day there was activity on the other side, where the trains arrived. People sent to the gas chambers must have entered the building there, for the only people I ever saw around that building looked like ordinary prisoners, shaved, dressed in uniforms, subdued and marching in columns, probably inmates coming from the showers as I had done, or survivors of the latest transport. So that evening, seeing those people behind the fence was such a shock that I couldn't fall asleep. The image haunted me the whole night, I cried and wailed for the unsuspecting, innocent people. In the morning I realized that the shadows I had seen by the dim moonlight were sunflowers behind the fence, swaying slowly with the breeze. It was a relief but I did not feel any better, knowing that what I had not seen this time was still happening all the time.

In late summer tens of thousands of Jews arrived from Lodz, the last Polish ghetto. For weeks, more and more trains arrived, more and more bodies were engulfed in flames and our feelings of despair and hopelessness knew no bounds.

In early November something happened that was so unusual it felt unreal. I was in Camp C at the time, and one morning we heard strange noises from the camp adjacent to ours, the so-called "Czech Camp", which had been empty for a while. A new transport had just arrived and the camp was full. To our amazement there were families, young people, old people, mothers with their children, all wearing clothes from home, all with their belongings, all with their heads unshaven. To hear children, to see elderly people in Birkenau was hard to believe, and even harder to explain. Was this a miracle? Had the Nazis changed their policy? Was this the end of the war? They came to the fences and talked. They told us they were from a camp in Czechoslovakia called Theresienstadt. After the war I learned that this was a family camp that the Germans kept for showing and passing off as a model to organizations such as the Red Cross. And now, because the Soviet army was nearing on the eastern front, the Germans started to evacuate Theresienstadt, sending its prisoners to Auschwitz. This was the last transport from there. Every day we talked, we threw them food over the fence -- for children we could always spare some, -- and they reciprocated with old but warm clothes. They were there for a week. Then one morning the camp was quiet. They were all gone. We stood there in shock. The silence was more eloquent than the human voices, the cries and the screams.

And again flames licked the sky, and clouds of black smoke rose over the camp and continued to tell us about the destiny that would eventually swallow us all.

Once in a while we dared to hope that this misery could end, that the war could be soon over. Late in the summer there were constant bombing raids nearby, the sirens blew wildly, the rumble of airplanes and explosions shattered the silence of the night. Rumors reached us that the Russians were close to Cracow, only about twenty-five miles from the camp. We hoped so fervently that the offensive would succeed, even if some of us had to die in the bombings, the sacrifice would be the price for liberation. But the place, the inferno would be destroyed, and many tormentors would also perish. It did not happen then. The next offensive on this front did not come for six more months, and by then most of us were not in Auschwitz any more.

How often can one be horrified? After months and months of those pitiful and dehumanizing conditions our reactions and our behavior had to change. We became numb. We went automatically wherever taken, to roll calls, showers, "selections", for whatever purpose, devoid of any thought or emotion, even knowing that death could be behind any door we were pushed toward. It didn't matter any more, we didn't care, we didn't react, we lost interest in living, our spirits were broken.

We became apathetic, unfeeling, unconcerned. I recall a grotesque image: we got out of the showers and were given only pajama tops to wear, and we had to wait outside for hours. Hundreds of us stood with bare bottoms while the SS officers guarded us and male prisoners worked around us. That aspect bothered us the least, we were beyond modesty. Degradation was so profound, humiliation did not enter one's mind. But we wondered whether we would ever react like human beings again. If we were liberated, would our old sense of pride and self esteem ever return? Would we ever be ashamed of such exposure?

My thoughts, if I had any, were foggy, nebulous. Nothing seemed to make any sense: the comings and the goings, the vanishing of whole columns of prisoners, some wasted and sick but others still healthy-looking; the way we were dressed, some in uniforms, some in odd-looking dresses; some with shaved heads covered by kerchiefs, others with hair; the unmatched pairs of shoes. What happened to the dresses, shoes, combs, toothbrushes, all the things that were brought by the truckload? Why were we awakened in the middle of the night for a simple shower? Why were some prisoners tattooed and others not? Was there a significance, a meaning or a purpose to all this strangeness?

With time the sense of reality started to leave me. There was no more connecting thread between my past and the present. The present seemed an eternity, as if I had always been a *haftling,* and always would be one, confined to barracks, surrounded by barbed wire and ditches, ordered about and abused -- yesterday, last week, last month, always. There seemed to be nothing outside this existence. Birkenau, the gas chambers and the crematoriums were the only reality. We didn't know of other camps. We didn't know the fate of other Jews. We never heard the expression "Final Solution", never knew the intent or extent of the operations the Nazis carried out. We didn't know about the rest of the world. Was the war still going on? Had the Germans won it? We didn't even know whether Birkenau was in Germany, in Poland, or somewhere else.

And still, very rarely, we rose above the gloom. Wasn't there a real world somewhere? Weren't there still places where people lived in houses, stayed with their families, slept in beds and ate at tables? Maybe my family was alive and together someplace, maybe someone was searching for me, waiting for me. If I vanished here would they ever find out where I had been or how I had perished?

So, when I was first told about the crematoriums I refused to believe it. Everything around us was so neatly organized, everything worked with such typical German efficiency and punctuality, with iron discipline, life was simple and reduced to bare essentials. We never saw shootings, only occasional hangings, blood was never spilled. It just seemed inconceivable and absurd that such mass destruction could be going on nearby. It was so much easier to believe the rumors about camps for families and for the sick. Some prisoners swore that somewhere they had seen old people, and even children with their mothers, and older women working in the fields outside the camp. All along, didn't we believe their intention of "resettlement" -- sending Jews to work camps to help the German war effort? When I began to realize the truth, some part of me kept crying out, "No, it cannot be!"

And when, after all I had heard and seen, I finally accepted the facts, it was too heartbreaking to apply them to the night when we arrived, to my own family. Illusions and foolish hopes lingered on. With the passing of time I started to have doubts about my parents' survival -- but never, never could the truth about the crematoriums have any connection with my brothers. Didn't I search for them on my way home to Sighet after I was liberated? Didn't I bring them two pairs of shoes for when we were reunited?

Today it seems so hard to understand why we did not simply accept what we were told, and why we did not see what was obvious. But up against that ghastly reality we were no longer the rational, intelligent, thinking and feeling human beings we once were, but what we had become: creatures functioning at the most elemental level whose bare necessities and day-to-day survival were all that mattered, who would rather grieve over a stolen bread ration or a spilled bowl of soup than reflect on the bleakness of the present. Torpor of body, mind and soul left no resources for anything beyond dealing with these essential needs, food, sleep, a bath, clothes.

Fleeting images come and go of those summer weeks. Occasionally a new one surfaces, perhaps fragmentary, but I am pleased because it fills in one of the many lapses in my memory of that time. I remember once, when I was doing road work, pushing a wheelbarrow with sand or helping other girls with the heavy roller to press the asphalt. Or I see myself on a sunny day in a blue cotton print dress I had just received that was clean enough that I could feel good wearing it. I see lots of girls around a pear tree throwing rocks and trying to catch some green, unripe pears. There are trees and green grass around me. Where could that be? I see myself months later, standing for hours at roll call barefoot on the frozen ground because my shoes had been stolen. Or standing or marching in heavy rains while the Kapos took refuge in the barracks, then returning to the *koyas* and trying to sleep in the cold, soaked dress, wet and shivering. I remember days when some or all of the chimneys rested. Then the air was calm, there was hope in the camp and our mood was more confident. Perhaps there was still a chance to get out alive.

I remember once when I had a pen in my hand. What a strange feeling it was to write. It reminded me of when I was still part of humanity, free and happy, and went to school and wrote essays. We were given printed postcards saying we were working in the town of Waldsee and doing fine. We had to sign the cards and write the address of a gentile family in our home town. We did not understand *Then* that this was part of the great deception, meant to fool the world. When was that? We had long lost track of time, rarely knew what the date was, and few of us could even remember the day.

And then it was winter, and bitter cold. The wooden barracks in Camp C had no heating, the harsh wind penetrated the buildings, and there was more crowding than ever. Transports no longer arrived, "selections" did not seem as threatening, and the chimneys rarely worked. Every day prisoners were sent from Auschwitz to Germany to provide what was left of the war industry with slave workers. With the Eastern Front so close we were afraid that everyone staying on would be killed by the departing Nazis. I wandered aimlessly around the camp, dressed in layers of tattered rags, my body covered with lice, my hands icy and my feet frostbitten, hoping I would be taken away for work, the only chance for survival.

The crematoriums were dismantled by the Germans as they attempted to get rid of the evidence of their crimes before the Red Army arrived. Just one was left working to handle the bodies of the prisoners who continued to die in camp. All was quiet and the landscape was even more desolate.

Too late, Auschwitz was coming to an end.

September 10, 1984

Leaving Hell

Today, December 12, is an important day for me. On December 12, 1944, I was still *There*, desolate and lonely. All of my friends were gone, Violet had been selected and taken away a few weeks before. The few girls from Sighet who remained in the camp were now scattered in various barracks. I had passed through many camps within the complex and I was still *There*.

Now it was Camp C, with its windy, wooden barracks with earthen floors and shaky three-tiered wooden bunk beds. It was chilly, we huddled close to one another, and shivered. So many girls slept on each level that often such a *koya* would collapse and crush those on the lowest level. The Russians were near and we all feared that before they reached the camp everybody would be killed. It was a very cold winter. I added more and more layers of dirty rags to my outerwear to keep warm. I had so many body lice I stopped trying to kill them. The large men's shoes I wore, filled with paper and rags, did not prevent frostbite. I had gone to the infirmary a few times, but they wouldn't do anything to help me.

There was no longer any work to take my mind off the freezing cold, the hunger and the bleakness. Every day prisoners still in good condition were being sent to factories in Germany. To stay on was to be condemned. I walked around aimlessly looking for a chance to leave. I was desperate to get out.

Every time when I saw groups of girls surrounding the guards who were choosing the lucky ones for factory work I ran over and pushed my way in as close to the guards as I could get, but I was always too late: they already had their quota. I was left behind again and again. It all seemed so hopeless. We were sure that if the Nazis were to relinquish Auschwitz they would leave no witnesses behind.

But on December 12, I saw a crowd and rushed into it. With hundreds of other despairing girls I waited in line for a chance to be picked for a transport. I saw two men dressed in civilian clothes choosing the girls by looking at their hands. I heard them say, "Enough. We have two hundred." There were at least ten other girls ahead of me in line. I figured that, since they were looking at hands this time, they might be choosing girls for fine hand work. In desperation I cried out, *"Ich bin eine Zeichnerin!"* -- "I am a draftsman!" They looked at me, called me out of line, said, "201," and sent me with the new group.

That day we were taken to the baths and given clean clothes. I got underpants, pajama tops, a short-sleeved dress, stockings, shoes with wooden soles, and a thin black coat with a red cross painted on the back, so we could be easily recognized outside if we were to run away. Of course I got no hat, scarf, sweater, gloves or any garters to hold up the stockings.

They took us to the tracks where we boarded a train. We were so packed into the railroad car that we kept each other warm. It was snowing lightly and a thin white blanket covered the icy ground. The whole landscape was frozen.

As the train left and I saw for the last time the hundreds of barracks and the fences and watch towers, I realized we were getting out of hell. We had survived it. What lay ahead, no one knew.

December 12, 1983

Weisswasser

It took almost a day by train from Auschwitz to our new destination. This was a new, small camp called Weisswasser, housing only a few hundred girls, all working at a nearby I.G. Farben factory producing war-related equipment.

The camp was on top of a hill. It had only a few buildings, encircled by barbed wire. There were dormitories, offices, SS quarters, warehouses, a kitchen and a large inner courtyard for roll calls.

You probably wonder if Weisswasser was different from Auschwitz. Oh, yes, very different indeed. Auschwitz was essentially a *Vernichtungslager* -- extermination camp; that was its purpose. The frequent "selections", the gas chambers and the crematoriums ensured that eighty to ninety percent of those who were brought *There* were disposed of, either upon arrival or after a while in the camp. In Auschwitz there was always the uncertainty, or rather the certainty, of where everyone would eventually wind up.

Weisswasser, however, was an *Arbeitslager* -- labor camp -- where people were sent to work. You were still confined, abused, worked and starved, but it appeared that your work was needed and that you would be allowed to live as long as you could work. Since there were no selections and no crematoriums, we even dared to hope that we would survive if the war ended in time. Still, the future remained bleak, and liberation so distant and doubtful.

When I was chosen for this transport I thought I would be the only girl from Sighet. I found, to my delight, that there were four others, who had lived in another barrack of the large C Camp. I was well acquainted with two of them. Hindi was the one I knew best, we were often part of the same crowd in Sighet. I had gone to a New Year's Eve party at her house and I had pleasant memories of it. We went to gymnastics classes together, which we both enjoyed. I also knew Baba, I already wrote to you how I tutored her at home when Jewish children could no longer attend the public high schools. Then there were Relu, Hindi's younger sister, rather difficult to have around, always arguing and quarreling; and Olga, their cousin, one year behind me in our high school. The four of them had been together since entering Birkenau.

About twenty girls from our transport were assigned to a rather small dormitory, the five of us with others from Greece and France. We had two-tiered bunk beds with straw instead of mattresses, and each girl got her own bunk and two blankets. There were no sheets and no pillows, but it was a vast improvement over the *koyas* we had had to share with eight to ten girls. The rooms had a stove, but we did not get enough firewood. It was so cold that we slept two in a bunk to keep warm; that way we could use three blankets as covers and put one underneath us to cover the straw.

Compared to us, the girls we found in Weisswasser were very well dressed. They were also from Hungary, but they had come from a camp other than Auschwitz, and all this, along with their familiarity with the place, gave them a "privileged" status vis-a-vis us new arrivals. They had warm long-sleeved dresses, good winter coats, huge wool shawls that must have been very warm, and high-top winter shoes, and they looked at us with pity and contempt -- or at least so we thought.

There was a dining hall, which was used rarely, but where we actually sat on benches and ate at tables. We received individual plates and utensils. There were lavatories and toilets that we could use without waiting in line. There was also an infirmary, but to go to the infirmary, to admit that one was sick, was still dangerous. Though there were no systematic "selections", sick people did nevertheless disappear from the infirmary. I had a deep, severe burn on one finger from the lye in the paint we used to whitewash the walls of our room. The wound was terribly painful but I didn't dare bandage it for fear of being discovered. But then I developed some boils, and the one over my eye was quite large and too visible to hide. I spent almost a week in the infirmary, frightened, hardly able to see, but it did get better and I returned to work.

We were sent to the factory to work. Those with a high school education were assigned to the *Gerate Revision* section -- quality control -- to check the finished hardware. We had to test some box-like containers with a panel of wiring and reject the defective ones (we thought these were airplane components). Baba and I worked at the same workbench. The other girls were sent to the workshops, in the carpentry, smithy or tool section. Hindi and her sister worked in the metal workshop with machine tools.

There were several hundred French prisoners of war working in the same factory, sometimes at adjoining workbenches. They were quartered in Schildberg, a small town nearby, and came to the factory every morning by train. They had some degree of freedom. Their camp was not guarded and they could go to the countryside and even buy food. They were also allowed to receive mail, packages and money from their families.

These young Frenchmen exchanged glances with the girls in the factory. Soon friendships developed despite the fact that they were not permitted to talk to each other; with the language barrier they wouldn't have understood each other anyhow. Their friendly smiles, their gestures of encouragement and their obvious sympathy helped the girls as much as the food parcels they dropped on our desks when the guards weren't looking.

They brought us toothbrushes -- we had had none for so long --, combs, soap, thread and needles. If it were not for them we might not have survived these months.

The presence of these young men and the attention they paid us made most of us aware of something new -- or rather, something we had long forgotten. We started to feel and look more like human beings again. Our hair had grown in and we combed it. The dresses we wore were real dresses, even if their short sleeves showed the long striped sleeves of our pajama tops underneath. In the spring we cut off the pajama sleeves and used them to make bras, belts, pockets, whatever. Even our coats and shoes were not grotesque anymore.

In the quality control section I worked with a soldering iron. Whenever I could, I melted pieces of lead, pressed them, smoothed them and cut them into round or six-pointed star medallions on which I carved names and patterns before giving them as pendants to my friends. It was our first jewelry.

We worked in a warm hall, each of us sitting at a workbench surrounded by real people, who looked at us with empathy. Some girls were pretty. No wonder the French prisoners fell in love with them. They slipped love letters to them and supplied news from the outside world. In their replies, all the girls wrote of home, of family, of freedom.

Most of the girls didn't know any French. Since I had studied French for eight years, I became a great writer and reader of letters for some of the girls, in return for which the Frenchmen occasionally dropped off a sandwich for me too. Baba and a few others who also knew French had their own "customers." To go from Voltaire, Corneille and the other French classics to a few simple love letters in exchange for a slice of bread is really a lesson in survival.

One Frenchman, whose letters I translated and answered for his girlfriend Pirike, asked me to memorize his name and address for after the war. I still remember it: Anatole Recoquillon, Rue des Deux Ponts, 52, Paris; but when I finally reached Paris thirty years later, the street no longer existed.

The winter lingered on. It was cold and the rooms at the camp were rarely heated. About once a week we got a few logs and could warm up some water. We took turns filling a basin with barely warm water and used it for a sort of sponge bath and to wash the underwear. In the washroom there was running water that we used to wash up in the morning but it was icy cold, and those who took baths with it were considered crazy, obsessed with cleanliness and in constant danger of catching colds and worse.

Morning roll call was relatively short, an hour or so, and then we only had to march a few kilometers to reach the factory. I still remember the relief I felt when entering the heated building. Even today when I come into the hospital from the cold parking lot, the warm air between the double entrance doors hits me with such force that it always reminds me of the welcome warmth of the factory after marching in the chilly, windy countryside.

That countryside! Between the camp up on the hill, and the factory down in the valley, was there anything else besides us marching in the freezing gusts? I don't remember anything else, but Baba does. Since arriving in Weisswasser, Baba and I shared not only a bunk bed but everything else we had, including our dreams. We had become good friends -- camp sisters, as she would say later. We were glad to have each other, to speak the same language, to reminisce about home, friends, family, food, warm clothes, food and again food. Now she lives in New York, and whenever we meet the most important topic is Weisswasser. She recalls having seen, during our marches in the dim, early hours, cozy peasant houses with lights in the windows suggesting some real life and real people behind the pretty curtains. And how she longed to be inside one of them!

She talks often about the most common sensation, hunger, about the anxiety we all felt every morning as we watched Hindi cut that heavy brick-shaped loaf of bread into the most equal eight portions she could manage, about watching me at dinner time agonizing over how to divide the kettle of soup equally into the twenty waiting bowls. The soup was usually a watery white concoction of turnips and cabbage which we most appropriately called *Weisswasser* -- white water --, even less filling than the soup in Auschwitz. Occasionally there were potatoes or beans, but almost never a piece of meat in that soup. I don't recall ever getting fresh fruit or vegetables. It was a time of slow starvation.

I am still mystified by how little one needs to survive, by how the human body responds to shock and starvation, and why some people are more resistant than others. It is really a wonder that more of us didn't get sick or die. There must be adaptive mechanisms: emotional lassitude to preserve sanity, physiological responses such as slowing metabolism or eliminating non-essential functions to maintain life. Indeed, all the girls stopped having periods a month after their arrival in Auschwitz (though it was rumored that this was due to medicine being added to the food).

For several months I was not used as a draftsman. I thought they had forgotten why they picked me as the 201st girl in the transport. Then one morning during roll call they asked for the draftsman, and I was transferred to the engineering office. It was quite a promotion. The atmosphere there was so different, it was almost congenial. I worked with French and Dutch prisoners who were engineers or draftsmen. There were a few civilians and the chief was a German engineer. It was never clear to me whether he was a prisoner or not.

In the office, I was the only girl from the camp and I had special privileges. Each morning I was brought in by a woman guard, who also took me to the bathroom twice a day, since I was not allowed to go through the workshops alone. Sometimes she talked to me, as did the people in the office. The German engineer, in particular, was very kind to me, he often asked about my home and my family and brought me food. At Easter he gave me a food package with cake his mother had baked. (Did they have mothers, too?). I took the gift to Baba and we savored it together. It seemed like a dream -- homemade food... how long had it been...? I was at a loss as to how to respond to this kindness from a German man.

Spring came slowly in 1945. I don't remember grass or trees or flowers, but the cold abated. Rumors that the Allies were approaching, whispered in passing by the French prisoners, made us optimistic. In the evenings Baba and I would stay outside, follow the moon rising in the clear sky, watch the bright, sparkling stars, and talk about our hopes, our yearnings, our boyfriends back home, and our dreams. Recurrent dreams, that someone would be home and waiting for us! But anxiety persisted: if the Germans were doomed, we could be too.

A new transport arrived at Weisswasser from an Eastern camp, evacuated because of the approach of Soviet forces. Our camp became more crowded and there was even less food. One of the newcomers was the mother of a friend of ours from Sighet, Mrs. Halpert. Seeing anyone from Sighet who was older than forty made a great impression on me because so few people her age managed to get out of Auschwitz.

Among the new girls was a draftsman who was assigned to our office. She was young, eighteen or so, and hardworking. She was noticed immediately. "See her?" said the German engineer. "She does such a good job and she knows less than you." I was ashamed for her. I didn't care to do a good job for the Germans, and I was sorry for us that we had to work so hard.

*

It feels strange to talk about Weisswasser. Everyone seems to have heard about Auschwitz or Birkenau, or other notorious camps, but Weisswasser? Nobody has ever heard of it. It must have been an obscure place, one of hundreds of camps built to house the slave laborers working in the factories sprinkled throughout Germany and its occupied territories. Weisswasser was in occupied Czechoslovakia. The town near the camp was called Schildberg in German, but I cannot find it on any map. Whenever I come across a detailed atlas I open it at Czechoslovakia, look at the province of Moravia and search for a similar sounding name. Once I found a place called Sumperk -- was that it? Then why did the Czechs call it

Silperku after liberation? No one has written about this camp; at times I myself am wondering whether it really existed or I only imagined it. But in 1944 it was real enough.

December 19, 1983

Brzezinka

Yesterday was a very difficult day: the weather, the visit to the nursing home, my brother coming to the hospital, -- and Bobbie.

Alter came to the hospital for his regular check-up. Every six months he has to see the famous surgeon who operated on him several years ago. This time they brought Bobbie along because after Alter's check-up we were all going to visit Uncle Herman at the nursing home in Rockland County.

Bobbie is the widow of my cousin Ezra, the only cousin on my father's side I knew here in America. He was Alter's generation, and the two came here around the same time, worked for a while in the same knitting factory, and were good friends. I often met Ezra and Bobbie at Alter's house in Brooklyn.

Ezra and Bobbie lived a quiet life in Borough Park among other observant Jews, and they were childless. They owned a bakery, and always brought some pastries when they visited us; on Vali's bar mitzvah they insisted on providing the cake, an especially delicious one with layers of fruit and white cream frosting. They were such nice, modest people, always grateful if you called on them, never critical of anyone, never showing any resentment or bitterness about the past. I really feel guilty when I think of how little time I spent with them. Sometimes I invited them to our house along with the family elders, Uncle Aaron and Uncle Herman. I always made sure to serve kosher food, even though Uncle Herman didn't trust me and brought his own sandwich in a brown bag. Ezra and Bobbie's sweets, however, were trusted by all of them.

Ezra died last winter at the age of 73. His death came as a surprise because Bobbie was the one who had been in poor health; over the years she had a number of major operations. After Ezra's death, Bobbie had only praise and gratitude for all those around her -- friends, neighbors, nephews and nieces: everybody had been so supportive and helpful; one nephew even traveled with her to Israel, where Ezra wanted to be buried. And Alter... there was no end to her admiration for him.

Before Alter and Sara drove to his doctor's office in a nearby building, they dropped Bobbie off at our cafeteria. I went down and had coffee with her. Of course she had brought along a box of cookies.

"But Bobbie," I said, "you don't have a bakery any more."

"And you think there are no bakeries around my house?"

"You look good, Bobbie. What do you do with yourself these days?"

"Since Ezra died, I often do volunteer work at the local hospital. I read a lot, I have many friends who don't let me get too lonely. And Alter, God bless him. He comes regularly every Wednesday and Friday to see me."

"And what do you two talk about?"

I had my suspicions, I know Alter's favorite topic lately. He retired some time ago and now, with too much time on his hands, he goes to a Hungarian library in Brooklyn and reads books about Hungary's history before and during the war. He is fascinated by Horty Miklos, the Hungarian regent who governed the country and was ousted by the Fascists. Alter tells and retells the story at such length that more than once I've gotten annoyed and said, "Who cares what happened to Horty? When everybody else is reading about terrorism in Israel or current efforts to hunt down Nazi war criminals, why are you interested in the politics of Fascist Hungary in 1940?"

Bobbie agrees that Alter is obsessed with these obscure historical events. "Yes", she said, "He talks and talks about Horty. Finally I told him I am bored with Horty, I don't want to hear about him anymore. A lot of good that did! Last week I got a lecture on Horty's imprisonment by Hitler."

"How long has Ezra been gone now?"

"He died a year ago January. I miss him so much! I can't tell you what a great marriage we had, what kind of person Ezra was -- how considerate, how honest, how appreciated in our community. He loved you all, he admired your father -- he talked so much about him. And he liked you -- he was so thankful when you came to visit us that Purim, he was grateful when you called or visited him during his illness."

I was embarrassed. "Well," I said, "he was too kind."

"Believe me, there was no one like him. Our twenty-five years of marriage were so harmonious that we never fought, never exchanged angry words, never disagreed."

"Why did you marry so late, Bobbie?"

She smiled. "I was waiting for him and he for me. It was written."

"But Bobbie, I know you were both married before the war."

"I was only married for a short time -- though I was very much in love with my first husband. At that time everyone thought that being married might save us from deportation. What did they know? We were married for less than a year before they sent us to Auschwitz. My husband didn't live beyond the first night."

"And you were lucky you were not pregnant," I said.

"Yes, probably that saved me. But you know, we did have a pregnant woman in our work squad who carried her baby to term. We hid her at roll calls; after she delivered, the SS guards threw the baby in the ovens."

"Now, Bobbie, how could you hide a pregnant woman? We could never do that."

"Because we worked in Brzezinka, where it was a little easier."

Brzezinka!?

Brzezinka was such a mysterious place, *There* and *Then*. It was somewhere between our barrack and the hell beyond the gates, between those still alive and those being gassed. That is where all those unspeakable things happened.

Brzezinka was in a forest near the crematoriums, close to where the trains arrived and the first selections took place, close to the showers and close to the gas chambers. Hundreds of inmates lived in special barracks and worked there sorting out the belonging left behind in the trains and in the gas chambers. These prisoners had plenty of food and enough clothing. But they had to see the worst of what went on. It was a dreadful existence, and yet how we envied them their "plenty!"

My cousin Serena worked there. Sometimes she would come to our camp and bring me whatever she could smuggle -- a bite of food, a piece of soap, a handkerchief. One night when we were near Brzezinka for showers I sneaked into her barrack. It was cleaner, less crowded, brighter than ours. But Serena wasn't there any more, she had been sent away.

I asked Bobbie how she got to work at Brzezinka in the first place.

"I was assigned there when we arrived."

"It must have been horrible to work there, Bobbie. Did you wear striped uniforms?"

"No. Those prisoners who wore nice clean gray-and-blue striped uniforms with a red pinafore and a white head scarf worked in factories in the town of Auschwitz. Don't you remember how every morning they marched to music out of the camp towards the city? Those were the well-dressed, well-fed, neat-looking prisoners the local population got to see. We who worked in Brzezinka wore polka-dot dresses."

"Polka-dot dresses? I never saw that," I said, surprised. Among the thousands and thousands of girls around I might have seen a few wearing polka-dot dresses, but I never would have suspected these were uniforms.

"Oh, yes," Bobbie said. "The day shift wore red and white polka-dot dresses; the night shift, blue and white, all with a red head band. We were even called 'the polka-dot commando'."

I had a hard time believing what she was saying. I had never heard of this before. I asked again what it was like to work there.

"Mostly we worked outside. The men from the *Sonderkommando* would bring us heavy bundles of clothing, packages of food, suitcases, albums, toys, and so many family pictures. We would sort them out and put them in piles. The new garments had to be neatly folded and placed in boxes to be dispatched to Germany. The old clothes were kept for the prisoners or were shredded.

"And do you know where many people hid their jewelry and money? Sewn in their underwear. The SS knew that and guarded us closely so we wouldn't steal anything. If they found us stealing, they beat us or took us away. Every evening we had to take showers, leave our dresses behind and get clean ones so we couldn't smuggle any valuables out of Brzezinka."

"Why would you do that? What could you have done with gold or jewelry?" I asked.

"We gave it to the men in the *Sonderkommando*. They used it to buy weapons from the partisans in touch with the Polish underground. You must have heard about their uprising. I was there. All the men were killed. We were used to them disappearing because the men of this team rarely survived more than six weeks. The father of one of our girls was part of the *Sonderkommando*. We talked often. He told us that all the men knew that one day they would be taken to the gas chambers and become victims themselves, they had seen too much. In the mornings, when we saw a new group of men working, we knew... "

"Did you ever see anyone from home among them? Relatives? Friends?"

"No, never. I'm grateful for that. It was difficult enough as it was. To have seen someone from home would have been unbearable."

"How do you feel about it today, Bobbie?"

"Now that I'm alone, I think so much about it. Brzezinka was so perfectly organized, by who knows how many devilish, monstrous geniuses. Just imagine -- a new transport would arrive, full of people starved and drained from days of traveling without food or water, scared and panicky. They would pass between us, clean, healthy-looking girls in gay, colorful uniforms on one side and on the other side musicians in white outfits with a red stripe on the side of the pants, playing some pleasant, fashionable tunes. The people would seem relieved -- they even smiled at us. Sometimes the SS guards would give them a piece of soap and a towel and they would march anxiously to the showers.

"After they all entered the crematorium building the lights would be turned off, silence would fall upon the whole place and then we knew that no one would come out. At first I cried, but sometimes I couldn't. I still have nightmares about it. Was it real? Could something like that truly happen? And was I part of it?"

"It must have been very hard. Could you help anyone?"

"I smuggled food into the camp whenever I could. Others did too. If you only knew what people had lovingly prepared and brought with them on that last journey to an unknown destination -- cakes, cookies, chocolates for the children, candied fruit and other delicacies. They must have been saving them for a long time. It was heartbreaking. When we had to go into the camp we would take in bits of food or give away our underwear and shoes to camp prisoners. But if we were caught returning barefoot to our barrack we were severely punished. Still, I wonder if I did enough to help others."

"Bobbie, you may not realize how much you and those working near the trains were able to help. I recall that my first night in Auschwitz a Polish girl working in the showers gave me a pair of sturdy walking shoes in exchange for my flimsy sandals. Those shoes only lasted a few months but I will never forget her kindness. And how many times have I heard about a member of such a *kommando* telling younger boys near the 'selection' point to say that they are over 18 and have a trade, thus saving their lives; or advising mothers to hand over the babies they were carrying to an older woman. One man from the *Sonderkommando* actually grabbed the baby from the arms of my distant cousin, Magda, in spite of her fighting, screaming and crying. She never forgave him, but had the baby stayed with her they would have both been sent straight to the gas chamber.

"How long did you stay in Auschwitz?"

"Till January 1, 1945. The Russians were closing in and the SS wanted to eliminate most of us. There was a big 'selection'. Out of about two thousand girls only two hundred were chosen to be sent away to work. I was sent to Leipzig and I worked there until the end of the war."

Our conversation moved on to her years in Budapest after the liberation. She came to America in 1956 after the Hungarian Revolution. She was still single then.

"How come, Bobbie, that you didn't marry in all those years?"

"I didn't care to marry."

"And Ezra," I kept on, "didn't he also lose his family?"

"Yes, his wife and two little children were killed."

"He also waited a long time to remarry, almost fifteen years."

"He loved his wife and children very much. It took him years to make peace with his loss. He put all of his energies into his work. He came to New York and bought a knitting mill -- just like Alter -- and worked day and night to build it up. After we were married he bought the bakery and we both worked hard to keep it going. In the last years, when he was getting older and didn't want to be bothered with the burdens of a business any more, he sold the bakery. But I kept on working there as a saleslady, you remember."

"Sure I do. You used to bring us cream puffs and all those kosher honey cakes. I will never forget that special bar mitzvah cake you brought for Vali, filled with fresh fruit and covered with white frosting."

"Ezra loved to come to your house. He was really happy to be able to contribute to such a joyous occasion."

When I finished my work in the hospital Bobbie and I picked up Alter and Sara in my car and the four of us drove up to the nursing home to visit uncle Herman. Along the way Alter and I chatted about his checkup. Then I asked him about his latest reading. He answered with a question: "Do you know when Horty Miklos died? And how?" Bobbie and I exchanged glances but managed to keep a straight face.

Herman is my mother's brother. During the war he lived in that part of Romania from where the Jews were not deported, and after the war he emigrated with his whole family to join his brother Aaron and his sisters Fannie and Goldie.

Uncle Herman has been in this nursing home since he had a stroke a few weeks ago. We found him sitting in the day room in his wheel chair, waiting for dinner. His wife Rachel, who had been in the same nursing home for a longer time, sat in another wheelchair, holding his hand. Herman was surprised to see us; he smiled, then started to cry, but his speech had improved and his mind seemed reasonably clear. He knew his age, 84, and knew that he was first married in 1926. He smiled when I exclaimed, "Married for almost sixty years!"

I wondered if Herman remembered our meeting in Bucharest when I returned from the camps.

"Do you remember the street where you lived?" I asked.

"No," he said.

"Not even if I tell you the first word? Fundatura..." (that means dead end)

"Fundatura Faurari," Uncle Herman remembered.

"You remember the courtyard? And the bedbugs in the apartment?"

He laughed. "Who in Bucharest didn't have bedbugs!" His sense of humor was returning too.

Dinner arrived but he had trouble eating. I asked if he wanted me to help him. He nodded "yes." I fed him.

What a feeling! Like feeding my own father or mother, a chance I never had. Nor did I have the chance to develop a relationship with any of the older generation of my family. How I wish to have had the fortune to be nearby and available as my parents became old, to be there when they would need me as they became children again, to help them and care for them as they once cared for me when I was a child.

That night I could hardly fall asleep. Bobbie's story haunted me. I could see how those girls in their polka-dot dresses might bring a ray of hope -- false hope -- to those arriving in Auschwitz after their ordeal inside the closed box cars. But it seems bizarre for the Nazis to have gone to this length, to orchestrate such a spectacle, just to deceive them. I was also troubled: how did it feel to be part of the deception, to stand there smiling or expressionless as so many marched to the crematoriums? And to be so helpless?

How did it feel to be well-fed and well-dressed while the rest of us in the camp were starving and freezing? And at the same time to be so unfortunate as to have to witness and understand the immensity of the crimes being perpetrated.

I feel lucky to have been one of the starving, shivering, frightened prisoners in the crowd of hundreds of thousands rather than one of the few hundred privileged but tormented ones. As I sank into sleep I drifted into a dream in which I found myself arriving at a place where cheerfully dressed girls stand smiling and soft music is playing. I reassure myself that I will only be confined for a while, and that all I have to do is work hard to ensure survival and eventual freedom.

May 22, 1985

Montreal

I have so much to write you about our trip to Montreal. We visited my cousin Feri, Uncle Yeno's son, and his wife and our good friends Shiku and Hannah, as we used to do when Vali was attending McGill University there.

Sunday we went sightseeing in the Old City, walking and talking, Tzali strolling with Shiku and I with Hannah. I said, "You know, Hannah, it seems amazing that I didn't know you at all in Sighet. Considering we're only a couple of years apart, we were practically of the same generation. Where were you?"

"Well, we lived on the outskirts of the city and I didn't go to high school."

So that's what it was. As a high school student I was in an "elite" category, and it was easy for me to lose contact with many of the other teenagers.

"So," I said, "you must have lived on one of the streets that became part of the ghetto."

"Yes," she answered, "We didn't even have to move. And I was taken to Auschwitz on the first transport."

"So was I. Unfortunately for all of us, the first transport was one of the worst.

"Yes, I know. I was the only one left out of eight children in my family. My cousins, who arrived on the second and third transports, were luckier. Many more of them made it into the camp."

I asked, "How long did you stay in Auschwitz?"

"To the end. You probably heard about the Death March during the last days, when the Soviet Army was so close, and all the 'able-bodied' were forced to march West. Not even half of us made it to the next camp."

"Yes. I was spared the march because I was sent away to Weisswasser a few weeks before. But where did you work in Auschwitz?"

"Brzezinka."

"Brzezinka?! Hannah, you're the second person I've spoken with in the past week who worked in Brzezinka. How was it? Colorful?"

"What do you mean?"

"Those polka-dot dresses that you wore there."

"I don't know anything about polka-dot dresses. We wore the same gray uniforms that everyone in Camp B wore. The only difference was that we got white head scarves.

"So you did not live in those barracks close to the crematorium?"

Would that explain it?

She was astonished by what I had said. I realized again, as many others must have before and since, that no two people came out of that inferno with the same experience. Perhaps one prisoner did not know, did not even care to know, where others worked during the day. Even those working in the same place, doing the same job, could have been there on different shifts or come at different seasons or entered similar-looking doors at other crematoriums and therefore have completely different and unique stories to tell now.

"The horrors that we saw *There* could not be imagined by a person of sound mind," she said.

I asked her if she could smuggle food or anything else into camp.

"I could only smuggle in tiny pieces of food hidden in my clothes or kerchief. There was tremendous pressure on me to bring back food. In the evening I had three cousins waiting for me to return to the barracks and bring them something. But after work every day we were checked by the guards. I was always upset when I couldn't bring anything back with me. I do remember putting on good shoes and underwear at work and then at night exchanging them for ripped ones. Then I wore those to work the next day and exchanged them again for better ones."

"Did you work inside or outside?"

"Outside when transports arrived. Inside the rest of the time. There was always so much work opening suitcases and bundles and sorting out all the belongings from so many thousands of people -- we had to work in shifts even when no trains arrived for days."

I asked if she had had any contact with the *Sonderkommandos*.

"Yes. Whenever a new transport approached, the men of the *Sonderkommando* would appear. They had some time to talk to us before the trains arrived and we all had to start working. They were the most unfortunate group."

One young man from Sighet told her of having seen his family as they marched toward the gas chambers. He didn't approach them, he couldn't face them, not until after they were dead... He told her he couldn't live with that experience; he was calmly awaiting his own impending fate.

But most of these young men became nervous and jittery as their time ran out. In their desperation they tried to escape, knowing full well that their chances were almost nonexistent. They were nearly always caught and hanged publicly.

Hannah also had a number tattooed on her arm: it was A-8100. I tried to figure out how many days or weeks had elapsed between the time I got my number and the time she got hers. Her tattoo has a deeper color, more even numbers, and more densely packed ink dots; obviously another scribbler, with more of a sense of symmetry than mine, had written it.

"Hannah," I asked, "did you work in Brzezinka until the end?"

"No," she said. "In the fall of 1944 I worked in the *Weberei*, the weaving workshop."

"But that's where I was working that fall. Were you at the weaving machines or making cords?"

"Braiding cords."

"Me too. Fabrics or plastics?" Suddenly I was remembering the time when I made braids with transparent plastic. The plastic sheets were so clear, so clean and glittery that I thought they looked like some sort of Christmas decorations.

"No, Dori, I worked with dirty rags."

"So did I, for a while. Who knows, we could even have worked in the same place at the same time. Isn't that odd? I was almost 'selected' then."

"How come?" she asked.

"Well, they thought I didn't do enough work. Actually my ball of braided cord was too small because I was busy helping the supervisor clean the place instead of making big balls of cord. But I escaped."

"How did you escape?"

"How did anyone escape? By sheer chance. It was really ridiculous but it could have been tragic. I was standing by the door with the other girls who were 'selected', waiting for the SS truck to make its rounds of the barracks and come pick us up. My mind went blank. The only feeling I remember was resignation. But do you remember the girls who worked near the door?"

"Yes, the old-timers at the individual looms, weaving those strange ribbons, the ones who had been there the longest."

"Exactly. The Polish girls. They were smarter and shrewder than us because they had more experience in survival. And they had guts! One of them looked at me with contempt and yelled, 'You, stupid! Why do you stand there and wait? Why don't you run away?' So I ran to the back, in among all the girls who were working, and sat down at my bench still trembling. When the guards returned they didn't check their list against the tattooed numbers, and didn't realize that one girl was missing. They just took the others and left. It seems so easy now. But at that instant my life depended on the jeers of a contemptuous Polish girl who saved me. Wasn't survival *There* a matter of chance?"

Yes, it seems so simple in retrospect, I still wonder why running away did not enter my mind. But we both knew that under those conditions one did not think clearly, nor could one see what should have been obvious.

Tzali and I left for home two days later. While the men were carrying our bags in the car, Hannah made a pot of coffee and we sat down at the kitchen table. She said, "You know, Dori, I believe in fate. I believe that what is written for a person will happen. Let me tell you a story. Before Auschwitz, before the ghetto, I had a boyfriend -- I must have told you about him. I was really in love with him, but my mother didn't like him because she said he wasn't educated enough and didn't come from a 'fine family'.

"One day I was sitting with Mother at our table -- just like we're sitting now -- looking out the window at the street and talking and arguing about my boyfriend. I was asking my mother what she really had against him. Suddenly a young man I knew passed by on his way to visit a friend down the street, and my mother pointed towards him and said, 'You see him? A young man like that I would accept for you.' And do you know who she pointed to? It was Shiku.

"Now," she went on, "so many tragedies had to happen -- our world crumbled and my boyfriend died. Shiku was taken to Russia as a prisoner. His girlfriend didn't wait for him to return. She got married and left for Israel. When Shiku came home in 1949 I wasn't married yet but I wanted to be. I was anxious to have a family.

"So Shiku and I were married, fulfilling my mother's prophecy. Tell me otherwise!"

While Tzali and Shiku went to get the car Hannah picked up the conversation again.

"I still have a score to settle, though," she said. "I'm the only survivor of my family and I won't die in peace if I don't settle it.

"After liberation I found out that my father and one of my brothers didn't die the day we all arrived in Birkenau. They made it into the camp. A Jewish man from Sighet, Isaak Stein -- you know him, he was one of the owners of the fancy men's store on Main Street -- became the *Kapo* of the barrack where my father and brother lived. I was told that Stein was mean, that he beat the prisoners, starved them and even tortured them. Both my father and my brother died while in his barrack. How can I forgive him? I would have killed him with my own hands if I'd met him then. But when I got home to Sighet Stein was already gone. I went to the Romanian police and they showed me a huge folder they had on him and they said they would track him down. Then I found out he was living in the city of Tirgu-Mures. I went after him but I missed him again. This time he had gone abroad. I still want to find him. I know he's living in Philadelphia now. I no longer wish to kill him but I feel I have to tell him to his face that I hold him responsible for the deaths of my father and brother. I have so much hatred accumulated in my heart!"

For Hannah to have carried such hatred for more than forty years must have been a heavy burden. And it was very disturbing for me to realize again that our own people could have behaved in that way, that evil, like goodness and forgiveness, can be part of human nature.

You should know, Miriam, that some war criminals were brought to trial in the years following the end of the war, even in Romania. The Hungarian collaborators who took an active part in the deportations, imprisonments, tortures or killings were charged with criminal behavior. So too were some Jews for their "crimes" in the camps. But by the time of those trials Tzali and I had left for the university in Timisoara; and when we left Sighet we left all that behind.

Yes, a few people were brought to justice. But that does not mean that justice was done. It could never be done.

June 1, 1985

A Tale of Passover

Last night we had Passover Seder. It's a holiday one spends with family and friends and we had about a dozen people gathered around the Seder table, including friends from Sighet. This was also our first Seder with a grandchild present and I was very affected by its significance. Vali and Debbie were so proud of Gabriel and he seemed to be proud of himself and smiled at everyone.

Maybe I ate too much or worked too hard, but for whatever reason I was wide awake when I went to bed. As you may have noticed, night is often the time when my memories are drifting back. For many hours I lay there remembering all sorts of things. I was searching the dark corners of my memory because what I could not remember disturbed me more than what I could.

No matter how hard I concentrated I couldn't remember the last Passover I spent with my parents forty years ago. I know that Passover that year came just before our world fell apart. Things were already quite bad, but not so bad that we would not honor Passover, the great celebration of the deliverance of Jews from Egyptian slavery. So why can't I remember that Seder? Wasn't it memorable? Or was it too sad to have stayed with me all these years?

I remember other Passover Seders. For the occasion, Father would be festively dressed in a *kittle* -- the white robe embroidered by my mother which was worn only twice a year, for Passover and Yom Kippur, and on wedding days. My mother prepared for weeks in advance. She cleaned and scrubbed every corner of the house until not a crumb of bread could be found to violate the Passover. It took her a whole week to shop and she filled an entire room with food: a sack of potatoes, bottles of Passover oil, a huge basket of homemade matzo, dozens of eggs, demijohns of wine.

On the night of the first Seder she would put on her best dress, adorned only with her pearls, and cover her head with a white silk kerchief. Then she would light the candles and say the blessing. Father would bring home a beggar or someone without a family from the synagogue to fulfill the holiday *mitzvah* -- the good deed. The children, dressed for the holiday and nervous with anticipation, sat eagerly around the beautifully-set table waiting for our little brother Yancu to ask the four questions starting with "*Ma nishtanah...* " -- "Why is this night different... ?" Father, reclining on an oversized pillow, would preside proudly over the entire ritual. A special dinner was served, with the most delicious Passover dishes, matzos, *chremzli* (potato pancakes), roast; and the four goblets of wine were drunk.

The atmosphere was of warmth, family togetherness, serenity. After dinner everybody sang traditional songs and read children's stories from the *Haggadah*. The melodies had not changed for generations. I still remember Father's voice as he sang the *Chad Gadyoh* (An only kid) and *Echat Elohenu (*Our only God).

But those Seders all took place in the good and peaceful old days. By 1944 times were turbulent. The war was in its fifth year. Nearly all my brothers were away and we had lost contact with most of them. Alter, the oldest, was in Budapest, where he had been working in a knitting factory. Moishi was at the front in the Ukraine in a forced labor unit. Miki was somewhere in Italy finishing medical school. Yossie had disappeared on his way to U.S.S.R. a few years earlier and my parents feared him dead. Ezu had been arrested in Budapest for printing bread ration coupons. Ebi, also in Budapest, was an apprentice in a trade school. Only Yancu, who was fourteen, remained at home with my parents and me. I was twenty-two, the only girl in the family, and at that moment the only breadwinner.

Sighet's Jewish community had suffered much hardship since Hungary annexed the northern part of Transylvania. Jobs were lost, stores were closed, Jewish children could not attend the high schools. Still, life went on.

It wasn't until March of 1944, however, that the Germans moved in. When they did, fear spread everywhere. Rumors were already circulating about pogroms and deportations in Poland. Now Jews had to wear a yellow Star of David sewn on their clothes when they went out on the street. There were frequent searches of Jewish homes during which valuables were confiscated -- although we didn't have much of value that the Nazis and their Hungarian collaborators wanted to take. There was an early curfew and no one dared to be on the streets alone.

The police requisitioned my room and a German officer moved into our house. He was so pleasant and friendly we could hardly believe it. To my father's worried questions about the future the officer replied reassuringly. "What do you think?" he would say, "The Germans would never do those things. We are human beings too."

Could we have celebrated Passover while the German officer was lodged in my room? This was the room where we usually had our festive dinners on Sabbat and holidays. It pains me so much that I cannot remember that last Seder with my parents.

Soon after Passover orders were issued for all the Jews in Sighet to move out of their homes into a ghetto. We got less than a day's notice. We were told to be ready to go by morning, to leave all our possessions at home, to take only folding beds or mattresses, one suitcase of clothing per person, cooking utensils and enough food for two weeks. And everything had to fit into one horse-drawn carriage.

I remember leaving our house with our few belongings and starting that journey that ravaged our family. We looked back for the last time to what had been our home and contained everything dear to us. It was like going to a funeral. I can see my parents walking alongside the carriage, and Yancu and I behind it. And I recall the neighbors watching. Some of them were Jews whose turn had not yet come and who perhaps thought that, because they were doctors, lawyers, pharmacists, they would escape what befell us. The family of our neighbor the pharmacist were at their window, watching and crying. They were spared only for another three weeks; they were among the last group to be evacuated to the ghetto.

We passed along the main street, surrounded by many other families with their carriages, all going in the same direction toward the outskirts of the town where a dozen small streets were designated by the authorities as one of the two ghetto areas into which more than one third of the population of the entire city was to be crammed. When we reached the entrance of the main ghetto we saw that it had been fenced in, and the gate was guarded by Hungarian gendarmes. The non-Jews living in that area had been moved out and in each of their homes eight to ten Jewish families were assigned.

We were led to a small house and shown our room, which we had to share with another family that had already moved into it. We knew them, years ago they had been our landlords. They had already taken the beds, so Yancu and I put our mattresses on the floor for our parents, and we slept on the porch with the other youngsters. Soon a third family was assigned to our room, and other families to the next room and to the kitchen.

After we unpacked and put our few belongings in the room, I went out to see who else was around. To my surprise, I saw Zsuzsi standing in front of the house across the street, looking at the new arrivals. I went over to Tzali's family, who would have become mine too if only the war ended, the young men came home, and there was time to marry and settle down. It warmed my heart that at least we would be close.

The very next day it was decreed that the houses on that side of the street were to be returned immediately to their gentile owners and the Jews had to move out. I helped Zsuzsi and her family carry their belongings to a house not far from us on our side of the street. They were so helpless. Zsuzsi was just seventeen. Her mother had been overwhelmed by her responsibilities for years, ever since she was widowed. Her sister Dori had four-year-old Yortzo to take care of. The grandmother was old, sick and bedridden. As in most other families, the men were away at forced labor camps, at the front, or in jail. Laichi, Zsuzsi's boyfriend, who was only seventeen and too young to be drafted, was one of the few young men who were around.

After the houses on the other side of the street were reoccupied by their former owners, access to those houses was changed. Their gates facing the ghetto were sealed and the windows were painted so they couldn't see what was happening on our side of the street and "they wouldn't know."

I spent a lot of time with Zsuzsi and her family. Her mother liked me and accepted me. I kept her company and helped her mend socks. I was impressed by her skill: for years she had been saving the boys' socks with holes on the heels. Now she had the time to fix them. She would unravel the hole to an even row, slip the eyelets onto a knitting needle, knit a whole new heel downwards, then sew the edges together. All her motherly love poured into this work as she eagerly anticipated Tzali and Bela's return.

It is so painful to remember and write about those times. Yet some of the last and most precious memories of my loved ones also come from the three weeks we spent in the ghetto.

It was spring, trees were in bloom, the lilacs and jasmine filled the air with a sweet fragrance. Behind our row of houses was a little creek where we young people would gather every evening to discuss what might happen to us and what we should do. Should we run away? Should we hide in the mountains nearby? And then what? How long could we roam the mountains? Who would feed us? How long would the war last? What would happen after the war? Obviously this was only talk. Could we desert our families?

The problems of day-to-day survival belonged to our parents. I still don't know where the food came from or how far down our supplies of rice, noodles and potatoes dwindled. We had been told to bring food for two weeks but more than two weeks had passed. Was there any milk in the ghetto for babies? There was no market, there were no shops.

All day long we walked around looking for our friends. Since I still had the job at the movie house I had a permit to leave the ghetto to go to work whenever they called me. On such occasions I found myself the only one in the center of the city wearing a yellow star on my chest. People stared at me. Once in a while a former gentile friend would approach me and give me some food to take to my family. But the theater manager found my presence too bothersome and soon let me go.

I volunteered to work in the infirmary. It was so dreary. The Jewish patients from Sighet's municipal hospital had been sent back to their families. A temporary hospital was set up in the synagogue at the entrance to the ghetto, but only the very severe cases were admitted -- patients with terminal tuberculosis, multiple bedsores, or others who could not be cared

Tell the Children

for at home. There were no medications. There were no clean dressings; the dirty ones had to be washed, boiled, ironed and reused.

Day after day we waited for something to happen. By the end of the second week the houses in the ghetto were bursting with people and the streets were jammed. The last ones to come had to sleep in barns, woodsheds, or in backyards, under the open sky. Then something unexpected happened: hundreds of young Jewish men who had been doing forced labor on the front in the Ukraine were recalled and brought to the ghetto.

Moishi was among them. We were so happy and relieved. He was very handsome, and lots of girls had been in love with him before he was sent to the front. He liked to court them, to go dancing, and to have fun. He liked to dress well. After the war began he was the only man in our family who ordered several suits from the tailor. After two years my brother was back with us.

Moishi was very creative. Out of any material he found -- shell fragments, shrapnel -- he would make drawings, cartoons, carvings, engravings or sculptures. He told me that at the front his officers kept him busy creating war mementos for them. This is how he survived while the other men had to dig ditches, sweep mines and live on near-starvation rations. It was so good to have a young, strong man to lean on. But he arrived with a severe toothache. There were no dentists available to treat him. Every aspirin we had or could find, Moishi took to ease the pain.

There was a great deal of speculation inside the ghetto. Why had these young, able-bodied men been brought back while the war was still raging? Their return strengthened our naive expectation that we would be sent somewhere to work, that we were needed indeed.

The week Moishi returned our house was raided again. The Hungarian gendarmes ransacked our belongings and took away the only good clothes we had left -- Moishi's three new suits. Moishi was in too much pain to react. Father suffered in silence.

The last image I have of my father before we were all taken away was of him in the backyard, sitting at a table in the sun, working on his manuscripts as he had done for years. It was as if he could express in his writing everything that he didn't dare say out loud. But none of us will ever know what he wrote, for those manuscripts were destroyed.

Rumors started circulating that the whole ghetto would be soon evacuated. One evening, after three weeks in the ghetto, we were told that we would be leaving the next morning. We were ordered to gather on the street in front of our houses and to take along only one piece of luggage per person. Everything else was to be left behind. Mother had found a hiding place in the attic of our small house where she hid what was left of the

- 127 -

trousseau she had been collecting for me: some embroidered table linens, lace curtains, a white silk shawl, a matzo cover; and some silky fabric for a dress, whose texture and grey-and-white paisley pattern I still recall. She had saved it for years for a happy special occasion that never came.

On the morning of May 14 the streets of the ghetto slowly filled with hundreds of people carrying bundles and suitcases. Some were helping the old and the sick. Others were carrying children. Everyone was dressed in his or her best clothes, the young ones as if for an outing, with rucksacks on their backs. There was so much fear and anxiety. The older people were arguing and speculating about what would happen to us, some were just praying. We waited and waited.

Against that backdrop of the mass of people worried about the unknown, an image haunts me: Moishi, tired, exhausted and in pain. We sat down at the curbside near a ditch and he put his head on my knees for a nap. Much else happened in the next few days, but this memory is the strongest. Moishi, the young man, my older brother, the strong, the handsome, so overwhelmed, needing me so much, resting his head in my lap. He alone is in that image. All the others have disappeared.

I wish, Miriam, I could explain it. Why is my heart now so heavy with this vision of my brother? Why does pain come from nowhere while I am writing this letter? Why does everything else disappear to bring out this one clear painful image?

By noon three thousand of us -- almost a third of the ghetto population -- were marched out of the ghetto and crowded into Sighet's Great Synagogue. Through the whole afternoon the gendarmes searched again and again through our belongings and took their share of jewelry or whatever else was left. My mother and many other women were taken a few at a time into a small room where they were stripped and searched internally by female guards for "hidden treasures."

Night fell. The searches ended and we were left in the synagogue without food or water. The doors were locked. People were sitting on benches or lying on the floor. Some were assigned to the balcony. The place was so crammed you could hardly move. The lights were on all night. It was noisy: children were crying, people were whispering, praying, coughing or sobbing. Our family sat together on the floor. Around were our neighbors from the ghetto. Little Yortzo was crying, "I want to go home!" We took turns resting our heads on our only suitcase. We were exhausted but couldn't sleep. The hours passed slowly.

The dawn brought noise and commotion from the outside. The gendarmes burst in and started to yell for everyone to get up and assemble in the courtyard for the walk to the railroad station. Carrying our few belongings, we started to march through the streets. I remember looking at the clock tower of the Roman Catholic church as we passed. It was six o'clock on a beautiful clear morning. Shouting commands, the gendarmes herded us together, clubbing anyone who wasn't moving fast enough. Some people who could not keep up were whipped by the brutal guards. Children and the elderly stumbled and had to be helped. Packages and bundles fell out of tired arms and could not be picked up. People cried, family members held hands to keep from being separated. Pillows and bags were scattered all over, baby carriages were left behind.

The streets were deserted. Where were the people of the city? Were they really sleeping, or were they peering at us from behind the shutters? How did they feel, witnessing this miserable spectacle, this mass of humanity being chased in front of their houses? Wasn't each of us a former friend, neighbor, schoolmate?

Finally we arrived at the station. As the crowd gathered on the platform, my parents, my two brothers and I tried hard to stay together. We felt strong and healthy enough to withstand whatever ordeal awaited us. Just as we had managed that two-kilometer march, we would manage whatever work the Germans expected us to do. Zsuzsi and her family were nearby, all waiting for the trains to come into the station. In the distance we saw a few freight trains.

Suddenly a train pulled in a few tracks away, a military train. When it stopped, a young man got off. He looked around at the thousands of us on the platform. At first I couldn't tell who it was, but then I recognized my brother Alter. I frantically called his name, I waved. He heard me and he looked in my direction until he saw us. He ran over, and hugged and kissed us all. He asked us where we were going. We said we didn't know for sure, but we suspected that we were going to a work camp in Germany, or to be resettled in Hungary, on the West bank of the Danube.

"And how about you?" I asked.

"To the Russian front," he said. He was en route from Budapest with a whole trainload of Jewish men drafted for forced labor.

There was no time for more words, only hugs and tears. His train whistled. He said goodbye and ran to catch the moving train. The whole incident must have lasted only a few minutes. Zsuzsi, who was behind me, didn't see any of it, and as she turned around and saw us all crying and waving to the vanishing train she was astonished. "What happened? Who is on that train?"

I wondered if I would ever see Alter again. Little did I suspect that Alter would be the only one of them that I would see again. When I think about that amazing encounter, it borders on the miraculous.

As for Moishi, you know by now that he never returned from Auschwitz. All my inquiries about him after the war ended in disappointment. No survivor I spoke to ever saw Moishi after our arrival *There*. For all these years I assumed that he had died -- rather, that he had been killed -- that first night, with Yancu and my parents.

Last April Tzali and I went to Israel. We visited the Museum of the Holocaust again. This museum leaves a strong impression on me every time I see it. It has exhibits on everything relating to what happened to the Jewish people during World War II. One exhibit has pictures and documents about the *Sonderkommandos*. These were those few young men who were forced to work at the crematoriums and help the SS herd people into the gas chambers. They had to shovel the bodies out of the gas chambers, remove whatever valuables they could find -- rings, chains, gold teeth, hair -- and stack the bodies in the ovens. Imagine the horror when one of the men of the *Sonderkommando* found his parents or relatives among the dead.

The work was grueling and the men lasted only a few weeks; then the whole team was gassed and replaced with other young men who had just arrived. Rarely did the men of this team escape to tell their stories -- but some did.

All the time I was in Auschwitz, very little was known about what went on at the gas chambers and crematoriums. After the war I learned a great deal about them, how they operated, how the killings were done, how the bodies were disposed; and that whole industries in Germany were based on the remains from the killings. Nothing went to waste: hair was used to stuff pillows and mattresses; fat to make soap, human skins to make lampshades for the officers. (Perhaps some gifted prisoners were forced to make nice drawings on these lampshades without suspecting what they really were).

As we saw the documentation of all this in the museum my heart sank. I was very quiet. On the way out Tzali said to me, "Moishi was also in the *Sonderkommando*."

"What do you mean?"

"Yes, I heard it."

"When did you hear it? How come you never told me!"

"I thought I did. Maybe I didn't. Probably I shouldn't have told you now."

"Tzali, I don't believe it. You knew about this and you never told me? all those years..." I was shocked, incredulous.

"Look, it was probably only hearsay. But what difference does it make?"

It makes all the difference in the world to me. For almost forty years I thought Moishi died an instant death with the others and this ended his suffering. Now I have to live with the knowledge of what he suffered and that he must have died a hundred times every day as he saw so many others die in front of his eyes. He knew then what was happening and that torture alone must have been unbearable. He also must have known that there was no hope for him or for the others working alongside him. How can I come to terms with this?

For many nights I couldn't sleep. I had nightmares about Moishi, forced to do all those terrible things. Wouldn't it have been better not to have been told? If Tzali had been trying to spare me this anguish, wasn't he right? I tried to convince myself that it was not true.

Would it be too much to expect that they would allow such a handsome young man to die without enduring his share of work, torment and suffering?

April 17, 1984

Part III: Expectations

Back to Life

Freedom!

This is the first word in the Journal I started on the day of liberation in Weisswasser. How can one express the feeling with one word only? A simple word, and yet so overwhelming, that to grasp its meaning I had to repeat it, reflect on it, share it, even if just with myself, in a diary.

It was May 6, two days before the German surrender. There was confusion in the camp, we were called for the morning roll call and then dismissed. We didn't know what had happened. There had been rumors for some time that the Allies were close, and that the Germans' defeat was near. The truth started to surface when we saw some SS supervisors come out in civilian clothes, others pack and load their cars in a hurry; we noticed that some had already disappeared.

I don't know how I got a pen and a notebook. As the guards fled, many girls rushed to their abandoned quarters and started to ransack the furniture, smash anything that was breakable, loot whatever they could carry. That is when I must have found what I needed most, a pen and something to write on. For the next two weeks I recorded everything in my Journal, thoughts, events, feelings.

There is excitement and anticipation. The camp gate is not yet open, and we are still prisoners in their power. We are afraid that the guards, in their defeat, will commit some ultimate, desperate act and destroy us. What will they do? Is the camp mined? Will they kill us? Drive us to some other place?

We rush to the fence, we scream and hug and kiss each other, we cannot contain our restlessness and happiness. We look down to the valley. The road is crowded, there is an endless stream of refugees on all kinds of vehicles, horse-drawn carriages, bicycles, trucks, jeeps. They make their way out of the village. Huge swarms of people follow on foot with bundles, backpacks and suitcases, some pushing carts. A train has just pulled into the station, passengers are getting out, and we recognize some of our French friends, the POWs who worked with us in the factory. They come to share this moment with us, to help us. They are as excited as we are. We wave to them. More former prisoners arrive, we talk through the fence, we shake hands, congratulate each other.

There is exhilaration and delirium as hundreds of girls storm the gate, eager to get out. The camp gate is finally opened. We all run out, we laugh and cry. Soon the men join us in the courtyard and in the dormitories and we all embrace. The food storage has been unlocked. We carry potatoes in pails to our rooms, we make fires in the stoves, we cook them. There is no salt, but they taste just as good with sugar or marmalade. We go back to the food storage and grab whatever is left, and fill our beds with more potatoes, bread, sugar, turnips and kohlrabi. Some girls cut blankets and start sewing backpacks, they are already preparing for the trip home.

I have this urge to run up the hill behind the camp. Baba and Henriette join me. The short climb exhausts us, but just being there, breathing the fresh and free air, is intoxicating. We look at the beautiful countryside and suddenly realize that everything around us is green, every tree is in bloom. We lie down on the grass sprinkled with wild flowers and look at the brilliant sky... memorable moments still vivid in my mind many decades later.

The first night we are anxious and worried because the camp is unguarded, we feel vulnerable. We are told that the Russians are three villages away from us. Some men join us in a vigil outside. It starts to rain. The gate remains open, and this heightens our sense of being free. When we finally go inside I jot a few lines in my journal:

> *I am in my bunk bed, I cannot sleep from the excitement. Camp commander Stanek's speech still rings in my ears. "I declare you free. The camp is open for you. Those who wish can still sleep here, but I warn you, if something happens to the camp supervisor, I will not refrain from retaliating accordingly. The key to the food storage was turned over to the Lageralteste. If you plan frugally, you will have enough food for a while. Try your best...You are free!" It seems so incredible to have reached this moment and to hear such words from the murderer's mouth! The girls whisper to one another, there is quiet outside, yet nobody is asleep. Is this really happening? Are we really free?*

The following day some of our French friends return and suggest that we move to their camp in the town of Schildberg, where it would be safer. Baba and I, along with a few others, go with them by passenger train. This is another new experience, sitting on benches, looking out the window, being among civilian passengers and part of the real world again.

> *To be free! To feel it so intensely! Sitting near us are Anatole and Michel, who are so generous, and I am so grateful for this trip. One station, another station, we can hardly sit from the excitement. The men laugh, we are like small children, we are in a frenzy, and for every little pleasure we are grateful to all of them, even to the fate that had been so cruel to us. No, this short trip cannot be forgotten.*

The dormitory is large and airy, the men are friendly and considerate. They give us corner bunk beds, they hang out sheets for privacy, and they feed us. They take us to their dining room, where we are served incredible portions of juicy roast beef, all red inside, with fried potatoes. I have never eaten anything so wonderful in my life. That whole night I am sick to my stomach, but I try hard not to throw up that delicious dinner.

Early the next morning we are awakened by a loud commotion from the street. We go outside. The Russians are marching into town to the acclaim of the newly liberated Czech population. The armistice has been signed, the war is over! Townspeople are lining the streets, they shout, they scream, they wave to the Russians. The French and Jewish former prisoners join them in the jubilation, happy to greet their liberators.

The Czech authorities, very protective of the hundreds of girls in their charge, decree that they cannot leave yet for their former countries -- the highways are destroyed, the bridges are demolished, there are no trains or buses, and the roads are full of soldiers. They assign the former prisoners little cottages abandoned by the fleeing German population. Baba, Itza and I move into one of them with some of the French men for protection and companionship. It is a small two-room house with a well stocked larder and closets, well kept and neat as only German houses can be.

I describe in my diary the plentiful meals, the strolls on the main street, all the warm water and soap we could wish for, privacy, a clean bed with white sheets, pillows and comforters, all unforgettable new sensations. Everything feels as if I experience it for the first time, as if I had never tasted such pleasures before. I revel in the new surroundings, I enjoy the freedom, I admire the landscape, I cherish human companionship, and I rejoice in living like a human being again. These are our dreams come true.

One day, while walking along the main street, we notice a crowd outside a shoe store whose German owner has fled. The store has been looted. Soviet soldiers are blocking the entrance and trying to restore order. When we tell them who we are, and that we need shoes, they check our tattooed numbers. Convinced that we are indeed liberated prisoners, they become very helpful and let us go in and take any shoes we want. There are no more women's summer shoes left, only high-top winter shoes, but there are lots of men's shoes. I take a pair of winter shoes for myself and I carefully choose two pairs of men's shoes, brown moccassins for my little brother Yancu and black shoes in a larger size for my older brother Moishi. I carried those shoes for hundreds of miles on my journey home to Sighet the same way I carried my hopes that my brothers might be alive and come home some day.

Another day, as we stroll in the center of the town I come across a group of German civilians working on road construction. Seeing them do forced labor as we had done until just days before, I become ambivalent. Maybe some of them are innocent? I recognize Godder among them, the engineer who had been kind to me when he was my chief in the technical office. He has a shovel in his hand, and there is fear and despair on his face. I stop to talk. "It was you then, now it is our turn," he says to me. He tells me about his family in Germany. I give him our address and invite him to come to visit. He is surprised. I am not sure he will come, but he does. I write about it in my journal:

We got up late today. Godder arrived as we were having our breakfast. The house was a mess. Everyone was still in nightgowns even though it must have been midday. Amid shame and embarrassment we invited him for coffee. Baba and Itza jumped at this chance to tell a German everything that had happened over the past year: every detail about Auschwitz, everything the Germans did to us, how they destroyed our homes and our families, how cruelly his 'civilized' people had behaved, about the crematoriums, the selections, Mengele. Poor Godder, he was so taken aback by this attack. He managed to say something like "Yes, yes, I believe it is as you say, but now those of us who are innocent have to suffer because of it."

It was very awkward, and I was sorry to see him so uncomfortable, yet I was glad it was happening. When I was a prisoner working in his office I could not talk this way, raise my voice and complain. And now, as a free person, I was unable to accuse him as the others did, because I would not forget his kindness to me. He was the only German who helped me. But he should know it all, for if he suffers for it, at least he will know why.

I would have preferred to invite him once for dinner. Then he would see that we can also eat, not only starve; that we can live nicely, that we too know how to dress, how to behave decently, that we are civilized and educated people. He would eat in our house as a guest, without the strained feeling I had when I accepted his help. But this was not to happen, for we did not act in a way to lead him to visit again.

Days pass and we are still not able to start our trip home, I become restless. I describe those happy and carefree days of liberation, the atmosphere of romance, love, and freedom. I mention couples who want so much to enjoy the present. We have dinner by candlelight, parties with dancing and singing and special food that the men bring from the countryside. All this makes me uneasy. I start to wonder, don't they have someone waiting for them at home, don't they care?

I confide in my diary my anguish, my doubts, my fear. As I reach the first anniversary of my deportation I begin to recall all the events of the year before with a freshness I could not evoke 40 years later.

> *I am home, writing. The whole afternoon I was lying exhausted, not from work, but from my thoughts, my expectations, my fears. My little room is cool, I hear birds chirping outside, somewhere an accordion is playing. It is a bright, sunny day, the trees are blossoming, like in the old song, "It is May and the lilacs are blooming, it is May and my heart is freezing." What do these surroundings remind me of? The summers in Sapantza? The nursery in Cluj where I visited Tzali during his imprisonment? It is so pleasant, so sweet and yet so painful.*
>
> *I am troubled. Maybe I should stay here and not go home. I am scared. Where will I go? To whom? Is there anybody waiting for me in Sighet? I will arrive on such a splendid May day, I will run home full of hopes, and who will be there? Mother? Father? No, I can no longer deceive myself with such illusions. My dearest parents! How much I loved you -- only now do I realize it. Why didn't I treat you as you deserved? Father, forgive me; Mother too, that I was not always considerate, that I caused you so many worries and so much heartache. I am afraid that I am ready to forget this past year, now that I am to embark on such a long journey into the unknown. It seems as if I am returning home from an excursion and I am expecting you to be there waiting for me with open arms. God, why is our fate so cruel?*
>
> *Yancu darling, maybe you will be home. Look, I am even bringing you a pair of shoes. You will like them, won't you? And you will be happy to see your sister who thought of you so often. Whom can I count on? Moishi, you are my only hope, the only one I trust has survived. I implore you, do not disappoint me, I don't want to remain alone in the family. Ebi, my dear, where are you? Look at the tears that I shed writing these lines. I will search for you in Budapest, where you were last time, even though I know that if you have survived these times you are probably home. But I dare not hope that I will find even a small family there... part of the family... or just one person waiting for me. Lord, look how my demands shrink, how heartbroken I have become. Dear Ezu, did you have enough strength to endure?*

Yossie, are you alive? You left five years ago, but we never found out if you reached Russia. Alter, will you be there? Maybe you are working for a Jewish newspaper or at a theater? Do you think of me? And Miki? No, no... I am not allowed to delude myself with such wonderful dreams of finding you home, because the disappointment will be so terrible. And it will be... oh, dear brothers, parents, my home, I am yearning terribly, and it hurts so much that I can hardly bear it.

Tzali, I don't know how to say it, but if I lose you too then I would rather have been taken to the gas chamber or have run into the electric fence. Today the memories are haunting me: our time in Cluj, the brick factory where we skied, all this was so very beautiful. You will be waiting for me, won't you? And you still love me!?

Wouldn't it be better to stay here, to listen to the birds chirping and to deceive myself that once I had a boyfriend, Tzali, whom I loved so much, whom I see when I look at any man and who is waiting for me with outstretched arms, to hug me, to hold me, to dance to the tune of Tango Bolero, "Come my love, I am waiting only for your coming." Maybe he even has a little room like this one, quiet and cozy, and he will love me as before... dreams of love... God, the disillusions are hurting me already.

Why is this May so beautiful and yet so painful?

The next entry in my diary is on May 13. This reawakens all the emotions of our last day in the ghetto, the departure from there, and the night in the Temple, a year ago to the day,

Thousands are gathered in this Synagogue, tired, exhausted, lying on the benches or on the floor, on one another, children crying. Our eyes are closing and there is nowhere to put our heads for a little rest. There is a suitcase and Zsuzsi, Laichi and I take turns sleeping on it. How hard it must be for people in love to see each other suffering so. It is barely two in the morning. Mother remained upstairs with the women after being body-searched. I look around. Father isn't asleep either. It takes a good hour for me to make my way to him through the crowd on the floor. "Come, take a little preserve, Father, why save it?" It is only three o'clock, only four o'clock and I have not closed my eyes the entire night.

Five o'clock. Movement outside. The guards have entered. We must get ready to leave! Where? Home? No, not after a day and a night like this. That would be too beautiful. We are taken to the railroad station. After the searches our parcels have dropped to less

- 140 -

than half.

It is a gorgeous May morning, just like those mornings when we used to gather in the square for our outings. The sky is painfully clear, the lilacs in full bloom. The tower clock on the Catholic church shows six a.m. Time seems to have stopped.

And we are marching to our doom."

The next few pages describe the train ride. Finally, we arrive at Auschwitz-Birkenau:

... the train stops again. I hear a terrifying scream in the night. Moishi and I are up and listening... There is another scream... cries... shrieks... "Mein Kind!"... "Mame!"... "Wie bist du?" We run to the little window and climb on suitcases to see better. Mother is frightened, even I feel that we have arrived at our tragic end: now, this night, here, in some hidden forest they will line us up and bang, bang! No, I won't let it happen, I want to live, do you understand?!

My heart is beating fast, but I try to calm my dear mother, "Mother, nothing is happening there, they are just carrying belongings of the people who are crying," or "they are getting off the train and they are being separated."

But the cries have intensified, there are some frightening shrieks, screams, loud orders are given, packages thrown out of trains are lying at random between the tracks. No, I cannot calm her anymore.

Our doors are opened abruptly and orders are given in German, "Heraus! Alle heraus!" -- "Everyone get out! Take some food with you. Leave all packages in the wagon!" We get dressed, the situation has become clear, it is now and here. Searchlights reach the wagon, "All out!" Around the train there are men in striped uniforms. Is there a jail nearby whose prisoners help out? We leave everything behind except a little marmalade that remained in my basket. There are blinding lights outside, we are driven alongside the train, others are getting off from the other track. "Where are you from?" But they are also from Sighet. We are all terrified. "Children, where are you, let's keep together so we don't get lost in the crowd. Zsuzsi, Laichi, Dori, come on!" We don't know where we are going, the crowd is pushing us ahead, we just drag ourselves along, all around us are familiar faces from our transport.

I hear on the loudspeaker that the men must form a column on the left. I cry out, "Mother, the men have to go a separate way." My dear mother is fainting. "Mother, Mother, please, I implore you!

Get hold of yourself!" Moishi, Yancu, Father, all are crying and holding her, I cannot see because of the heavy tears. "Dear Mother, we two will stay together. Don't worry, the men are only going to the baths. Mother, look at me!"

I was so happy that I would be with her. I felt so close to her, I hugged her and kissed her, my tears dropped on her face. Did I foresee that we too would be torn apart? Mother's instinct was right though, she knew, she felt the upcoming tragedy. She hardly opened her eyes and stumbled again in my arms. In despair we shouted, we cried, the crowd passed us by and moved ahead. "Mother dear, don't leave me alone." I know she didn't want to, the murderers took her. We again hugged my father and my two brothers and kissed their tear-soaked faces, and they disappeared in the crowd to follow the men.

I held Mother tightly by her arm so as not to lose her and we followed the multitude of women and children. Our happiness lasted a few steps only. I soon realized that in front of me the young girls were being sent in one direction, to the right, and the mothers to the left. "Mother, they are separating us!" I panicked. She cried out "No, no!" What should I do? A wrong instinct advised me that there would be trouble for the young people, so I had better stay with Mother. I pulled the kerchief over my forehead, I walked stooped, I limped, but they could not be fooled. As we got in front of the selecting officer, a stick appeared between the two of us. I was motioned to go to the right, Mother to the left. I muttered something about going after her to say good-bye, but a club hit my arm and I was sent after the other girls. I looked back, Mother had stopped and stood as if petrified. I looked back again, and I did not see her anymore. Zsuzsi was coming behind me with tears in her eyes.

And what happened thereafter? You know the rest, Miriam, that's when the hell of Birkenau started.

I end the journal at midnight of May 17, exactly one year later,

It is after midnight now. So it was then. If someone had shown me a picture of the present, or had told me, "Don't worry, silly, within one year you will be a free person, you will look good, grow fat, live in the romantic Sudeten region, you will fry potato pancakes, you will enjoy the company of men, you will bake cakes for your trip home," I would have thought him crazy. And I still don't believe it. What? The present or the past?

And all day long we have been preparing, for we are leaving

Tell the Children

the day after tomorrow. I am so restless and impatient... I have to find out what happened to the others.

Home... what is the meaning of this word now? My heart sinks at the thought of it...

1993

Home Again

It was a long trip home through the war-ravaged countryside, crossing parts of Czechoslovakia and Hungary before reaching Sighet, now again part of Romania. The roads had been bombed and left impassable, ruined tracks forced trains to stop before their destination. We had to walk long distances. Soldiers were eager to give us lifts in their trucks or jeeps. We slept in open wagons or on benches in train station waiting rooms. We received food from the civilians on the trains or from local peasants, sometimes by bartering the clothes or other things we had picked up in Schildberg.

I was with a few girls from Weisswasser intent on getting home. Many others went to Prague or to nearby liberated camps to find family members, or stayed with the Czech families who had given them shelter. Around us there were hundreds of POWs and liberated prisoners from other camps, all trying to make their way home. I remember an instance when we were sitting on the platform of such a wagon together with some Italian POWs before reaching the station where they would change trains and continue towards Italy. We had talked along the way. When they heard that my brother, Miki, was in Rome they tried to persuade me to go with them to look for him. It was tempting; since liberation all of us had this dilemma, where should we go, where would we find someone from our family. But no, I told myself, I had to go first to Sighet. My brothers might be there waiting for me, and Tzali should be there. They wouldn't know where to look for me if I went somewhere else. Many girls, however, switched destinations and went West, knowing that they wouldn't find anybody if they went home.

Whenever my train slowed down or stopped I asked those crowded on the neighboring trains or waiting to board, "Have you seen any of my brothers anywhere? Have you seen an Apsan in Germany, in a camp?" For days I found nobody who had seen any of them. When I got closer to Budapest, one man finally said, yes, he had been with a fellow named Apsan who must be on one of the trains going home.

"Which one? What is his first name?" I cried. But the train moved on and I never got an answer. I became very excited. Someone was alive, and coming home! It seemed to me it had to be Yancu or Moishi.

Budapest was one of the few places in Hungary where most of the Jews had escaped deportation. By the time their turn came there was a change in the government's policy due to the rapid advance of the Soviet Army. Also Raoul Wallenberg's efforts on behalf on the Swedish Embassy saved thousands. Now relief organizations were set up to help the hundreds of refugees arriving daily. All over the city rescue teams waited to welcome former prisoners like me with food, and to guide us to the central shelter, where a school had been turned into a dormitory and clothing and food were being distributed.

When I arrived at the Center I rushed to the main office. I recognized a few men and women from Sighet. I kept asking everyone, "Have you seen any of my brothers?"

"Yes," someone said to my great relief. "One is around here, looking for you."

"Where? Which one?" I was told to go behind one of the buildings. I ran around the building and bumped into Ezu coming from the other direction. We dropped into each other's arms, crying for joy, the first happy tears since it all began. I had not known that he had also been in Germany. The last I knew of him, he was in a Hungarian labor camp for printing fake food coupons. He told me that from there he had been deported to a concentration camp in Germany and had worked in a coal mine in the Upper Silesia.

And now he was here. I had a brother who was alive! And more good news was in store for me. I soon found out from a man who had came from Sighet to meet his cousin that Tzali was there, waiting for me. He was the one I most hoped would be there. Suddenly everything looked brighter.

I reached Sighet on June second. It had taken two weeks to travel the few hundred miles from Schildberg. It was a sunny day, and the carriage that brought Ezu and me to Sighet stopped on the main street, in front of the Crown hotel. How strange, to be in this town again, after all that had happened this past year! It felt as if a century had passed since I had left. A small crowd surrounded us, pressing us with questions. I was looking for Tzali, but he was not there. His brother, Bela and their friend, Sanyi showed up soon. They told me that Tzali had heard a few days earlier that I was coming home, and had gone to nearby Slatina, where a train with refugees was rumored to arrive. They took me to their place. Finally, in the late afternoon, Tzali returned. His joy in our meeting again was only clouded by his disappointment that he hadn't been there when I arrived. He looked so haggard. We went out into the garden to be alone, but it was not the time or place to talk about all that had happened since we had seen each other so long ago. Besides, words were not needed to express the feelings that overwhelmed both of us.

Tzali had been in Sighet for several months. He had returned from the prison in Cluj in September 1944, when Romania allied itself with the Soviets against Germany. Earlier that summer he had escaped deportation by a thread, through the shrewdness of the prison's benevolent lieutenant

Czikkora, the deputy commander. When the decision was made by the higher authorities to deport the Jewish prisoners to Germany, he went to the commander and argued with him forcefully that these people should not be taken out of the country, for they were political prisoners who might carry secrets with them. Then, when the authorities agreed, he came running to the train station, where his prisoners were already in locked box cars. Czikkora put on a whole scene, swearing and chasing them out and beating them so the other guards wouldn't suspect his real reasons. But his men knew, for he had always been sympathetic to them.

When Tzali arrived home the town was deserted, a ghost town. Most of the Romanian population had abandoned Sighet when the Hungarians occupied the city, in 1940. The Hungarians fled when the Soviet Army reached Transylvania in their advance against the retreating Nazis and their allies. The only Jews in Sighet were the few men who had returned from the Eastern front or from the prisons. No one knew what had happened to the entire population who had been deported. Jewish houses were dilapidated and the interiors had been vandalized, Tzali's home among them. Peasants from the countryside and gypsies had moved into those still in habitable condition. Tzali was able to get a furnished room in what had been his Uncle Alex's house. The rest of the house was occupied by a gypsy family.

For months, he had no hope that anyone in his family was alive. Alone and depressed, he went to work for what was to become the civilian administration in Sighet. Then, in April, a few people from the eastern camps liberated by the Red Army began to make their way back to Sighet and the neighboring villages. They told horror stories about the death camps, about the mass killings. But their return also rekindled hope. If they had survived perhaps some members of his family had survived too. And indeed, Bela and Sanyi returned from a forced labor detachment in May. Also around that time more former prisoners came from the liberated camps in Czechoslovakia. Among them was Tzali's cousin Yutzi, and the four of them stayed in the same room and waited impatiently and with great anguish for more to come.

Ezu soon went back to Budapest, but there were still five of us in one room, with no other place to move into. We had little money, no clothes, no possessions. But we reveled in our freedom, and we lived only in the present, still hoping that more members of our families would return any day. For the moment we didn't even think about the future.

Eating continued to be a major preoccupation. Yutzi and I did the cooking but we were very clumsy at it. Neither of us knew how to cook, so we just tried to remember how our mothers did it. The men made fun of us when the noodles boiled over, the meat burned, the vegetables overcooked.

But we all continued to eat as if afraid of hunger and starvation. Since the liberation I had put on about twenty-five pounds and looked quite plump. I was still wearing high-top laced shoes, a man's shirt with rolled-up sleeves and a gathered peasant skirt I had found in the house in Schildberg, and I was often taken for a peasant woman. The boils on my chin had not healed yet. I must have looked awful; but Tzali did not care. Not that he looked better himself: he was very skinny and had lost some teeth in prison, which the dentist was to fix before our wedding. It all didn't matter, we were happy just to have found each other.

But we couldn't get married. We still had no home, not even a room for ourselves. I had no clothes except some dresses and shoes handed out by relief agencies. We didn't even have identity papers. To earn some money Tzali joined some friends in exporting salt from the nearby salt mines to Hungary. He went to Budapest with his merchandise while I stayed in Sighet.

Every day I went to the Jewish Community Center to find out who had just returned. New people arrived all the time, bringing information about those who had been with them in camp. They knew about some who had disappeared through selections, others who were alive and on their way home. We examined hundreds of notices posted on the bulletin board by people searching for relatives, and letters from abroad addressed to people who had not returned, and might never return.

The Center served hot meals, offered clothing donated by American Jewish organizations, and provided dormitories for those who had nowhere to live. It was always crowded, bustling with people and intense activity. In the courtyard one could witness the despair of those who had just learned the fate of their loved ones, or the joys of a few happy, emotional reunions.

I continued to search for my brothers. I knew only about Ezu, who was now in Budapest working for a relief organization. I spoke to dozens of young men who might have been with Moishi and Yancu, but no one had ever seen them in any of the camps. I read the notices avidly, hoping someone was looking for me. Then one day -- unexpectedly, amazingly -- I found a postcard from my brother Yossie, sent from a Russian prison camp in Siberia. Then another one came, and yet another one.

I was overjoyed. Yossie was the last one I thought could be alive. For years my parents had mourned him. They believed he had perished in the snowy Carpathian Mountains in the winter of 1940 when he had tried to escape to Russia with many other young people. He had been in Siberia for all those years, was still there, and knew nothing about the family he had left behind. Since the end of the war he had been sending desperate letters to all our former addresses, to the city hall, to the police: "Where is my family?"

"Where is my dear sister?" "Please write me if you know anything about the Apsans!"

He was still very far away, but he was alive, and I knew that he would come home some day. I wrote at once to let him know I was there waiting for him, and to tell him about the rest of the family.

A few weeks later I found another letter on the bulletin board. This one was from my Aunt Czili, my mother's younger sister. She lived in Medias, a small town in Transylvania just outside the formerly Hungarian-occupied territory. The letter came as a shock. I had completely forgotten that Czili's family did not live in the occupied areas, and thus they might have escaped deportation. For years my aunt had lamented that she lived so far from her sisters; and now, precisely because she did not live in Maramures, she was the only one to have survived with all her family.

Medias was a main railroad crossing on the way to Bucharest. Every day Aunt Czili went to the station, desperately trying to find anyone from Sighet who might know something about her large family. Crowded trains passed through Medias carrying hundreds of refugees from one place to another, following sometimes uncertain leads and false rumors, also hoping to find someone who might have been in camp with a husband or a brother. Many went as far as Bucharest, where the central office of the Jewish Agency collected more complete information about refugees, and they could even get assistance with emigration. One day Aunt Czili found out that I had returned and she wrote to me.

I was bewildered and distressed that the thought of Aunt Czili had never entered my mind. Where was my judgment? How could I have forgotten? It seemed as though a dense fog had settled on my memory, as if everything that I had experienced before deportation had belonged to someone else's life, or perhaps to another life of mine. I could hardly connect the two. My mind had become blank. For weeks the only thing that had mattered was that I was alive, that I had found Tzali and that I was waiting and hoping for my deported family to come home.

I took the next train to Medias. It was wonderful to see my red-headed Aunt Czili again. She was such a warmhearted woman. I had been her favorite niece, and had visited her in Medias when I was 14. She always loved me and now she loved me even more, knowing how much I needed it. Czili, her husband Ignatz and their three daughters lived modestly in a small two-room apartment. Their only son had emigrated to Palestine to help build the Jewish state, and the girls planned to join him soon. I don't remember how we all fit into their little home but I had a couch all to myself and I was pampered. I stayed there a couple of weeks.

Not without sacrifice, Aunt Czili had a new dress made for me, my first one: a blue print cotton dress with ruffled white collar and cuffs. She also got me my first pair of sandals. It was so unusual and marvelous to again be wearing clothes and shoes that fit. I thought I looked beautiful in them, and felt proud. I enjoyed her excellent cooking, sunbathed in her tiny vegetable garden and continued to feel free and happy.

Aunt Czili kept asking me about the rest of the family. One day she and I found some quiet time to talk about it. She could not believe all that I told her about the camps, and my suspicion that all those who had not come yet would never come. For the first time I myself realized the enormity of the losses. We counted about forty relatives who had lived in Maramures and had been deported. Only a handful had come back so far, Ezu and I in Sighet, and cousin Faigi in Borsa. Not one of the relatives from Sapantza or Remetz returned, not one of Esther and Pearl's families survived.

One Friday, when my aunt was cleaning the house in preparation for Sabbath, she covered the freshly scrubbed kitchen floor with newspapers. As I was walking on the papers I looked down and suddenly a headline caught my attention: "A new medical school has opened in Timisoara." This was a revelation! For the first time since we had been taken away from Sighet I remembered that I had wanted to go to medical school. In the camps I had lost every ambition except one -- to get out of that hell alive. Now it hit me. This was it! I had a goal! What was I doing here, eating, sunbathing, absorbed with new clothes and other unimportant things.

Suddenly I was in a hurry to return to Sighet, to plan my future with Tzali, to get married, and go to the university. One cannot stay idle and wait forever. I wanted us to get on with our lives. I took the next train back.

Tzali returned from Budapest having made enough money to last us for a while. Soon cousin Hedi's house became available and was assigned to us. We could all move in with the few pieces of furniture that Tzali had acquired. It had plenty of room for our whole impromptu "family" and a separate bedroom for the two of us. We were delighted. By August we were ready to get married.

All of our friends came to the party, bringing home-made cakes and pastries. It was a great celebration, one of the first weddings after the war. From Budapest Tzali had brought me a brown georgette dress and fashionable platform-sole sandals, which weren't yet available in Sighet. This was what I wore. I had neither a wedding gown nor a wedding ring. No one brought presents. We ate, we drank, we sang and danced the whole night. We all rejoiced together. Most of our friends didn't want to leave, it was not safe to walk at night, there were too many Russian soldiers around. At dawn the exhausted guests fell asleep on the beds, on the couch, even on the floor. The next morning more friends arrived. Usher, Tzali's brother-in-law, who had survived in a labor camp and had settled in the city of Satu-Mare, was late catching the bus from there. He brought more food and more liquor, and the celebration continued.

From Budapest Tzali had brought back a china coffee and tea set for our new home. It was our only wedding present. The pieces were beautiful and unusual. We arranged them in the cabinet and often admired them. Over the years, as we moved from one place to another, and later from one country to another, cups and saucers were broken, but in our china cabinet we still have a few of the original pieces, now patched together. We cherish them as a precious reminder of that wedding in the summer of 1945.

And our wedding picture? One day, Miriam, I will show you a tiny snapshot in our picture album. It's less than an inch, and it shows a fat smiling girl in the middle of a happy crowd. On her left you can see a skinny guy. Those are your grandparents on their wedding day.

Aunt Czili was not happy that we had only a civil marriage ceremony. We promised her that we would be married by a rabbi under a *chupa* on our first vacation from school. And indeed, one year later we were married again in her home in Medias in accordance with Jewish law. She was satisfied, and I believe that our parents would have been, too.

August 12, 1983

Getting into School

I know, Miriam, that you would like to hear about how we managed to start a new chapter in our lives after the war, how we moved away from Sighet, started school, started a family, and dealt with the new realities of Communist Romania. The beginning was very confusing, and it seems even more so as I look back on it today.

Everything was happening at once. There were the financial and economic problems inherent in a post-war era, the privations and scarcity of basic goods, rampant inflation, the upheavals caused by the struggle for control among the numerous political parties, and the uncertainty and adversity brought about by the eventual Communist takeover. Young people like us, who had gone through war and deportation, felt displaced, uprooted from our native towns, and were often isolated from the few surviving family members who had not returned to Romania. Studies, work, the demands of politics, the lack of financial support, all added to the hardship.

Yes, peace had arrived. The new society that we had hoped for and struggled for during the early war years, that had promised justice and equality for all, was within our grasp. We faced that new world with confidence, but also with ignorance and naive expectations that our beliefs about an ideal society could ever be fulfilled. To explore the path from our initial idealism to our gradual disillusionment over the next few years, our awakening to the new realities, and our inability to change the increasingly oppressive conditions may be beyond my capacity. But I will try to shed some light on it.

After terrible years of separation Tzali and I were together again. We had just married. Tzali wanted to study mechanical engineering and my dream was to go to medical school. The money Tzali had made exporting salt to Hungary was enough to support us for a while. We bought a few clothes, shoes and other basic necessities and we were ready to pursue our interrupted education, settle down and start a family.

We knew we had to move to a large university city, and we rejected the efforts of some local political groups who tried to persuade us to stay and work for the Romanian Communist Party or other organizations. At the end of summer we went to Cluj, the capital of Transylvania, an old academic center with many famous universities, Hungarian as well as Romanian. It had a well-known medical school, and there were rumors that a new polytechnic institute would soon open. It had always been my dream to study in Cluj. I had applied repeatedly to its several universities during the war years, but Jews were not admitted. And now I was here, free and with

Tzali, and all the schools seemed to be open to us.

I remember our first night in Cluj. It was wonderful. We had a nice hotel room in the center of the city. In the evening we came down to the bar and an elegant restaurant where soft music was playing. A couple of Tzali's friends from the years he was imprisoned for political activities joined us for dinner. I wore a grey wool dress made from a fabric that Tzali had brought me from Budapest. My cousin Serena, who had returned from camp and reopened her dressmaker's shop in Sighet, had sewn it with great care, and on the skirt she had embroidered a colorful horseshoe and a four-leaf clover, both for good luck. I thought I was quite elegant. Tzali had a nice suit on. The atmosphere was romantic. We danced. We were very happy and hopeful.

We knew very little about admission requirements, scholarships, applications, student aid organizations or necessary documents. We joined a large group of Jewish students at the community center, all in the same situation. For years, under the Hungarian occupation, they had not been permitted to attend high school or go on to higher education. They were much better informed than we were. They told us that the new Secretary of Education had issued a decree allowing applicants who had suffered discrimination under the Fascist rule to enter universities without admission examinations. It applied to those who had been deported from Northern Transylvania under the Hungarian rule, those from Romania who were shut out of higher education by the quota system, and also to former soldiers who had served at the front. This was a great relief for all of us.

The new admissions policy, combined with the lifting of restrictions on class size, had brought to the universities thousands of people, qualified or not, from all over the country. By early summer in 1945, freshman classes had already started at some schools to help students make up for lost years. Each applicant needed only the standard personal documents and a high school diploma -- the baccalaureate. But those like me, who had been deported, didn't even have these papers.

I joined the other candidates for medical school in the effort to register for the next first-year class, which was to start in late September. We held frequent meetings. We were militant, demanding not only admission rights but dormitories, cafeterias, scholarships. We also socialized.

At first we ate at university cafeterias called *mensas* that were organized as soup kitchens, or in cheap eateries. But Tzali and I soon realized that our financial reserves wouldn't last much longer, and we looked for even cheaper places. We found one where for very little money one could order *mamaliga* -- corn meal polenta, the Romanian national dish, a poor man's dish -- with milk, sour cream, or cottage cheese, or even sausages, though that was more expensive.

Although we both liked Cluj very much, it soon became clear that we wouldn't be staying there because the promised opening of the new engineering school never materialized. We decided to go to Timisoara, where there was a long-established polytechnic institute, and a new medical school had opened that spring, the one I had read about at Aunt Czili's.

We arrived in Timisoara in the fall of 1945. Timisoara was the capital of the province of Banat, with a population of Romanians, Hungarians, Germans, Jews and even Serbs. We had never been there before, though I had heard a great deal about it from my brother Miki, who had gone to high school there in the early 30's. To us, who had grown up in provincial Sighet, the city seemed like a cosmopolitan metropolis.

Tzali and I checked into a hotel near the railroad station and went to look up some relatives, my cousin Yankl and his wife Bertha. Yankl, Aunt Esther's oldest son, was the only member of his family who had remained in Romania; the others had emigrated to Palestine before the war. Luckily he and his wife had moved away from Sighet before the Hungarians marched in in 1940. That spared them deportation and possible death in Auschwitz.

Yankl had lost one eye, who knows when and how -- to me it always seemed that he had been born that way -- and was known in the family as "Yankl, the one-eyed." He never received an artificial eye, he probably couldn't afford one, nor did he ever use a patch. His two eyelids were just sewn together over the empty eye socket. Otherwise, though, Yankl was not bad-looking. He was in his thirties, stocky and muscular, and was a hard worker. Here in Timisoara he was living in utter misery with his wife and five small children in a rundown section of the industrial district called Fabrik. They had a small apartment, with a bedroom and a tiny kitchen that opened onto a large courtyard shared with many other tenants. At the far end of the courtyard were common utilities and running water. There were two beds in the bedroom, one for Yankl, Bertha and the baby, and the other one for their other four children.

Yankl had a stall in the nearby marketplace. All of his merchandise was contained in a deep baby carriage that he kept in the kitchen overnight. In the morning he would push the carriage the few blocks to the marketplace and arrange the combs, brushes, hairpins, ribbons, notions and trinkets on the table and side panels. The market square was surrounded by rows of such stalls owned by other poor Jews, selling much the same merchandise and keeping each other company.

Bertha was overwhelmed with the housekeeping chores, the cooking, cleaning, washing, and looking after the children. She complained all the time and was always sick with one thing or another. It pained me to see such misery and their struggle to put food on the table, yet, having come from a place where there were no more Jewish children, Yankl's large family gave me a strange sense of both loss and comfort.

We also got in touch with Mrs. Taussig, whose son Pista had been Miki's best friend when he was going to school in Timisoara. He used to come to study with Pista, and usually stayed over for meals. He was like part of the family. Mrs. Taussig had loved Miki and she had so many stories about his high school years. He had been recruited by a cantor in Sighet at the age of 13 because of his good singing voice, and had been brought on a scholarship to Timisoara to sing in the temple choir. Mrs. Taussig told us what a good student he had been, how he struggled after his voice changed and they no longer needed him in the choir, and how he supported himself by tutoring. He was spending his vacations in Sighet, and every time he returned to school he would tell them about the new baby in his stepmother's arms. She and Pista welcomed us with open arms and became good friends of ours during our stay in Timisoara.

Tzali and I went to the universities to gather information. His acceptance in engineering school seemed assured once he procured a few more documents. But there were unexpected hurdles for me at the medical school. I was late for the new freshman class that had just started, and the dean, Dr. Yagnov, had decided not to accept anyone else for the coming school year without the standard entrance examination, in spite of the open admission decree.

More than five hundred students had entered the first class in the spring of 1945. Most of them were of poor academic caliber and almost half of them failed the final exams of the shortened school year. The new freshman class, which began in late summer, had to carry not only the new students, but all those from the first class who had failed. Meanwhile the new school was having difficulty acquiring buildings, space, offices. Equipment had to be found, classrooms and laboratories had to be set up, and faculty had to be recruited. Yagnov decided to return to the traditional entrance policy to limit the number of entering students and improve their quality.

We were a group of about thirty to forty applicants very affected by this decision. We were upset and angry. We believed that the open admission policy had been created specifically for people like us who for years had been discriminated against and barred from schooling. When the university opened that spring we were still in the Nazi camps so we couldn't take advantage of the new policy. Now we had just missed the deadline for the summer class to which the policy still applied. The candidates who had benefited from this policy had, for the most part, not been deported, and had not even suffered discrimination. It seemed very unfair. And taking the entrance test after years of being shut out from learning, and after the trauma of concentration camps, seemed almost hopelessly futile. We sent delegation after delegation to Yagnov, to the president of the school, to the Department of Education in Bucharest, all in vain. Yagnov was adamant.

It was late October when the date of the entrance examination was posted. Our group decided to fight Yagnov, but time was running out. I realized that I had no choice. Having already lost five years, I couldn't risk losing another one. I would have to take the exam, no matter what. The others argued with me and told me I was breaking ranks. Only one other young man joined me in registering for the test.

I was worried, afraid that I had forgotten everything I had learned in high school, that the five years of war and those twelve months of horror had rendered my mind unable to concentrate and assimilate academic material. And I had only three weeks to prepare.

Meanwhile Tzali had to return to Sighet to get some of his transcripts, not an easy task, since most had been destroyed by the retreating Hungarians and it was quite difficult to obtain new ones. I couldn't stay on at the hotel; not only was it expensive, but it was unacceptable for a woman to stay in a hotel alone. So I moved in with Yankl's crowded family. Since I had nowhere else to go, I especially appreciated the sacrifice they had to make to accommodate me.

Some of the children slept on a bench in the kitchen so I could have a whole bed to myself. It was noisy, the children cried, they were dirty and malnourished, and bedbugs and flies kept me awake at night. There were at least a dozen other families who lived around the courtyard, and during the day the lives of the tenants spilled into the courtyard, in front of their crowded apartments. Men sat on little benches, talking, arguing, and reading newspapers, women washed the laundry and did other chores, children played, screamed, ran and chased each other. But I kept on studying, and Tzali returned after a week and started to look for an apartment.

I put in an extraordinary effort to review the required subjects in those three weeks. I took the test and waited anxiously for the results. To my great surprise and relief I saw my name on the "passed" list. As usual the candidates were listed in the order of their grades, the maximum score being 10, with a cut-off point after all the available openings were filled. That year there were 250 openings and I was accepted with a grade of 7.85. I was very satisfied. Under normal circumstances I would have thought this grade rather low, but this was anything but an ordinary situation. The other student from our group who took the test did not pass.

I was surprised at how the rest of the group reacted. I had been admitted to the new class on my own merits, and I was glad about it, but those who had boycotted the test resented me and that bothered me. In any case, a few weeks later their request was approved in Bucharest and Yagnov was ordered to accept them without an exam.

So, everybody was in and it was time to relax and start studying.

January 5, 1988

Sighet central square with high school on the right

My Mother with her parents and
sisters Goldi, Esther and Czili 1920

My parents with Alter, me and Yossie
1925

Me, Yancu and Yossie
1936

My Father
1930

Moishi
1943

My older brothers Moishi, Alter and Miki
1935

Yortzo and his mother Dori
1943

In front of the movie house
1943

High school friends on the Corso:
me, Hedi, Hindi and Olga on the right
1938

Sugatag: Tzali's first photograph of me
1939

Picnic in the Carpathians
1940

With Zsuzsi in the park in Sighet
1941

Tzali, my boyfriend
1940

My high school
graduation picture
1940

Soon after we were married
1945

The family at a resort in Geoagiu, Romania
1960

Vali, Silvia and Yancu at the Black Sea
1960

In Rome with
Miki's family
1961

In Belo Horizonte, with Bernardo
1963

In Queens, New York
1966

My brothers and their wives in New Rochelle
1981

At Silvia's wedding: Dan, Pista, Zsuzsi, Tzali, Silvia and Paul
1982

The extended family celebrates our 40th
anniversary with us in New Rochelle
1985

Our 45th anniversary with our children's families in Santa Cruz
1990

My 70th birthday with my grandchildren:
Olivia, Miriam, Rebecca. Madeleine and Gabriel
1991

In Los Angeles at 70, still young and happy
1991

Our 50th anniversary cruise to Mexico with our children
Vali, Silvia and Yancu among those who accompany us
1995

All of the family on a cruise to Alaska
1997

We settle into our new home in San Rafael, California
Zsuzsi, Bela and Irene visit for the housewarming
1997

The Freshman Year

Let me tell you about our first home in Timisoara. It was a furnished room in old Mr. Schiller's apartment. Mr. Schiller was a *Schwab*, as the ethnic Germans were called in Timisoara and in the province of Banat. He was in his eighties and was relatively rich; he owned several apartments around a large courtyard -- not unlike Yankl's, but in much better condition, with middle-class families as tenants. He himself lived in a three room apartment near the street entrance, and since he was a widower he agreed to rent us the room between the entrance hall and his bedroom. It had once been the living room, and its large windows overlooked a noisy main artery with a busy trolley line.

What I remember most about him was his avarice. He was so stingy that Moliere could have written another play entirely about Mr. Schiller. He had no family. His late wife, who must have been a good housekeeper, had left him with a well-furnished apartment and a larder that was full with preserved foods she had prepared over the years, and which he didn't dare to consume himself. He sold her unique home-made preserves of quince, green nuts and watermelon to neighbors who appreciated their fine flavor, and bought himself the cheapest prune butter sold in grocery stores. He made his own bread and would walk miles to a bakery where yeast was sold a little cheaper. He heated the house as little as possible, and he kept the drapes pulled to keep out window drafts. He cleaned sparingly for fear of wearing out the carpets and upholstery.

One day we got a food parcel from Aunt Czili in Medias. She usually sent us delicacies -- cookies, goose liver and cracklings, salami, smoked turkey and such, especially in winter when food kept better because of the cold. This time, among other things, we got some meat balls. I offered one to Mr. Schiller. He took it and I assumed he ate it, but the next day I saw it on a plate on a shelf in the larder. A slice had been cut off. Every day he would cut himself another slice of it. I really don't remember how long that meat ball lasted.

We stayed in that room only the first winter. Mr. Schiller let us use the other rooms for studying and went out of his way to be helpful, for fear that if we left he would have to take a less desirable tenant. But the apartment was too cold and uncomfortable, and we had no privacy.

The start of our freshman year had been postponed because of shortage of classrooms and laboratories at the Medical School, and I was idle for months. I went to visit Aunt Czili while Tzali remained in Timisoara to attend his classes. Finally, around January, my school started, and I immersed myself in lectures, laboratories, dissections, etc. By the time classes ended it was late summer of 1946 and I was pregnant. I had constant morning sickness and I threw up almost every day. I had great difficulty studying, but somehow I managed to prepare for and take the exams in all the basic sciences except anatomy, which was the most difficult. I got permission to postpone the anatomy exam until the fall, and spent the summer at Aunt Czili's, where I studied leisurely while she took care of me. When I returned in the fall, I was rested and very well prepared.

I presented myself for the test at the anatomy laboratory with about fifteen others who had all failed the first time. This was an oral exam with professor Yagnov, the chairman of the department. The president of the school, Dr. Lupascu, happened to also be present. Yagnov asked me the first question, then the second, then the third. When he realized how well prepared I was he became animated and kept asking me more and more difficult questions. He was very pleased, and proud to show off with a good student in front of the president. I got the highest possible score.

This success gave me the courage to fight for what I considered my right -- to make up some of the lost years. This was particularly important to me because in Romania medical school lasts six years. There is no "pre-med" -- students go to medical school right after high school. If I couldn't get ahead somehow, by the time I graduated I would be past thirty.

A few days later, I returned to see Yagnov, this time in his office as dean of the school. As he smiled benevolently, I explained why I had come: I had arrived in Timisoara too late for the first and second entering classes. Having lost years because of the war, this would have been a chance to recoup some of that time. I had taken and passed the entrance examination as he required. He had seen my competence in anatomy, and could check my other grades, which were also very good. I was there to ask him to allow me to make up at least one year. Another long vacation was coming, and while my class was on vacation I would have no difficulty taking second year courses and exams and move ahead into the third year.

His smile became mocking. "Come on," he said, "What's your hurry? You're a woman -- go, get married!"

"I am married already," I said. "I lost five years because of the war, I couldn't get to Timisoara sooner because I was liberated from a German camp only a few months earlier..."

"You're married?" he interrupted. "Go and have a baby." I was losing my patience.

"I will have one soon. I am pregnant. And that hasn't kept me from being a top student."

He dismissed my arguments and rejected my request, leaving me idle and frustrated for the whole long vacation. I stayed angry at him all

through my student years. I could have graduated a year or two earlier if he
had let me try. What a tremendous difference it would have made in
supporting our growing family, in making our lives easier, in starting my
career. And it was short-sighted on his part, too. The school had a pressing
need for faculty members, and many recent graduates were recruited for
teaching positions. I was a good student and I might have been one of them.

My being married was itself a novelty for my classmates, most of
whom were much younger than I, teenagers just out of high school. There
were some older students too, who had fought in the war. I recall a 46
year-old former colonel who had probably dreamed of a medical degree for
a long time, and finally had the opportunity to enroll. But he had a hard time
keeping up and the professors teased him, saying, "When you finally
graduate, you'll be ready for retirement."

My pregnancy was pretty easy after the first two months. I was able
to go to classes, take exams, attend dissections and work in the physiology
and chemistry laboratories. I didn't even miss a day of class -- Silvia was
born during spring vacation. When classes resumed two weeks later and I
arrived, slender again in my elegant gray woolen dress, my young
classmates looked at me in wonder.

February 3, 1988

Yossie

Another memorable event of late 1946 was Yossie's return from the Soviet labor camp of Vorkuta, one of the northernmost towns in the European USSR, bordering Siberia. Learning about the existence and the horrors of the Stalinist camps, the Gulag, was a great shock. Many years later, Yossie wrote up his story and titled it "Slavery in the Twentieth Century in Russia." The story never ceases to impress me, because there are so many similarities, yet it is so different from what we went through in the Nazi camps.

Yossie was the oldest of my four little brothers. In the camp he was known as Yasha. Later on, in Brazil, his name was Jose. Now he lives in Brooklyn, and is known as Joseph, or just Joe, though his wife Riva calls him Yossl, his full and authentic Jewish name. And what is in each of these names but a place, a time and a history? I will relate to you, Miriam, in my own way, very much shortened, his account of the war years, because I think it is a very moving story and I wanted to share it with you.

The story starts in September 1940, in Sighet, when the occupying Hungarian army marched into Northern Transylvania. Yossie was seventeen years old then, a year and a half younger than I, and he didn't know what to do with himself. He had always fought doing things the conventional way. He dropped out of school early. At thirteen he ran away from home, went to Bucharest and worked at various jobs. (In our album we used to have pictures of him as a *piccolo,* a bus boy, in a fancy hotel, looking charming in his uniform.) Now, back in Sighet, he found himself in this new Hungarian world, cut off from the Romania he knew, with no schooling, no skills, no job and no future in sight.

He thought, as did many young people around him at the time, that the best solution would be to escape to the USSR, the land where Communism flourished, where "everyone had equal opportunity, education was free and guaranteed, and discrimination and anti-Semitism had long been abolished." The war had redrawn the borders of the countries covering the Northern Carpathian mountains. With the Hungarian occupation of parts of Romania and Czechoslovakia, and the Soviet annexation of eastern Poland, what had previously been a junction of the Polish, Czech and Romanian frontiers became the boundary between Hungary and the Soviet Union, bringing the Russian border to no more than 40 or 50 miles from Sighet.

Yossie made his decision. Without telling anyone, he found a connection, gathered the money the smugglers demanded (50 pengo), and took the bus to the last Hungarian village, up in the mountains. From the bus station he was to walk a mile to meet a Ukrainian peasant who would guide him across the border. He was surprised to find that there were six other young people heading in the same direction -- five men and a woman, all from Sighet.

The peasant was waiting at the appointed place. They all climbed the steep mountainside, crossed dark pine forests, and reached a ravine where the peasant showed them the path to the unguarded frontier and left them. It was late fall. It was cold, the passes and peaks were covered with snow, and they didn't see any sign of life on the other side of the border. They walked and walked for days, climbed and descended rugged hills, and slept in the snow under the trees. Their food was soon gone and still there was nothing in sight. Finally, after six days of walking in deeper and deeper snow, hungry and exhausted, they found a hut. An old woman took them in. She appeared friendly; she made them hot tea, let them remove their boots from their frozen and swollen feet, and allowed them to stretch out and sleep on the floor. It was an enormous relief.

The following morning, however, the border patrol, whom the woman had notified, arrived and arrested them. They were taken to the nearest police station, registered and questioned. Within a few days, they were moved to a large jail in the city of Stanislav, the former capital of Galicia, a Polish province. There, to their great astonishment, they found other young men who had left Sighet months earlier on the same journey. Back home there had been rumors that they had been warmly received in Russia; that some were going to schools, others had joined the army, and yet others were encouraged to develop their artistic skills. They told the newcomers about the bleak future that awaited them all and asked for news about their home town and their families.

What followed were months of transfers from one transitional prison to another, with renewed interrogations by the secret police, then called the NKVD, about their affiliations and their mission. Did they have information about activities of any political groups? Had they been Communists at home? Did they know any Communists? Some of the young men had indeed belonged to Communist youth cells, but Yossie had not even been aware of any Communist activities in Sighet.

They were beaten, tortured, and deprived of food and sleep to extract confessions. The Soviet interrogators dismissed their naive explanations of why they had come, and concluded that they were all German spies. The sentence was forced labor for "subversive political activities." They were examined, x-rayed, vaccinated, and given uniforms with special code numbers. Then they were dispatched to forced labor camps.

They boarded long trains with thousands of other prisoners and started their journey across the USSR eastward, with no idea of their destination. After weeks of traveling they woke up one August morning to find that it was snowing heavily. This is when they realized that they were headed not only east but north. As they continued further and further north, the climate became harsher and colder, the days shorter and shorter. They reached the end of the railroad tracks and continued further north on barges on the Pechora river, on the western slopes of the Urals.

It was winter when they arrived at their destination, Vorkuta, in the northernmost part of the continent, well above the Arctic Circle. The temperature was below freezing, the days and nights almost equally dark, the ground barren and covered with snow. Yossie entered a whole new universe: the world of the Gulag, the Stalinist system of concentration camps where prisoners worked in the harshest conditions, having been sentenced, without any trial or recourse, to years of hard labor. Yossie was informed that he was to spend there ten years for spying for the Germans.

Vorkuta was one of the largest camps. Hundreds of thousands of inmates, mostly men, were divided into numerous smaller units, and provided workers for the coal mines of the Urals. Since the German invasion this industry had become vital for the Soviet war effort. New trains arrived often, unloading thousands of new slave laborers. The cold was unbearable, the winds blinding. There were no trees, only tundra grass in the summer and endless snow field in the winter. There was no need for fences because no one could survive outside.

Work in the coal mines was exhausting, with long hours and hundreds of armed guards everywhere. The food rations were apportioned according to one's productivity. Very often the prisoners became drained, collapsed and died. Yossie had to learn how to survive, how to get more food, how to exchange stuff on the black market and how to work less without being caught.

The camp population came from many levels of Soviet society. Russian Jews were deported for their "counter-revolutionary" activities, charged with following outlawed Communist factions like Trotskyism. Russians were arrested and deported for the most trivial indiscretions, for having voiced opinions, told jokes or simply because informants disclosed "facts" or just suspicions about them. Priests were considered "parasites". Foreign refugees were caught trying to get out of the country to join their families. Ethnic groups like the Volga Germans, who had been forcibly shipped east during the war years, were often accused of being enemy sympathizers and sent to camps. Fervent Communists from abroad, who had fled their Fascist countries to escape persecution and imprisonment, and had come to Russia seeking a safe haven, were called traitors for having abandoned their comrades and also ended up in Vorkuta.

It was common knowledge that some civilians were arrested simply because of the need for their particular skills in the camps, for there was never a shortage of doctors, engineers, or architects at Vorkuta. The secret police would appear one day, usually at dawn, at the house of such a specialist and knock on the door. People lived in dread of such a knock. The individual would be taken for interrogation, and then would disappear. If he returned, sometimes fifteen or twenty years later, his label of "former convict" would cause suffering to his family, hardship, suspicion, and even threats. Most never returned.

Besides the political prisoners there were also common criminals and murderers in the camp. Ironically, they had an easier time than the others: they already knew how to cheat, steal and rob to survive and did so with impunity. They often ended up as supervisors of the work teams.

At one time Yossie got sick, ran a high fever and was hospitalized. He became so weak and thin that the prison physician felt compassion for him and arranged to relieve him from hard labor in the mines. After being discharged from the infirmary, he was assigned to workshops, where he worked as a tailor. Later he became a nurse in the clinic, checking the patients' temperature, urine samples and stools, and often accepting bribes for excusing prisoners from work. By then his life was better: he spoke pretty good Russian, was liked by his superiors and was able to get good food rations and better clothes.

Eventually Yossie was assigned to work as a waiter in a restaurant for high camp officials and visitors. He turned out to be very good at it, having worked as a busboy in a Bucharest restaurant when he was fourteen. He was hardworking, charming and very clever. He served the camp elite and courted them; they befriended him and depended on him for special services. One day, one of them, the director of the theater, needed a new administrator and asked to have "Yasha" assigned to the job. Yossie was very pleased, he finally had work he could enjoy.

Theater in Vorkuta seems like a strange notion, but the need for entertainment was great, considering the hectic industrial activity and the thousands of bureaucrats sent to supervise the camp and the work, their families and the official visitors. People were hungry for diversion and cultural activities. There was no other theater in the whole province of Komi, not even in Syktyvkar, the capital. And there was a wealth of talent among the prisoners. There were famous artists, writers, musicians and singers, conductors and designers. An architect prisoner built an imposing wooden theater building, almost a palace; I still remember its picture on a postcard that Yossie sent me to Sighet. Numerous popular works were produced -- some Verdi and Puccini operas and almost all of the Imre

Kalman, Franz Lehar and Johann Strauss operettas. There were concerts and recitals by accomplished performers, and when there were no musical programs or the company was off touring the province, movies were shown.

Yasha/Yossie became indispensable at the theater. He organized performances, procured sets, arranged for skilled workers from the camp administration and handled the distribution of the much-desired tickets. This brought him connections, influence and extra money. There was a hierarchy of seat assignments: generals and their families sat in the first rows; behind them were camp administrators, secret police officials and the many visitors, delegates and supervisors; then came prisoners with special privileges, and finally local civilians. Vorkuta had been a town of about 20,000, but its population grew constantly as prisoners, released but not allowed to move away, brought their families and settled there.

Yossie now had a good, challenging job and prestigious, interesting friends. He saw all the performances and rehearsals, had a decent room, good food and nice clothing, and could save money. He even had some freedom of movement, and at one time he had a girlfriend, Larissa, the daughter of a camp official. For a prisoner, it was a dream job. The war was far away. But he suffered from the confinement, the isolation, the lack of information about his family and the hopelessness of ever getting out of there. He longed for his hometown, his parents, brothers and sister, and freedom.

The years went by. The tide of war turned. Soviet military victories were proudly announced over the radio and loud speakers. Russian soil was being liberated from the German invaders and Russian prisoners of war were being freed. New people arrived in the camp from the war zone: soldiers arrested for black marketeering at the front, civilians suspected of having collaborated with the enemy, and even former prisoners of war charged with treason for allowing themselves to be captured by the Germans. All the new arrivals brought with them news of Nazi atrocities against the Jews, of deportations and death camps, of complete devastation of Jewish communities.

By 1944, the Eastern European countries were being liberated by the Red Army and more rumors were reaching Vorkuta about the Jewish deportations. Late that year, Yossie found out that a girl from Sighet was being set free and allowed to go home. He became very excited and asked to be seen by the Commander. He was told that the girl was from Czechoslovakia and that there were new orders to repatriate displaced, non-political prisoners from the liberated territories. Yossie gave him a lecture in the geography of the Northern Carpathians, brought in a map, and argued that Sighet had been on the Romanian border with Czechoslovakia and might even be considered a Czech outpost. He must have been convincing, for the process was set in motion for his release.

A few more weeks passed, a few more hearings, expectations, excitement, and then finally, in December 1944, he got his release papers. He was now a "free man", allowed to join the civilian population of Vorkuta and settle there. But he could travel only with a pass and only to certain destinations. He was forbidden to go to Moscow, and could not leave the Soviet Union.

It was a bitter kind of freedom. He felt trapped. He continued working at the theater and dreaming and making plans for getting away from there. He still had no information about his family or what had happened back in his home town, only those grim rumors that he could not bring himself to believe. His worries deepened, his anguish about his loved ones intensified.

As the war was coming to an end Yossie started to write letters home, sending them out of Vorkuta with people who left or with visitors, knowing that they wouldn't get out of Vorkuta's post office if he mailed them. He kept writing postcards, dozens of them, to the Sighet city hall, to the Jewish Community Center, to old acquaintances in Sighet, to schools, begging them for information about his family, asking them to notify any one of his relatives, to post them on bulletin boards. There was no reply. It was as if everyone had vanished, as if Sighet itself had disappeared from the surface of the earth.

When I came home in June 1945, I found some of Yossie's postcards on the bulletin board of the Jewish Community Center. I already told you, Miriam, about the relief to find out that another one of my brothers had survived. His cards, his distress, his crying out, and his hope moved me profoundly.

I wrote him immediately. I told him about my surprise and my joy in hearing from him, and how our parents had mourned him as long as they lived, believing that he was lost, probably frozen in the mountains in that brutal winter when he left home.

I told him about what had happened to the family, about the ghetto and the deportations, about Auschwitz and other camps, about our loved ones who perished there -- Father, Mother, Moishi and Yancu. I wrote him what I knew about the others, that Ezu had come home at the same time as I did, Alter must be somewhere in the USSR but I hadn't heard from him, Ebi had left Switzerland for Palestine, and Miki had probably stayed in Italy, but again I didn't have any concrete information about him. I could only hope that they were also alive. I told him about my plans, how fortunate I had been to find Tzali home, and how we would soon get married and go to the university.

Years later Yossie told me the impact of the revelations in that first letter of mine. It was the first news about his family he had had in five years and it described the whole tragedy. He cried for weeks for all those who had been killed. At the same time he was happy that I was home and was waiting for him to return. He showed the letter to all his friends and read it over and over again. It was the fall of 1945 and he was determined not to spend another winter there, to use all his resources, all his wit and all the skills he had acquired to get out.

His identification papers said clearly that he could not travel to certain large cities, but he thought that if he could obtain a valid traveling pass he would try his luck, hoping that his papers would not be checked. The odds were slim and the risks enormous. NKVD agents were everywhere. But he had to take his chance and he seized the opportunity when it arose soon after.

The theater was preparing for a tour of the province and Yossie had to get travel passes ready for all the performers. He wrote the destination on all the passes but left it blank on his own. The omission escaped unnoticed; all the passes were signed without suspicion. Then he filled in his own destination -- Moscow. When the train carrying the theater troupe left the station, he jumped off at the last minute and boarded another train, going south. A friend stood waiting with his luggage and put it on his train.

Yossie traveled in fear for more than a week, avoiding officials. Luckily conductors only checked his 30-day pass. He looked and talked like any other Russian, and no one asked for his identification card.

When he arrived in Moscow, he was dazed. He had never seen such a large city before. And it was crowded. Soldiers were returning from the front, and war refugees were passing through on their way to the western frontiers for repatriation. He had a few addresses in Moscow from people he had known in Vorkuta. He looked up the family of the director of the theater. He had met them during their visits to Vorkuta, and had helped the director send them food parcels. Now they welcomed him in their home.

He hoped to find the Romanian Embassy and ask for repatriation but that turned out to be very difficult. There was no telephone directory and he couldn't ask strangers for fear of arousing suspicion. He imagined everyone to be a secret agent. Once he was deliberately misdirected to an address that turned out to be the central offices of the secret police. Two people were following him but he managed to disappear into the crowds. Days passed. He became desperate. His pass would soon expire and he hadn't made any connections.

Then one day he heard two people speaking German. He followed them, listened to their conversation and realized they were diplomats. He approached them with a simple question: did they know where the Romanian Embassy was? They told him that it was temporarily housed in a hotel close to theirs and took him there.

Seeing the consul Yossie was relieved to speak Romanian again. He poured out his heart about the years of imprisonment and his earnest wish to go home. He even showed him my letter, hoping for sympathy and understanding. The response was very official. The embassy would give him a visa if he had a passport, and that could be obtained only in the capital of the province of Komi where he was registered. He broke down, to no avail.

When he left, he was followed again. There was another chase through buses, subways and public buildings. By then he was suspicious of everyone and decided to return north to obtain the passport. It took another week to travel back to the Arctic Circle. When his pass expired he forged a new date.

In the passport office in Syktyvkar, the secretary asked to see his papers. From the expression on her face he realized that something had provoked her suspicions, perhaps the inconsistencies in dates. She asked him to wait. He said he was going across the street for a coffee and would bring her some and left, realizing how foolish he had been to return there and risk arrest. The penalty for having left Vorkuta without permission was the firing squad. He hurried straight to the railroad station and took the first train out without even bothering to check where it was going.

More traveling followed and more weeks of idling in Moscow. By now he had no pass. He started to run out of money. He became more and more restless. He finally persuaded the Romanian consul to give him a letter stating that he was a Romanian citizen from Sighet who had asked for repatriation. Yossie forged the Ambassador's signature so as not to lose more days in getting it. Every day counted. Time was running out. With that official paper and with information from a few helpful Jews who paid for his fare, he boarded a bus that took him to the city of Chernovitz.

Chernovitz (*Chernovtsy* in Russian) was the capital of Bukovina, an eastern Romanian province before 1940, now part of the Soviet Union. It was on the Soviet-Romanian border and thousands had come there to try to get out -- Romanians separated from their families, western nationals who had been stuck in the USSR during the war, displaced people and ethnic groups. More and more people arrived daily. Jewish families came from Birobidjan, the region the Soviet government had once designated as a future Jewish republic. They had all discovered relatives in the United States and were anxious to leave. The city was crowded, the boarding houses were jammed, and people slept in private homes and in train and bus stations.

Yossie had to register at the repatriation office where thousands of others were waiting in line. It took him several days just to get registered and then the wait for the visa started. His spirits were low. He had no money left, so he started selling his belongings, the better clothes that he had acquired in Vorkuta. One day he gave a peddler a package of new winter underwear to sell at the market. It turned out that the garments were marked with the prison code. A policeman recognized the mark and arrested the peddler. Another day, he helped a drunken soldier get home and then exchanged clothes with him. In a uniform he was less likely to be suspected. When he found a discarded officer's jacket covered with decorations, he picked up the medals, just in case. He has many more stories like these that show the kind of resourcefulness and ingenuity it took to overcome the never-ending hurdles that rose in his path.

Finally, he obtained the visa. Hungry and exhausted, he boarded the bus, still apprehensive. He had heard rumors about whole busloads of people heading to the frontier post being diverted and taken away to a camp. He didn't trust the Russians, no matter what they promised. But he crossed the border safely. He was out of the Soviet Union.

How did it feel to breathe the free and fresh air on the other side? To leave behind the "Freedom land," the "Workers' Paradise" that had lured so many innocent and naive young men from other countries with its false promises? He was neither innocent nor naive any more, nor was he so young, though he was only twenty-three. He had suffered, learned, grown. He had had experience enough for a lifetime. The relief he felt was intoxicating. He could hardly believe that it was over.

On the Romanian side of the border there were crowds waiting for their relatives. People stopped every new arrival to ask for news. There were booths set up by various organizations, serving food, offering clothing and even pocket money. Yossie was given ten American dollars -- he had never seen dollars before -- and a great deal of advice and encouragement. There was joy everywhere.

Yossie wouldn't wait for the next train to Bucharest, the only possible destination. He put on his chest all the medals, buttons and decorations he had picked up, stopped a Romanian truck going southward and asked for a lift. The Romanians feared any Russian, more so when he displayed military decorations, and Yossie knew that this was the surest and safest way to travel. He didn't reveal any knowledge of the language. The drivers also felt safe with a "Russian" officer aboard. They shared their food and drinks and they all became friendly.

He stayed in Bucharest just long enough to look up some friends and register with the Refugees Clearing House. His goal was to get to Timisoara, where he knew Tzali and I were studying, spend some time with us, then head on to the West. It was October when he reached Timisoara. We were on vacation at Aunt Czili's in Medias. Our landlady, Mrs. Deutsch, told him about our cousin Yankl, and he found him in the market at his stall. Yankl knew the exact time our train was due to arrive. He went to the railroad station and waited for us.

As he tells it, I got off the train and walked right by him without recognizing the young uniformed Russian as my brother. He called my name. We fell into each other's arms, overcome with happiness and tears that did not stop for days. There were so many stories we had to tell each other. The tragic events that had happened since we had last seen each other nearly six years before, the deportations, the deaths, the camps, the sufferings. His years of captivity in Siberia and his adventures on his long trip home. He brought me a present, a fur hat of black astrakhan, the only possession he had left, that he would not sell.

He wouldn't stay more than ten days. His adventures, his disillusionment, his distrust of the Russians and of Communism drove him further to the west, to get away as soon as possible and as far as possible from the USSR. And we never discussed how we would meet again. He realized that we saw our future in the new Romania, that we were happy being married and attending universities, and he did not even try to persuade us otherwise.

That's where Yossie ended his story. It is amazing to think that at that time these Stalinist concentration camps, which had been around for years before Hitler established his camps, were totally unknown outside of the USSR. The news about these camps began to trickle out as former prisoners, like Yossie, returned. But it took someone with the experience, knowledge and stature of Solzhenitzin, to reveal the full extent of the Gulag to the Western world.

October 28, 1985

Students with a Baby

By the time Silvia came along we had moved from Schiller's to a new place, a nice furnished room in the apartment of Mrs. Deutsch.

Housing in the post-war Timisoara was a huge problem. With new universities opening up the city became very crowded. There were few dormitories for students, mostly at the old, established universities. Office buildings were confiscated from their former owners and hastily furnished for the thousands of students flocking to the city. The girls' dormitory of the medical school, close to the administrative building, looked like a large hospital ward. In each room there were about twenty cots along the walls, no closets, no dressers, only pegs on the walls full of dresses on hangers. Suitcases were on the floor, books piled up on makeshift shelves on stacks of bricks. There were no cooking facilities. The bathrooms were at the end of the corridor, serving several hundred students. The men's dormitory was a similar building on the other side of the plaza, with the same inconveniences. Those who could afford it took better lodgings in private homes. This was also the only choice for the few married couples like us, who couldn't claim space in the cheap campus dormitories.

The Deutsches, an elderly couple who had been well-to-do before the war, owned a large apartment. Under the new regime, they were not entitled to so much "living space" and were required to rent out all rooms that had separate access. A long hallway led from the front door to the kitchen and bathroom. On the right side, facing a busy street, were the Deutsches' living quarters, a living room and a bedroom. On the left, toward the backyard, were the rented rooms. Ours was small and narrow, with two single beds, which allowed us a good night's sleep. There was a wardrobe closet and a desk for study, and later we added a crib for Silvia. The room was not too expensive, and, most importantly, it provided us with the privacy we longed for. We found this arrangement quite satisfactory.

The room next to us was rented by an obstetrician, who became our friend and delivered our first two children. He used the room as a clandestine office where he performed abortions, which were illegal at that time, though fairly common, as contraception was never available in Romania. At night we often heard women moaning and groaning. Later on, as he became more prosperous, he moved to a larger office, and Lica, one of my fellow medical students, moved in his place. One of Lica's legs had been amputated above the knee during the war and his prosthesis was so clumsy and noisy that it woke us up whenever he had to use the bathroom at night.

At the end of the corridor, between the bathroom and the kitchen, there was a little window. As the Deutsches did not share their kitchen, I was allotted the space under that window for a gas burner, where I could heat water for all the necessities, boil the milk, and make some simple food for the baby.

Cooking dinner at home was out of question. The market and the grocery stores were very poorly stocked. One could usually find the most basic foodstuffs, which were rationed, but there were long lines whenever anything else was available, and we didn't have time to shop. We were grateful to cousin Yankl, who occasionally brought us some hard-to-find produce from the market.

The city had a large number of government subsidized factory cafeterias, where at noontime a pretty substantial dinner was served to the workers. For a small price students could purchase meal tickets at those cafeterias. Very soon it became apparent that important people, students with Communist Party or Student Union affiliations, were assigned to choice factories where meat dishes were served almost daily. But we were pleased to be assigned to a cafeteria which permitted us to take food home in a lunch pail, so I could stay home with Silvia while Tzali bicycled over to get the food. Then the three of us would make a meal from the two portions.

When we had some extra money we subscribed to a boarding house for dinner, where there was more variety, meat was served regularly, the food tasted better, and we even got dessert. We also had a few friends in the city, the Taussigs and some well-to-do acquaintances from Sighet, who often invited us, the hungry students, for holiday feasts. Occasionally we would cook some noodles or potatoes on our gas range. For a small monthly fee, Mrs. Deutsch's maid would wash our few dishes.

For a few months after Silvia was born we had a helper to take care of her. I was nursing, and was lucky to have enough milk, because formula was not available and preparing baby food was quite a task. In the morning I went to classes. At 11 I got up, left the classroom discreetly (though the teachers knew where I was going), took the trolley, rode the three stations to our home, and returned within an hour. The morning classes ended in time for the next nursing. Life was easier when we had the helper because she also did some cleaning and the laundry, took the baby out, and made a fire in the wood stove in the winter so the room was warm when we came home.

But we didn't always have money for help, and when Silvia grew older, and could sit on the bicycle baby seat that Tzali had built, we took her to a day care center at a nearby factory. She didn't seem to mind. Every day we had to wash baby clothes and diapers. Tzali would warm up the water and carry it to the room, I would wash the diapers, Tzali would rinse and wring them, then we would hang them on three or four clotheslines strung between the window and the door. They would be dry in the morning. Friends coming to see us had to dodge between the drying diapers.

Our scholarships covered only tuition, and the funds we had brought with us from Sighet were soon used up. My brothers sometimes sent us packages, but no money, because getting foreign currency was illegal. Nevertheless we were able to obtain some through clandestine transactions. Occasionally Tzali earned some money tutoring high school students in math and physics. Zionist organizations from abroad also sent clothes and food packages for poor Jewish students, but the Communist Party and the Students' Union ruled that these would be accepted only if all the students could benefit. This was in keeping with Communist ideals of equality, except that the Party officials, who controlled the distribution of these packages, got to pick the choice items for themselves, leaving the rest for the other students. It became rather amusing to see them all dressed alike in fine American shirts and slacks, as if in uniform.

But whatever clothes we got were helpful, and the fabrics were always special. If the clothes didn't fit we had them altered -- there were many good seamstresses around and they were not expensive. We made a skirt from a jacket, or baby clothes from children's items, and we unraveled sweaters to knit them again to the right size. We were very resourceful. Packages seldom contained baby things, but when they did, these were distributed among the few students who had children. I still remember the wonderful blue snow suit we got for Silvia. She wore it for a couple of seasons, and when Yancu came along we had it reversed and it was like new again.

Adding to our financial difficulties was the severe inflation of the post-war years. The economy was in shambles. Merchandise and agricultural products were scarce. Prices soared. Speculation and corruption pushed up inflation even more. In late 1946 and early 1947 prices went up by the hour. All income had to be spent immediately, because the next day prices would be higher. There were times when we needed a pocketful of money, hundreds of lei, to buy a loaf of bread, and a suitcase of money to buy a pair of shoes. Savings lost all their value. Apartments were rented for the equivalent of two kilos of butter a month and the black market thrived.

Tzali's classmates wanted to buy a baby carriage for Silvia. In the couple of weeks it took them to collect the money, with the value of the Romanian lei dropping every day, they were only able to buy us an electric iron. Luckily we found a used baby carriage at the flea market.

My dearest girlfriends, Rolla and Klari, were several years younger than I. They had always lived with their families in Timisoara, and each was an only child. I felt they belonged to a separate and privileged category of

Jewish students who had never lost their homes and families, had never been deported. When the quota system was enforced in the public schools in Romania, they were able to attend the prestigious Hebrew High School where my brother Miki had once studied. And now, even the medical school came to their hometown.

Klari's father was a retired businessman, a former jeweler. It was he who sometimes helped us out with a loan when we were in need; he was our 'banker'. Rolla lived with her widowed mother, who took care of everything. They were among the few Jews of Sephardic origin and even spoke Ladino. Rolla and Klari respected our troubled past without ever asking questions about it. They looked up to us for being older, having more life experience, being married and having a child. They were always available if we needed their help, and we often ate in their homes.

And we also studied, although not as much as we wanted, or even as much as we needed to for the exams. We had difficulties in some subjects. Tzali hadn't studied calculus in high school and had to make that up. I didn't do well in the laboratory subjects because I started working and could not attend the practical sessions. And it took time to get used to the many compulsory 'philosophy' courses, whose only purpose was indoctrination in dialectical materialism, Marxism, Leninism, Stalinism, and the rest of the socialist dogma. When the finals approached we had to cram all the material in one or two weeks, studying day and night, leaving all the chores for later. The day after, instead of resting, we had to catch up with the cleaning, the basket full of dirty diapers, laundering, scrubbing the floor. Then, finally, we could play with the baby, and occasionally go to a movie.

February 28, 1988

Family Dispersion

What little family we had left after the war did not stay around for long. The old way of life, with its traditions, the Yiddish language, the community, the grandparents and children, were all gone. Only a few young people were around, and even they, after brief reunions, often left, searching for new family ties and a new life. Sighet, our birthplace, had become a memory, a reminder of recent tragedies, evoking images of its pre-war liveliness superimposed on empty houses, burned synagogues, and deserted streets and schools, devoid of familiar faces. It would fill me with great sadness to think of it, and for a long time I didn't feel like visiting. I tried instead to turn my mind to the present and future.

When Silvia was born, in 1947, my surviving brothers were already scattered all over the world. I didn't really know their whereabouts, but they sent us messages as they moved from place to place in search of a new home. I was happy just knowing that they were alive. Only Miki had a permanent address, in Rome, and we were able to correspond with him. He was finally established as a dentist (father would have been proud of that).

Ezu, whom I had found in Budapest on my way home from camp, spent about a year working for a relief organization, traveling back and forth to Austria and smuggling Jews out of Romania as the borders were closing. The last time I heard from him was in the fall of 1946 when we had our *chupa* wedding in Medias. He gave us a fantastic wedding gift, a complete set of cookware. A manufacturer from Medias wanted to thank Ezu for helping his brother escape to the West, and Ezu told him, "Send my sister some cookware from your factory." He obliged. I had never seen so many blue enamel pots and pans. I had nowhere to store them, so we took a few with us to Timisoara and left the rest with Aunt Czili.

By the end of 1946, with the new restrictions imposed by the Communist government, it became too risky for Ezu to travel across the border. He went to Vienna where he met and married Olga, and from there they went on to Rome to meet Miki and to find a way to emigrate to Palestine. They stayed in a Displaced People's Camp in the Cinecitta, (the Movie City), where old studios and warehouses had been transformed into living quarters for the increasing number of refugees.

Yossie, on his way back from Vorkuta, stayed with us in Timisoara just a few days. But he was restless to move on further to the West. He hated everything Russian and anything that reminded him of Communism, and there were still plenty of Soviet troops in Romania. He still remembers going out on the street with us on November 7 to see the parade celebrating the Bolshevik October Revolution and loathing it, even though, he says, we were offered free frankfurters. (I think he is probably wrong about that, because the great sensation on such a holiday, the workers' great day, was that frankfurters were *available* at all; they were for sale but everybody rushed to buy them as eagerly as if they were free.) So Yossie, too, soon left for Vienna and Rome, hoping to get to Palestine. He was a dutiful letter writer and sent us a photograph of himself with Ezu and Olga, and later on with Miki and his fiancee Mantzi.

I wish, Miriam, I could explain to you what Palestine meant at that time to the thousands of Jewish refugees returned to their unfriendly neighbors, or languishing in Displaced People's camps. The land of Palestine had been the home of the Jews for thousands of years, until 70 AD, when the Romans destroyed the Second Temple in Jerusalem, and chased them away to the four corners of the earth. Ever since then, Jews have ended their Passover celebration with an expression of their most fervent wish, to meet "next year in Jerusalem," and they have always prayed facing in the direction of the Sacred City. Zionist organizations that started to appear in the late nineteenth century looked upon this dream as a feasible reality, and began to advocate the actual return of Jews to the land of the Bible, the land of Israel, and the building of a modern state there.

In 1918 this region became a British Protectorate. Arabs were the main inhabitants, but there were also Jews and Christians guarding their sacred shrines.

At the conclusion of the Second World War, it seemed that the only viable solution for the magnitude of the refugee problem was to establish a Jewish state, which would stand for and defend all Jews. There was a strong current of support from the Allies and the United Nations for the idea of partitioning the land of Palestine between the Arab and Jewish populations. Yet while the fate of the future state was being argued, the British had greatly restricted Jewish immigration to Palestine and refugees had to be smuggled in.

After a few months of waiting in Rome, Yossie, Ezu and Olga went to Brindisi, a port city at the Southern tip of Italy, to board a ship that would take them to Palestine clandestinely. But the boat was intercepted by the British and they returned to Rome disappointed. A relief organization offered them Brazilian entrance visas and boat tickets, and they decided to renounce Palestine and go to Brazil instead. That is how a part of our family came to settle in South America.

My youngest surviving brother, Ebi, was already in Palestine. He was working in construction and was planning to join a kibbutz. His letters were very sparse because he was being continuously drafted. I did not know yet how he had escaped from Budapest, where he was enrolled in a trade school at the time of the deportations, how he had survived the war, and how he had gotten to Palestine.

All I knew about Alter was that for years he had been in a prisoner-of-war camp in the Soviet Union, and was still there, waiting for repatriation. I was hoping he would return to Romania.

Aunt Czili came to be with me in Timisoara during my confinement, as my own mother would have done if she were still alive. It must have been very hard for her family to be left to fend by themselves, but they all did many more sacrifices for us. She arrived more than a week before I delivered and stayed at Yankl's place. When my labor pains started we took a horse-drawn carriage and picked her up from Yankl's to come with us to the hospital. It was Friday night, and the first time she violated the Shabbat rules. She stayed the whole night with Tzali outside the delivery room, trying to impress on him "how much she must be suffering!" And she came to the hospital every day for the whole week I stayed there.

The birth of a new baby in our family, the first one after the great devastation, was a momentous event, and Zsuzsi and Bela came from Sighet as soon as they heard the news. Zsuzsi had recently returned from Sweden, where she had been taken after liberation from Bergen-Belsen, emaciated and sick with typhus. One year later, recovered in health, but homesick for Sighet and her brothers, she declined the Swedish government's offer to grant citizenship to refugees from Germany, and decided to come home. Her two cousins, Hedi and Livi, with whom she had been together since deportation, stayed behind, and eventually married and settled there for good.

Bela, back from a forced labor detachment in the Ukraine, was ready to settle in Sighet, and had bought a drug store on the main street. With the Soviet occupation, and so many Russian soldiers still around, it seemed like a good idea to give the store a Russian name. I remember how we debated whether to call the store "Volga" or "Balalaika," and picked "Volga" because it was shorter. Bela managed it with his friend Sanyi; later on, when Zsuzsi came home, she also joined the business. She was happy to be back in Sighet, she enjoyed working, she made new friends, and she soon met Herbert, her future husband.

From Bela we learned how unsettling the future was for store owners in Sighet, where the Communists were beginning to take over, seizing private businesses and forming large, nationalized cooperatives. Most of his friends and acquaintances had left for the West. The stricter control of the borders was a signal that if one was considering emigration, that decision should be made without delay. So now Bela, too, was joining the few remaining friends in emigrating to Palestine. This was his farewell visit. He still remembers the pride with which Tzali showed him his new daughter. The next time he saw Silvia, she was already seventeen.

It meant a lot to us to have Aunt Czili and her family around. Spending vacations in Medias those years was like going home. Tzali's school had a different schedule than mine so quite often I went alone or just with Silvia. With Aunt Czili's three daughters and 16 year-old Faigi to play with the baby, I could relax. Aunt Czili was a good cook, and she went out of her way to prepare special foods for us. When Tzali came with me she found us a room at a neighbor's and kept the baby overnight. Ignatz, who was so quiet and self-effacing in comparison with Czili's exuberant energy, went about his business, procuring all the necessities on the black market, bringing an occasional toy for the baby or an old bicycle for Tzali, saying very little but always smiling.

But this serene family sanctuary didn't last. Soon after the state of Israel was established in 1948, Czili's daughters left to join their brother there. Czili and Ignatz followed a few months later, leaving a great void in our lives.

Around the same time Czili's brother, Uncle Herman and his family, who had lived in Bucharest until the end of the war, departed for America, where his sisters Fannie and Goldie and his brother Aaron waited for them.

Yankl and his family left, too, to join his sisters and brothers in Israel. The move was a blessing for them. Once in Israel, Yankl began to thrive and his children grew up with all the opportunities of Israeli citizens. After Bertha died, he married her widowed sister. He is about eighty now and is surrounded by grandchildren and great-grandchildren who don't have to sleep on benches in the kitchen. When I last saw him he looked fine, and did not pass any chance to tease us about our youthful beliefs and trust in the Communist regime.

And so within two or three years after the end of the war, the only relative we had left in Romania was Zsuzsi, and even she lived far from Timisoara. We did not think at the time that the separation from the others would be forever. We were so absorbed in the present, our studies, the baby, the party and our unreasonable expectations that it took us years to realize that we would be stuck there for a very long time, perhaps for a lifetime.

February 25, 1988

Easier Times

I want to tell you about some of the easier times we had as students, when it was not all struggle and hardship.

At the beginning of my third year in medical school, the department of histology needed a full-time draftsman and posted a call for applicants. Since ours was a new school, the department didn't have enough visual educational materials and buying them would probably have been more expensive than hiring a draftsman to create them. They needed charts, posters, drawings of microscopic specimens, slides.

Here, I thought, was a job for me. I was not an artist but I was good in lettering and lines because of my work in the movie house in Sighet and my experience with technical drawings in the camp. I applied for the job and was quite surprised to see ten other applicants showing up to be tested for their skills, all medical students who probably needed the job as much as I did. I became anxious. We were given a chart to copy, we were requested to write titles in large and small print, and finally to make a drawing from a microscope slide of some colorful specimen.

I got the job and I was elated. I started to work in the laboratory immediately. I sat at the microscope for hours, I drew large posters of tissue structure, I titled and framed them and hung them on all the laboratory walls. My professor liked to watch me work. He was impressed to see me draw nerves and tracts and marveled at how I could draw circles and parallel lines with a free hand. I wonder whether, if I went back to visit the histology department today, my drawings would still be on the walls.

From then on we had a steady income and, financially at least, life became easier. Studying, however, became more and more difficult. I had less time to attend courses, and while the students who had jobs in the school were exempt from regular attendance, the make-up became more strenuous, particularly during these years of clinical subjects, of hospital clerkships, of bed-side rounds. My great academic record of the first two years started to fall and I almost failed one subject.

As I look back, it seems like a great deal of struggle and hardship, but we didn't think about it that way. Everyone around us had similar problems and I knew few who were more comfortable. In spite of all the difficulties, we did not complain. And I felt so privileged to have a job. We had little leisure time and few entertainments, but we were satisfied with simple pleasures like having a good meal, a warm room, and a winter outfit for our child. Passing an exam was always a great relief. Being invited for a special dinner was a treat. Going to a movie on a free evening or occasionally taking a vacation was a luxury. We loved being students and living in Timisoara.

When I reached the fourth year of medical school, the government policy makers decided that the medical institutes were producing too many internists and surgeons, and that the country needed more public health specialists and pediatricians. Since there was no time to publicize the new policies and let students make their own choice, it was decreed that for the rest of our training the entire fourth-year class would be assigned one third to public health, one third to pediatrics and one third to general medicine, including surgery. That way, by the time we completed the six-year program, we would already be specialized.

The assignments were made pretty arbitrarily, and in great secrecy by the Party and Student Union leaders of the school. Some students were probably asked about their preferences; most were not. When the placements were posted on the bulletin board, I found my name under public health. It took but a couple of minutes to notice that all the officials and their friends had obtained their assignment of choice.

I was extremely upset. The Party secretary knew of my preference for internal medicine. I had already left the draftsman's job for a clerkship in medicine and was working in a hospital. I felt wronged and I was determined to do something about it.

I really don't know if I was the only one who dared to fight this new injustice, or the only one who thought she had a chance to win, but I was the only one who tried. And I must admit that not all of the students assigned to public health were unhappy. That section included all the laboratory specialties and the fields of infectious diseases, tuberculosis and dermatology, and it appealed to people interested in research. But I knew of many who were unhappy; it wasn't what we had worked so hard and made so many sacrifices for.

First I went to argue with the school administration. I had interviews with the dean and the president. When that didn't work, I went to Deleanu, the Party secretary of the school, and the most powerful member of the student body. He agreed to try to help. After months of meetings, applications, arguments, and interventions by the Party and the dean, I was finally promised that in the next school year I would be back in internal medicine, but I had to take all the exams in the clinical subjects that were not taught in public health. So I did a rotation in pediatrics in my free time, and I studied the extra subjects during vacation -- and in my fifth year I was back in medicine.

Another windfall came our way around the same time, when we moved to the Savoy Hotel. In the late forties, most of the hotels in the city were pretty empty: people weren't traveling much. So the small Savoy was claimed by the student organizations and was turned into a student dormitory for the elite. It was an old and elegant three-story building, with a large central lobby, an impressive circular staircase, and large rooms, some with their own bathroom. It was located on a corner, near the charming center of the city, with the imposing opera house at one end and the splendid Orthodox Cathedral at the other, close to the river Bega and a riverside park. Between them was a promenade along Lloyd Lane, an exclusive row of old-fashioned buildings with stores, casinos and restaurants. In the riverside park were a cinema and an open-air theater where many summer festivities were held.

The takeover of the hotel was handled with great secrecy to avoid a strong reaction from dissatisfied students. Overnight all those with important positions in the medical school -- the new elite -- moved in. Tzali and I realized that there was finally a student dormitory with individual units which could accommodate married couples, and we could claim the right to move there. A new battle started with the same officials. A group of married students joined us, including two other couples with babies. The authorities seemed to find the idea of babies in student housing inconceivable -- but then, never before had a hotel been taken over by student organizations. We won.

We moved in and it was wonderful. Tzali and I got a corner room on the second floor. The other couples with babies got the same room on the floors above and below us. The room had a curved wall with windows facing the street and a door opening onto a balcony. It was well furnished, with a double bed and built-in closets, and it had central heating and a private bathroom with warm running water! We installed our little gas range in the bathroom, which became a kitchen too.

Everything was convenient. Hospitals were nearby. We could go out in the evening for a leisurely stroll on Lloyd Lane as far as one of the bridges over the Bega. The other couples volunteered to baby-sit for Silvia so we could go out to a movie on a rare free evening. Tzali got a part-time job in a vocational school teaching math and physics. The Student Union even gave us tickets to summer resorts and we spent two vacations in the Carpathians.

We had finally settled into a life that was more tranquil, at least for a while.

March 20, 1988

The Party

At some point I *had* to write you about "the Party" -- the Communist Party -- and its overwhelming presence and influence in our lives, how it governed our activities and demanded our time, our energy and even our souls. And I had to tell you what happened over the years, how things changed surreptitiously, and how ideology and optimism gave way to incompetence, repression and power struggle. And how our expectations and our confidence in the new rule evaporated.

Right after the war there was still a hint of democracy and human rights in Romania. The monarch, King Michael, was in his palace, there were many parties, and the country was run by a coalition government. Elections were to be held in 1946. The most influential organizations were the Communist Party and the Socialist Party, bolstered by the continued presence of Soviet forces in Romania. The fascist and reactionary parties who had ruled Romania in the early forties had been outlawed in 1944, when Romania joined the Allies and turned against the Germans. There were also many youth organizations and the supposedly apolitical Student Union. Young people were expected to belong to some or all of these groups to demonstrate loyalty to the new regime.

The leadership recruited actively, demanding that everybody contribute his efforts to achieving a society with social justice and equality. There appeared to be peace, freedom, choices, and a future. Those of us who had been discriminated against before were admitted to the universities and were given financial help. What else could one ask for? Responding to the promises implied by these opportunities never before available to them, the majority of students became members of these organizations. After I began medical school I also joined the Communist Party.

But things were much more complicated for Tzali and other "old-timers," the dreamers and idealists of the war years, the activists who had joined the anti-Fascist resistance, and had been arrested and sentenced to years in prison for it. At first these old-timers were accepted into the Party. However, they were soon suspended because of "their past," which could be tainted. They were told that their behavior during their prison years had to be "verified." Those who had suffered for the cause during the Fascist regime, who had the courage to resist under the most adverse and dangerous conditions, were now under suspicion of having collaborated with the authorities, informed on their comrades, and dragged them into prison. They felt hurt, humiliated, and resentful.

I still don't understand how the "verification" process was conducted nor why it took so many years to finally say to Tzali and the others, "You are cleared." By then their initial anger and resentment had faded, and they had become disillusioned with the new regime. They no longer wished to be rehabilitated; they actually hoped that the verification would never occur and that they would be left alone, even though the stain of having been labeled "illegalist" -- member of the outlawed war-time Communist Party -- remained.

I was not one of them but I could have been, if my political consciousness had been aroused just a little earlier. Tzali knew about my ideals and my intentions. He was my boyfriend and my best friend, and I confided in him. I suspected that he had joined the Youth organization of the Party, though he had never said so. With the war raging, and discrimination, hardship and suffering of the Jewish population seemingly at its height, every bright, conscientious young person who was looking for a cause, for a way to respond, to show concern, found the most obvious way: to join the resistance.

One evening, as we were walking alone in a dark alley, I told Tzali my great secret. I had decided to join the Youth division of the outlawed Communist Party and contribute my share in the fight against Fascism. He was surprised, excited and glad that I trusted him with my decision, and proud that I had reached it on my own. He said he would put me in touch with a Party cell.

But it was not to happen, for the crackdown came just a few days later. I already told you how dozens of young people, Tzali among them, were arrested by the Hungarian gendarmes -- some for organizing subversive activities and "plotting against the regime," others for participating in meetings, printing pamphlets, owning and distributing banned books (mine were hidden under the firewood in the woodshed), or for collecting money to help those already in jail. I later learned from Tzali that I was already assigned to a cell, and that the meeting had been scheduled. But I never met my connection or learned anything about the Party's secret operations. I was spared arrest, torture, and political camps and prisons, and I felt fortunate to be able to stay with my family during those trying times.

And years later, after the war, I was not designated an "illegalist," nor did I suffer the suspicions that this term created. It was strange and disconcerting to see how the old-timers were mistrusted by the Party leadership, while everyone else was accepted into their ranks, no matter how opportunistic their reasons for joining. The Party especially courted and welcomed into its ranks the offspring of workers and peasants, the presumed previously exploited classes, those of "healthy origin." That became the yardstick for all those seeking to get ahead, to win a prestigious position: were they of "healthy origin," or were they of "bourgeois origin," sons and daughters of former landowners, factory owners, or other "exploiters"? The same criteria were applied to admissions to higher education. There was a quota system, with 70% of the university openings reserved for students of "healthy origin," and many poorly qualified students got in. This system lasted into the sixties, when the new doctors, teachers, and engineers had evolved into the new "middle class," and their children didn't have their parents' "healthy origin": they were now discriminated against and had difficulty getting into top schools -- how ironic!

A new elite class began to take shape in this "egalitarian society." The newly recruited party members moved into leadership positions, obtained recognition, became the privileged ones: they got special material rewards, access to well-stocked, exclusive shops in this world of scarcity, the best factory cafeterias, tickets to special events, and vacations at top resort stations where previously government officials splurged in elegant villas. Party secretaries had the best positions available, they passed exams with flying colors, and learned to live in luxury.

The ideology now was quite different from the idealism, even romanticism, of earlier days; the new Communism was pragmatic and opportunistic. The old-timers among the leaders in the government and institutions were slowly eliminated. In our school the cadres changed, and more and more of the new breed were recruited, mediocre members, whose only qualifying criterion had been their background. Those of "unhealthy, bourgeois origin" were looked down upon, even considered enemies of the people, and were barely tolerated.

The ideological Bible was *The Short History of the Communist Party,* which contained the dogma according to Stalin. All the so-called philosophy courses, even in medical school, started with this booklet. For every exam it was compulsory reading. We all read it so many times that a colleague told us one day, "I've read this book over and over again. I know it by heart. If the manuscript were ever lost, I could dictate it perfectly word for word."

Stalin was worshiped by many as an idol. We did not know at that time about the political terror in the Soviet Union, about the concentration camps. We were inclined to believe that Yossie's story about Vorkuta was an aberration, an "honest mistake," an overreaction during the early stages of Communism in the USSR; it could not be the officially sanctioned policy. Much later, when Tzali and I read the Sakharov memoirs, we were surprised at his admission of how he trusted Stalin and how he cried at his funeral. It is embarrassing for us to admit today that we, too, trusted him at that time and mourned his passing away.

The indoctrination emphasized the superiority of Soviet

contributions in the development of art, culture, and science. The Russian language was now compulsory, replacing French as the most important foreign language. We were fed a constant fare of Russian and Soviet literature, movies, plays, concerts, and ballets, and were practically cut off from contemporary western culture. There were occasionally French or Italian movies on classical themes, and socially conscious Indian movies. But an American movie was a rare and much anticipated event; there was mobbing at the ticket window and intensive scalping.

Russian contributions to medicine could not be omitted from any lecture. Lysenko was now paid more attention than Darwin, and traditional procedures and tests got new Russian names. There were some ignorant lecturers who, after discussing the classical and well recognized discoverers of diseases, syndromes, or vaccines, took out a list from a pocket and started to enumerate the Soviet greats in that same field, lest they be considered heretics.

Public monuments were torn down and replaced with others dedicated to the founders of Communism. Streets, institutions, and even cities were named for important Russian personalities, like Maxim Gorky Theater, Pushkin Plaza, Stalin City. If and when these personalities fell from favor, the old names were reinstated.

The most threatening aspect of those student years was the power the Party displayed, controlling all aspects of our lives, demanding that nothing else be as important as the "cause of Socialism" -- not family, studies, or work, not to mention the trivial social life (if one had any). We had regular meetings, and we were constantly summoned for extraordinary meetings and indoctrination sessions to discuss the party line in relation to every new decree or strategy, economic change, or agrarian reform. We were sent to factories as "propagandists" to instruct workers in Marxist philosophy. We had to participate in all kinds of rallies to show support for new policies or to denounce the enemies of the working class abroad.

All this forced participation in political activities was very boring and time consuming. It was also frustrating. Timisoara was a lovely city with parks, riverside promenades and picturesque surroundings, a cultural center with concerts and an opera house, and we had acquired an appreciation for cultural events. But whenever we bought tickets to some performance (standing room, of course), something always came up to keep us from going: an "important" meeting, a discussion of tactics for the upcoming elections, another shake-up, or just some new esoteric topic from the Party's endless list of political trivia.

We didn't dare to question or to discuss the policies. We knew of people who had been arrested for telling a political (anticommunist) joke; and of party members who had been denounced for attending a Christmas mass. We came to live in fear, suspicion and frustration. We felt helpless in the face of this powerful force of lies and deception. What if I couldn't go to a meeting? What would they suspect? We didn't trust our colleagues, for anyone could be an informer. An atmosphere of hostility and paranoia was pervasive.

I remember an unpleasant incident with Zoia, a colleague from my medical school. She belonged to a group of girls from Moldova. They lived in the dormitory and struggled hard to make ends meet. They were all devoted Party members, and Zoia was the most zealous. She was also a "propagandist" in the factories, and an eloquent speaker at Party meetings. On one occasion, in her eagerness and perhaps for other motives as well, Zoia announced that I was of "bourgeois origin", that my father had been a grain merchant. I don't know what motivated her or where she got that information, but it could have been very damaging. I had to take great pains to prove to the Party that Father had never been an "exploiter."

I can't forget our dread of the Party purges, which came in quick succession, as if the Party had to cleanse itself periodically and thus be absolved of its mistakes, economic failures, and ineptitude. The Party line changed often, new ideology emerged, what was right one year fell into disgrace the next. There was infighting, and the old leadership was replaced. No one was immune. One could be expelled for ideological heresy, opportunism (what a dirty word in that society!), dishonesty, or joining the Party without disclosing past errors or the parents' social status. Showing indiscretion, having an affair was considered unacceptable anti-socialist behavior -- the list seemed endless. Whenever an extraordinary plenary meeting was announced we knew something was coming. The surprise was only the identity of the casualties; the end result was always public denunciation and expulsion with great fanfare, decided by a majority vote based on a show of hands that were never counted. If the accused were prominent people, expert ideologues versed in the dogma of Marxism, Leninism and Stalinism and the rigid Party line were sent from the Central Committee in Bucharest. No one could match their eloquence and self-righteousness. And who would dare? These special prosecutors could accuse anyone of disloyalty, of misinterpreting the Party ideology, of poor judgment, opportunism and even treason. This was the Communist Inquisition and expulsion was equivalent to burning at the stake or excommunication.

This is what happened to Yagnov, my former Anatomy professor. Since he had been a department chairman and dean of the medical school for several years, his purge became a grand show, a "cause celebre." Yagnov's case might have been started by someone pursuing a personal vendetta or wanting his position. But we knew the real cause of his disgrace and downfall: he had been a Social Democrat before that party and the Communists merged into the new "Workers' Party," run mainly by the Communist faction. The merger was followed by a stiffening of ideology, increased rigidity, more isolation from western influence, and repression. Suspicions were cast on the former Social Democrats: they had to prove that they were as devoted and as radical as the former Communists. Like many before him, Yagnov was stripped of his Party membership in a very arbitrary and autocratic way, and was publicly exposed and deprived of respect, pride and integrity. It was embarrassing even for the Party members who had no choice but to participate in the act. After that Yagnov continued as a professor but was removed as dean. He lost his spunk and he became subdued. I felt sorry for him, a dedicated man who had been destroyed by the system.

The revolution was over. Now the Communist Party was in power, the King had been ousted, and no other parties, no dissent were allowed. It had become totally corrupt, greedy, and power hungry, and was able to act with impunity, autocratically, with only the fear of being overturned by another internal faction, by new and more orthodox groups. The propaganda against the former bourgeoisie and against the "American Imperialism" was at its loudest. And for the countless rank-and-file members, as repressed as the rest of the citizens, the only way to survive was to submit, to listen to the demagoguery, and avoid voicing any opinions, and grudgingly participate.

In retrospect even today, in spite of what Communism turned out to be, I am glad that I cared to take a stand and to join the only movement that offered some hope. Yes, I was an idealist. I am only sorry that it took such a long time to learn the facts and to try to return to the real world. I wish that you too, Miriam, have high ideals, pursue them, and fight for them. Sure, times change, causes appear and disappear. But you should never regret that you fought for something that seemed right at the time. Trust your judgment.

March 12, 1988

Voices from the Past

Recently I found a box of old letters exchanged between Tzali and me that brought forgotten memories back to life. It was a revelation. We have very few pictures or other souvenirs from our student years. We had a camera, and we even went to professional photographers to have formal pictures of the children taken, which we sent to my brothers. But recording events was not important. Meeting the daily challenges was. And the few reminders we did have -- Silvia's rhyme and song booklet, the baby diary I kept for Yancu, the children's notebooks, school reports, the usual family mementos -- we were not permitted to take with us when we left Romania in 1961. So today I reflect on what I kept in my memory from those days, and what I have forgotten, and why.

Those letters were written between 1945 and 1950. Then the school years started irregularly and exams were given at odd times. I would often visit Aunt Czili in Medias or Zsuzsi and Bela in Sighet after my exams, to rest up and recover, while Tzali stayed behind to take his exams. That's when we wrote to each other. Reading these letters reopened a whole chapter of our lives. Events long forgotten or even repressed come back to life, sometimes with a significance we didn't recognize at the time. The letters contain all the trivia of everyday life, the little pleasures and miseries, the preoccupations and the feelings, the expressions of love and longing.

Letters from 1945. I am a young bride, visiting Medias for a week. I feel terribly guilty that I left my husband behind in Timisoara, that I'm eating so well, that I am being pampered by my aunt's family, while he has to take care of our household problems and stand in line for food. I keep asking myself, is it right to be apart just so I can get some rest and comfort? Weren't all those years of separation enough? I write about the textbooks I need, I ask him to go to my school and find out the dates of my exams, which are constantly being postponed. I ask about his finals and worry about him. He writes about his problems with the inflation. Bread isn't always available and when he finds some, it costs 10,000 leis a loaf. A pair of shoes is 350,000; we can't afford it.

I am in Sighet in July 1946, in the house that Bela now shares with his friend Sanyi. Bela went to Budapest to pick up Zsuzsi, who is finally coming home from Sweden. I am lonely and don't know what to do with myself, so I go to the nearby town of Viseu to visit my uncle Yeno, my mother's brother and the only one from that generation to return from the camps. Aunt Czili has come from Medias to see him. Faigi, from Borsa, is there too. So are Yeno's son Feri and his new bride Hailu, who has also just returned from Sweden. She is urging him to go to the university. I am impressed with Hailu's clothes, with the way her relatives in Sweden took care of her, and the presents she brought for Feri and his father. I write about a beautiful orchard behind the house.

Today I cannot recall anything about that reunion, and I wonder why. What is most amazing is that except for my brother Ezu, everyone in my family who had survived the camps was there at that time -- Yeno, his son Feri, my cousin Faigi and myself. With aunt Czili there too, it must have been a momentous family gathering. I can't understand why I am unable to recall it, even when I read all the details in the letter. Wasn't it important? Didn't I grasp its meaning? Or was I still hoping that more family members would return, and then we would have a real reunion?

Another letter from 1946. I am back in Sighet. Zsuzsi arrives. She looks healthy and happy, prettier than ever, and is surprised and delighted to find me there. She is wearing a beautiful embroidered green dress that Bela bought her in Budapest. Her excitement, her enthusiasm, her cheerfulness, all remind me of the way she was before we were deported. But she has grown, she is nineteen, and her experiences have profoundly affected her, though we do not talk about them. She tells lots of stories about Sweden and her cousins, Hedi and Livi, who decided to stay there. As if forbidden, we never mention the time we last saw each other, when we were separated in Birkenau almost two years ago.

Three days later I write again. The house is different with Zsuzsi around. She has moved furniture, put flowers in pots and vases, covered the tables with colorful tablecloths, hung paintings and pictures on the walls. I repeat Bela's comment: "Sure, a woman has come to the house, not a student". But she also has anxieties and doubts about the future. We talk and talk.

I am back in Medias. I am pregnant and very excited about it. Tzali writes me letters full of tenderness and affection, he urges me to take care of myself, because it is not only me... I am concerned about his exams in Technology, I even dream that I failed my exam but he passed his. Since we have no telephones, I ask him to send a telegram after the test. The mail is late; I am worried.

I talk with Czili about baby clothes. She gives me some old woolens, which I start to unravel for the yarn to make a new baby outfit. Tzali's letters exude love and devotion. We cling to each other with a certain fear and apprehension. Behind the excitement of the forthcoming event there is some uncertainty and anxiety. We don't yet feel sure of the future.

I am in Sighet again, late in the fall, exhausted after my Anatomy exam. I am thrilled as I feel the first movements of the baby. I am full of anticipation about the great event. This joy overshadows my annoyance with my brother-in-law Bela and the old housekeeper, Mariska (I have no idea over what, probably Mariska catered only to the men in the family, the 'masters'). Tzali writes about his intense studying for yet another exam in Descriptive Geometry. He has no money and will try to borrow some from Klari's father, so he can come to Sighet. The gypsy woman had sold the old clothes he gave her, but the money is just not enough. I always look forward to letters from my brothers, and I write to Tzali, "Don't forget to leave a large envelope with Mrs. Deutsch before you come, so she can forward us the letters without opening them". (Sometimes there were dollars in them!)

The first letter from Alter from a prisoner-of-war camp in the Soviet Union has arrived. I knew from others that he was alive, but had not heard from him before. Even now, there is no return address.

It is August 1947. I am at Czili's with Silvia, who is almost five months old. Oh, the universal, ageless, feelings of motherhood, that overwhelm a woman and drive out all other preoccupations! How easily does one forget them! Did I ever remember that I felt the same way as my daughter does now with her babies?

My aunt cries when she sees me arrive at the train station, tired, exhausted and skinny. She makes me go to bed while she prepares hot chocolate. She buys butter and a chicken, and bakes a cake, all for me. She won't let me get up even to nurse, she brings the baby to me. And how everyone takes care of the baby! The older girls have left for the *Hachshara* to prepare them to join their brother. (The *Hachsharas* were agricultural farms set up by Zionist organizations which entitled young people to a "certificate", a requirement for emigration to Palestine under the British mandate.) But Czili, her younger daughter Rochi, and cousin Faigi cook and take care of the baby. They collect rainwater to bathe her -- it is soft and better for babies, -- change her often and with much pleasure. They find a cradle in some neighbor's attic and make a straw mattress for it. They hire a young peasant girl to do the laundry, and to wash and iron the diapers until they look white as snow.

Silvia, the first baby after the Holocaust and the only one so far, is cherished as if she could replace all the children who were lost.

Every day Ignatz brings something new for the baby from the hardware store where he works: a pan, a strainer, a grater, a potty, all important acquisitions. He goes to the postmaster early each morning just to bring my mail a few hours earlier. He arranges a fellowship for Tzali at a factory in Medias for next summer, so we can spend the summer with them. We assume it will pay 1100 new lei and we will be able to contribute to the household expenses.

Ignatz comes through in these letters very different from how I remember him. He is so devoted and concerned, so attached to us, yet reserved and unpretentious. I am impressed and remorseful that perhaps I did not reciprocate his love. Aunt Czili meant so much to me that I might have ignored him.

And how much I write about the baby! How she laughs and chuckles when the girls play with her. She looks so adorable in that new flannel outfit that she got from her godmother, Czili's neighbor. My constant problem is that she hates the vegetable soup that I prepare so laboriously using the pediatrician's recipe to make sure she gets her vitamins and minerals. I write in more than one letter about the fuss she makes when we try to feed her her soup: she spits out everything but a few teaspoons of mashed potatoes. Now that I am weaning her, she is so finicky that I worry about her health.

Sometimes I mention the need to study, but then I go over my daily activities with the baby; when they are all done, the day is gone. I am a mother only and a happy one, and the baby is my sole preoccupation. I don't even appreciate the luxury of having time for this. Had my application been approved, the one to advance a year in my studies, I would have had to take extra exams at that time, and I couldn't have done it.

I get a telegram from Rome on my birthday, signed "Miki, Yossie, Ezu and Olga". It makes me so happy to hear from my brothers and see how thoughtful they are. Ignatz brings a bottle of wine to celebrate.

Back in Timisoara Tzali is studying. He has many problems. The baby carriage, where Silvia used to sleep, had to be repaired again, but he couldn't pick it up because he had no money. And anyway, it had become too small, and there is no money for a crib either.

He has arguments with Mrs. Deutsch over the new rent. Since the "stabilization" that followed the inflation, the rate of exchange for the new currency is supposed to be one new lei for 2,000 old ones. We had been paying 350,000 old lei, so it should now be 175 new lei -- but she wants more.

There is no bread to be found, but he was able to acquire 20 kg of flour. (I don't remember what we did with the flour. I know I didn't make bread. Maybe we gave it to a baker in exchange for bread?) He got coupons for oil and sugar. He will arrange for me to eat at the best factory cafeteria when I return. He has an upset stomach. The day before he passed by a long food line, he got in without knowing what they were selling, and got three ears of corn; they made him sick. Another day there is milk and even salami at the grocery stores. He writes that, since he eats dinner at the cafeteria, all he needs at home is bread, milk, butter, tomatoes and grapes. Looking back I wonder when he ever had time to study.

Again I am at Czili's. A huge food package has arrived for all of us from Aunt Fannie in New York. With amazement I list everything she sent: sugar, cocoa, chocolate, sardines, tea -- abundance for a time. The relatives in New York correspond with Aunt Czili and that is how we keep in touch. Uncle Herman, on the way to his sisters' in New York, just sent a telegram to tell us he has arrived in Le Havre and is waiting for the ship. Before he left he wrote me that if he reached America, I would have no more money troubles. I don't remember what happened. But reading these letters today I am overcome by affection for him, my only uncle who is still alive. I call him at the nursing home. He's 87 now, has had a stroke and doesn't remember anything any more, not even what happened last month. But I felt better after calling.

Oh, how I wish now I had more than this handful of letters! They are priceless. They enable me to glance back at our life then, the daily problems and worries, the little incidents that were important then, the joys that made life happy, the small achievements. The letters evoke so much feeling, warmth, concern about each other, joy. Somehow memory is more inclined to preserve sad or tragic events.

And yet, nowhere in the letters is there any mention of the past. Does that say something? It just seems that the whole year spent *There*, in that inferno, had to be erased, obliterated, to make room for the strength needed to build a new life.

Today rarely does anyone write letters: communication is by telephone. Can you imagine not having letters in your old age, having to rely only on your memory? You see how flawed memory can be? Miriam, do write letters, to friends and cousins, to parents and grandparents. Express your feelings in them. Describe the momentary problems, preoccupations, the daily pleasures. Maybe you will learn from my experience what a pack of old letters can do for you, when your memory has long forgotten those events that once meant so much to you.

January 14, 1988

Graduation

As we both approached graduation it became clear to us that we were not going to be able to settle in Timisoara, that our decisions about our future, family and careers would take us somewhere where housing and jobs were more available than in this crowded metropolis.

By 1950 the dominance of the Communist Party in the People's Republic of Romania (RPR) was almost complete. The Party line became more rigid and the expression of individual ideas was suppressed. One didn't dare to complain, even to someone who was presumably a friend. We had become more disillusioned and discouraged. Our initial optimism and confidence, our dreams of a better life and a just society, were all but shattered. We had learned not to believe the promises, the decrees, "the great economic plans."

The first "five year economic plan" promised a 92% reduction in the cost of living. Five years later, the situation was worse. True, as the official newspapers told us, the prices of a large number of items had indeed been lowered: notions, buttons, brooms, books, chalk, paints and building materials, vinegar, toiletries, liquors, etc. Meanwhile essentials and necessities -- including basic foodstuffs like bread, sugar, oil, and meat, train tickets, clothing -- increased in price and decreased in quality. We learned how figures like '92%' could be manipulated, and how to read between the lines. We started to distrust everything we read.

Tzali, now in his senior year, worked hard to complete all the courses for graduation. This was an event we both looked forward to and dreaded, because the decisions regarding job assignments were arbitrarily made in Bucharest according to the government's policy and plans. There was never any consideration for family or personal needs. Husbands and wives were frequently assigned to cities far apart, in rural areas and distant industrial cities, and it could take years for them to find jobs close to one another.

This almost happened to us too. When Tzali graduated, he received his job assignment in the mail. It was in Moldova, in eastern Romania, across the country from Timisoara. No one cared that his wife was still a student in Timisoara, that he had a child, that he would be a ten hour train ride from his family. No questions were asked, there was no discussion -- and most significantly, there was no recourse. Luckily he met a student who had the same problem, but in reverse: he had been assigned to Arad, a city not far from Timisoara, while his fiancee was working in Moldova. He and Tzali applied for a swap, which turned out to be lengthy and complicated.

They had to go to Bucharest, where they were shuffled from one office to another, wrote new applications, waited for weeks for approval from the respective companies, and after a great deal of red tape and the customary *baksheesh* (bribe), they were allowed to exchange positions.

We were fairly satisfied. Arad was only two hours away by train. Tzali found a furnished room there, and he came home every Saturday night, after work, and returned on Monday at dawn. The travel and his living expenses almost exceeded his earnings, but Tzali had no choice. He had to accept the position he was offered. He couldn't look elsewhere -- the state was the only employer. He couldn't stay home, idle, even if he had chosen to. That was labeled "parasitism" and was considered a most severe infraction, close to "hooliganism".

Since my husband was working we couldn't keep our room at the Savoy any more, other students were waiting for it. We were expected to be able to afford rent outside of student housing. We started again to look for suitable accommodations.

We found space in a three-story house in a very nice secluded area. The street that had once been called Nightingale Street was now renamed Kutuzov street after the famous Russian general of the Napoleonic wars. We were the third tenants in what used to be a one-family apartment on the second floor.

The owner, Dr. Kaufman, was a dentist who was forced by the authorities to share his family's flat, and he made no attempts to be gracious about it. He had been allowed to keep two rooms for his family and for his office. A narrow hall served as a waiting room for his patients. Another room off the hall was already rented to a woman who worked at a bank.

Our room had once been a second bedroom of the Kaufmans'. It was spacious and sunny and we fit in pretty well. We had a convertible couch, a table to eat and work on, a cupboard for our clothes and a crib for Silvia, and when Yancu was born we added a bassinet. From the hall we had to go through the bathroom to reach our room. If it was in use a curtain was drawn, leaving a narrow passage for us. The toilet was in a little cubicle with its own door. And we could use part of the kitchen, though we could eat there, on our own little table, only when the Kaufmans had finished their meals.

Behind the house there was a vegetable garden, with flower beds and an apricot and a walnut tree. We could pick the ripe apricots, and even make preserves, but the walnuts were 'off limits' -- they belonged to the Kaufmans.

There were two or three families on each of the other floors of the house. One of them was a security officer and had a telephone, where Tzali could call me from Arad if he had something important to say. As he called at pre-arranged times, I often sat on the staircase listening for the ringing. Across the street a Romanian family had a daughter Silvia's age who went to the same kindergarten, so she had a playmate. And there were only two other houses on this short block.

On the left end of our street was the entrance to the Rose Park, on the bank of the Bega river. In spring, roses of all colors and shades blossomed, and the sight and scent were delightful. We often went for a stroll there. In summer, an open air Music Festival was held in the park. Even if we did not buy tickets, we could walk around or just stay in front of our house and listen to operettas by Franz Lehar and Johann Strauss, most often *The Gipsy Baron* and *The Merry Widow*.

That was our entertainment. We gave no parties, were rarely invited to one, and had no visitors. Since Tzali wasn't home during the week, work as an intern in the hospital, Silvia, Party meetings and the household took up all my time, leaving very little for studies.

Shopping for food was a constant, time-consuming task. There continued to be shortages of practically everything. If butter became available, the lines to buy a half pound were sometimes three blocks long. I would get in line repeatedly to get enough butter for two weeks. Silvia helped too. She was perhaps six years old when she started to wait in line on her own. If potatoes or other vegetables arrived at the grocery store, she would take her little scooter and the ever-ready string nets, and proudly return with five pounds of potatoes on one handle of the scooter and three pounds of onions on the other. Then she would go back for a second load. Many essential food items were rationed. Others could be found only on the black market, but we had no time to go and search for them.

Soon after we moved to the Kaufmans' I became pregnant again. We told Silvia about it in December while we were preparing for the "winter holidays." This was a very important official holiday season, as the Communist regime tried to discourage Romanians from celebrating Christmas. The school vacation was called Winter Recess, and its major event was the celebration of the New Year with great pomp and spectacle. This is how they tried to make the holiday secular. Christmas trees became "Winter trees," Santa Claus became "Old Frostman," and everybody exchanged gifts on the New Year. Fir trees were not sold until December 26, and then everybody bought them. We had always celebrated New Year's Eve (called the night of Sylvester) and now we even had a fir tree like everybody else. It was nicely decorated with colorful globes, candles, sparklers, walnuts dipped in gold paint, and our own home-made candies and star-shaped cookies. (Although chocolates and decorations could be found in the shops at that season, they were expensive.)

By the time Yancu was born, in June 1952, Tzali had obtained a transfer to Timisoara and we were finally all together. We hired an old German woman, called Hoffman neni (Hungarian for aunty), to take care of Yancu. She often took him to her home, where she and her husband, who were childless, overwhelmed him with love and attention, just as grandparents would. She also cooked for us, and made all sorts of delicacies on our gas stove in the apartment kitchen.

The Kaufmans were unfriendly and complained about us all the time. When a neighbor had asked Mrs. Kaufman who were her new tenants, she had answered scornfully, "Ah, some poor students. They arrived like gypsies, with their few belongings in a small carriage." That was true, our furniture hadn't yet arrived from Sighet. But they resented us because we were forced on them, and they did not appreciate having a new-born cry at night.

Anyway, we tried to have nothing to do with them and go about our daily business. There was no refrigerator, but there was a cool larder where we kept our cooked food, vegetables, jars, canned goods and other provisions. The walls were lined with shelves, but every time I put our food there, Mrs. Kaufman would place it on the floor and tell us not to use their shelves. We asked for some space to build our own shelves, but they refused. Finally we filed an official complaint in small claims court to get storage space. Our case was rather simple, as similar skirmishes were typical when so many families had to share facilities. The judge quickly decided we were entitled to one wall for storage. The Kaufmans took down their shelves, so until we built our own, the food still stayed on the floor -- but at least it was in our space.

April 6, 1988

Yancu

Today is Yancu's birthday, and my thoughts take me back to the events surrounding his birth. It evokes so many endearing memories.

When Silvia was almost five years old, during the New Year's celebrations, we prepared her for the big surprise. Then we told her that a new baby would be coming. She was very excited, but then she started crying.

"Why are you crying, Silvia, aren't you happy?"

"Yes I am happy," she said, "but I didn't even notice that you are pregnant."

After that she counted the months, then the weeks and finally the days. I remember how embarrassed I was when the chairman of my department, who lived across our street in a furnished room, recounted at a round the conversation he overheard between Silvia and her friend, his landlady's daughter. It went like this:

"Doina", Silvia said, "do you know how many more days are until our baby will be born?"

"Ten days" Doina answered.

"No, only nine more days" was the reply.

He enjoyed hearing these daily exchanges. Anyway, it was common knowledge by then. But when I was six months pregnant, the same absent-minded professor was extremely surprised when I told him about my condition.

We were expecting the new baby in June and we were hoping for a boy. I told myself that if the baby arrived on June 15 and if it was a boy, I would name him Yancu in memory of my youngest brother, who was also born on June 15. It is a Jewish tradition to name children after lost loved ones, and Silvia -- Zissel in Yiddish -- had been named for my mother.

My good friend Rolla and I were preparing together for the State Board examination, which was posted for June 20. She, too, was pregnant, and our due dates were just one day apart. It was one more thing we had in common. We were both in our last year of medical school, and her husband was an engineer like Tzali. We were constantly comparing the experience of being pregnant: who showed first? who was bigger? whose baby kicked first? Every day we would walk over to the Rose Park to sit on a shaded bench and study. But as the months progressed I realized that without parents or relatives to help I wouldn't be able to handle a new baby and an examination in the same week, and so I decided to postpone the exam. Rolla, who had her mother to help her, chose to go ahead. We continued to review our courses together anyway, particularly Marxist Philosophy, an important required topic that I knew pretty well.

When I arrived at the hospital, in the evening of June 14, I called Rolla from the public phone between two contractions.

"Aren't you coming, Rolla? Didn't we plan to have the babies at the same time?" But she wasn't ready.

I gave birth the next morning, on June 15. It was a boy, so we called him Yancu. Everything was as I had hoped, and I was happy, relieved and exhausted. So was my obstetrician, but he couldn't go home because Rolla had called, and she was on her way to the hospital. Vera was born a few hours later.

Our beds were in the same room. Her mother visited us and brought goodies for "her two daughters." When Silvia came to see the baby, we showed her both and asked her to guess which one was her brother. She hugged each of them, and then chose Vera.

Rolla continued studying and nursing her baby, but she was nervous. The first exam, in Obstetrics, was to be held in our hospital five days later. When the day arrived, Rolla got dressed and went downstairs to the classroom, while I joined the other students in the audience. She was sitting on the bench waiting for her turn. At noon she glanced at the clock on the wall, then turned around and looked at me with apprehension; it was feeding time. I gestured to her that I would take care of things and went upstairs to nurse the two babies. By the time I returned she had finished with the top grade -- no wonder, after experiencing Obstetrics live! But in every subsequent exam, about two days apart, she did a little worse. She had returned home, the baby was crying a lot, and she was tense and did not have enough milk. For days her mother would come to get some mother's milk from me, as formula was not available. But Rolla managed to pull through in all the subjects and graduate.

As for myself, I was happy just to be a mother, with no other preoccupation than home, family and children. I had a six-week leave from my new job as instructor in Internal Medicine in the hospital, and I had postponed my final exams to the next semester. When I returned to work and studies we took Yancu to a day care center. He had become a beautiful child, charming and absent-minded, and all his teachers were in love with him. Every year on May 1st all the schools had to participate in a huge parade to demonstrate public allegiance to the Communist regime. When Yancu was about four, the children of his kindergarten also marched. The last one, at least ten steps behind the others, was my little blond boy, looking to the right, looking to the left, forgetting where he was. And everybody admired him.

***

Watching our baby son with his soft, golden curls I would often think of my little brother Yancu, the youngest of Father's eight children, and the darling of the family. He was rather short, but cute and intelligent, with inquisitive green eyes and beautiful blond hair. He was the only one of my father's sons allowed to let his hair grow out after it was first cut off, and the first who did not have to wear a cap all the time. This is how modern Father had become over the years.

Yancu surprised all of us with his interest in books and learning. Most of my brothers had taken up various trades, only Miki and I graduated from high school and went on for further studies. When the schools were closed to Jewish children and I tutored many of them at home, Yancu was one of my pupils and among the best. He liked to study, and I predicted a great future for him. He also kept me company when I worked, did errands, and joined me for strolls on the Corso when I had just broken up with Tzali.

He was the only one of my brothers to stay home in the last years of the war. After we moved to the ghetto Moishi returned from the front, and the five of us were all in the same train going to Auschwitz. Yancu didn't make it, just like Moishi, not even into the camp. He perished before he was fifteen.

There is so little I remember about him. I have so very few pictures of him. I wish I knew more about his short life.

But I did learn something a few years ago when we went to see Tzali's cousins Hedi and Livi in Sweden. For many years they had been asking us to visit, but other commitments always seemed to intervene. Now Hedi and Livi decided to have a party for us and invited all of their friends from the camp who had ended up in Sweden.

It was Midsummer's Day, the longest day of the year, which in Sweden never turns into night and is celebrated all over the country. It was a lovely party. We met their friends, talked, ate and drank until dawn. During the evening a tall, fat woman approached me. She looked much younger than I but she said she remembered me. She told me that she and my little brother Yancu had been in love.

I was astonished. I stared at this large middle-aged woman and tried to recall my little brother at fourteen. Was he in love? Why not? But with this big woman? Even as a girl she must have been tall, and Yancu was short. Then she said that in fact Yancu didn't want to go out with her because she was too tall for him.

The two of us talked about Yancu, about those years, and the last days in the ghetto. She had never returned to Romania because there was no one in her family left. I wondered, if she was the same age as Yancu, what saved her in Auschwitz? Did her height make her look older? So very, very few kids of Yancu's age group survived.

It had never occurred to me that at fourteen Yancu could have been in love. But the thought that in his short lifetime he had known love made me very happy.

***

At the time of our new baby's birth, we again had money problems: there was a second wave of inflation, more severe than the one five years earlier. The prices of all the basic necessities were climbing daily and we could hardly keep up. We also needed baby articles that were unavailable in Romania or were of poor quality, nylon panties, bottles, pacifiers, diapers, rubber sheets, and so forth. So we asked my brother Alter, who now lived in New York -- he was finally given an entrance visa after waiting for years in a DP camp in Germany -- and he promptly sent us a package. We waited for it eagerly, anticipating all kinds of wonderful American things in it.

Then a new "stabilization" came, as suddenly and unexpectedly as the first one. Once again, in exchange for some of the money they had, everyone got the same 150 new lei to last for the next two weeks. But now this was much less than the equivalent of a minimum salary. One could hardly pay bills with this amount, and people struggled until their next paychecks. Overnight all savings, whether hidden away or deposited in the bank, were lost. Paper money became worthless, it filled waste baskets or was used to start fires.

A few days later I was notified that my long awaited package from America had arrived. The customs duty was 900 lei and we were informed that if the package was not picked up within three days, it would be returned to the sender. We were in a panic. If it had not been for some of the items we needed so badly for the baby, we would have left it there; and we couldn't even be sure that it contained any of them. By now we had grown so cynical that we suspected that all packages from abroad had been held back at the post office until after the stabilization.

But we borrowed money from any friend who could spare 50 or 100 lei and collected enough to get the parcel. It contained some nice shirts, silk ties and blouses, and a few other articles which we sold to pay our debts. We kept only the baby clothes, the nylons panties, the fine diapers, and one bar of chocolate for the children.

With the new baby, and with Hoffman neni coming daily to take care of him, our small room became very crowded, and getting a new apartment in Timisoara appeared impossible. Nor were we too satisfied with our jobs, which were dead-end positions that did not advance our careers; and our salaries were too small to support a family decently.

Meanwhile our colleagues who had moved to the provinces or to new industrial centers were doing quite well, and urging us to join them. There was a strong need for engineers and doctors, there were better salaries with fringe benefits, and newcomers were accepted with open arms.

We loved Timisoara, but we had to realize that our expectations could not be fulfilled in this crowded academic center. It was time for decision, time to move away and settle somewhere else where life would be easier.

June 15, 1984

Part IV: Behind the Curtain

Father

Dear Miriam,

Has it really been one hundred years? I don't know exactly when he was born but by my calculations Father was about fifty-eight when we were taken away, and that was forty years ago. But I just learned that a long article appeared in an Israeli newspaper commemorating the hundredth anniversary of my father's birth.

The author of this article is Schon Dezso, a writer from Cluj. He knew my father before the war, admired his talent for storytelling and encouraged him to write. In those days Schon was the editor-in-chief of the *Uj Kellet* -- the New Dawn -- the main Jewish Hungarian language newspaper in Transylvania. In 1938, when Father's book was published, Schon wrote a long column about him and his book, and referred to my father as the only spokesman of the Jews from Maramures. After the war he emigrated to Israel, where he continued publishing his newspaper, the only Hungarian language periodical there.

Surprisingly, just a few weeks ago I had another unexpected reminder of my father from Rabbi Schnitzler in Rego Park. He had found out that the daughter of Apsan, the "raconteur," lived here in New York, and wanted to tell me what an impression my father had made on him. Rabbi Schnitzler is younger than we are, and he was born in Sighet. After moving away with his family, he returned every summer to visit his grandparents. He remembers vividly how on Saturday afternoons, he and other teenagers would hurry to our Synagogue where "Mr. Apsan was telling his amusing stories." It was so inspiring to talk to someone who knew my father!

Father published only one book, *Vizhnitzer Rebbe's Hoif* -- The Court of the Vizhnitzer Rabbi, with bittersweet stories about simple folks who lived in the surrounding villages, worked hard all year, prepared joyously for the holidays, and kept the Jewish tradition alive, passing it on from generation to generation. When Schon wrote the eulogy for Father's hundredth anniversary, he also reprinted the 1938 article about him, where he quotes from some of Father's stories, praises his talent, recognizes his historical importance, and mourns his loss and that of his writings. Schon says my father never realized what a great gift he had nor how important he could have been for posterity. I was deeply impressed and moved by this tribute.

I often try to revive forgotten images of Father, Mother and my brothers. I recall so little about the times when we were together. And so I was startled when Debbie, my daughter-in-law, asked me one day, "Did your mother love her three stepsons?"

"I don't know" I answered.

"Did she love you?"

I told her I didn't know that either but I thought so. Then I told her that I was the only one in our house whose birthday was celebrated.

"You mean they did not celebrate the children's birthdays?"

In those days and in our community, I explained, birthdays weren't usually celebrated, nor were Bar-Mitzvahs. But I was an only girl with seven brothers and that made me special, if only in mother's eyes. This is why, even to this day my brothers remember my birthday. Theirs I didn't learn till much later.

Since my birthday fell at the end of summer, it was always a celebration with lots of fruit, candies and cookies. Mother prepared one of her specialties, called "non-plus-ultra," two round cookies glued together with raspberry jam and topped with whipped cream or whipped egg white. It was the ultimate delight. I always invited my friends to my birthday parties.

Did I invite boys? No, boys were not allowed to come, until and unless they had "serious intentions." I do remember though that one boy sent me a bouquet of red roses on my 17th birthday with his sister. (What was written on the note? "I hope these few flowers will whisper to you how I feel about you." How romantic! And how funny that I should remember to this day every word of that note!)

Did my mother love me? Do you know that song from *Fiddler on the Roof* where Tevye asks his wife, "Golda, do you love me?" and she answers, "I suppose I do!" We did not talk much about love or other feelings. I recall very few moments when affection was expressed between Father and Mother. Nor do I remember Father ever hugging one of the boys. Even for me, Mother's embraces and Father's caresses were so rare as to be memorable. We just didn't kiss and hug and tell each other "I love you," as people do so much today.

And yet, how can one question their love, their trust and their devotion to each other. I can still feel Mother's anguish when Father would get up in the middle of the night with one of his frequent asthma attacks, open the window and smoke his medicated cigarette. One time Mother was admitted to the hospital for a minor procedure. To keep Father from worrying she wouldn't tell him the time of the surgery. When we went to visit and found that she was already in the operating room, Father became apprehensive. He went over to the window of the waiting room and prayed fervently until the surgeon came out and reassured him.

As I start looking back the images become clearer. Now I hear her early on Friday mornings as she returns from the market with two heavy baskets of groceries and three live chickens. She stops at the gate and calls me to come and help carry everything up the stairs. Before the holidays, with more to shop, I go to the market with her and watch her carefully inspect and haggle with the peasants for every bit of produce, a bunch of radishes, a dozen eggs, a well-fattened goose, a ripe watermelon. At the end of the summer we bring home large baskets of prunes, apricots, currants, quince, tomatoes, and cucumbers, and spend days preparing and cooking them for winter storage in huge kettles on a specially built outdoors fire. The children are all delighted to help stir the thick paste in the simmering kettles, taste the jams in the making, and eat fresh fruit to their heart's content.

I see Mother on a Sabbath, when I come home from school, too late for the festive dinner. She has kept the food warm, she serves it to me, then sits down while I eat. She looks pretty, a few blond locks have escaped from under the embroidered silk kerchief. I hungrily devour the spread in front of me: chopped eggs with onion, challah, cholent, roast chicken with prune compote, sponge cake. I tell her everything that happened in school that day. She watches me and listens, her love and pride barely concealed. This is one of my particular pleasures of the Sabbath.

In winter I see her embroidering tablecloths and wall hangings, or crocheting that fancy curtain with a huge peacock in the middle surrounded by a floral pattern. But when a particularly fine piece is finished she says, "No, I am not going to use it, it's too nice. We'll save it for when Dorika gets married." And she adds it to the drawer already full with my future dowry.

I recall one of the rare occasions when she went on vacation alone -- to Aunt Czili in Medias -- and she left me, then about thirteen, in charge of the household. She made certain that our neighbor would come to help me prepare the Sabbath meals, the only ones with chicken or beef, but during the week I was on my own. And since I had never learned to cook, it took but a few days to run through the things I knew to prepare. How the boys made fun of me, that all I knew to make for dinner was potato soup and green beans for vegetables, or bean soup and potatoes for vegetable! When Mother returned after two weeks and saw me so distraught, she hugged me as never before and held me as I cried bitterly on her shoulder.

Doesn't everything she did for me express her love? Doing all the household work, so I can do my studies or my work? Letting me have all the presents Miki sent her from Italy? Looking the other way when I acted like a rebellious teenager, going on excursions with boys, attending Saturday night dances and staying out late at parties, or declining to accompany her to temple for special events. And how eagerly she prepared the dinner when Tzali finally came to visit officially, wearing a hat for the occasion. As Tevye said, "If that's not love, what is?"

My parents remain carved in my memory at the ages when they died: Mother was forty-six and Father fifty-eight. And a part of me stopped growing at that time; in my mind I still relate to them as a young girl cherished by and needing her Mom and her Dad.

How I missed my parents over the years! When I returned home to Sighet after the war there was no cemetery, no tomb, no grave where I could go to meditate, remember, cry, and pray for them. No place to some day take my children and grandchildren and say, "This is where your grandma and grandpa lie." There was nothing left of our home to remind me of the past. All of our clothing, furniture, photographs, books, letters, school mementos, medical and legal documents -- everything was gone.

Imagine, Miriam, a fire in your house. You escape but lose everything in your home, in your room. All your clothes, albums, pictures, diaries. Your awards and diplomas, your graduation dress, your favorite dolls, the locked box containing all of your secrets that you hid under the bed. Wouldn't that be a disaster?

The photographs in our albums -- I still miss them so much. You probably know already how during the war Tzali kept with him a little pocket album with pictures of his family; of our first outing to Sugatag, of me performing the Tango Bolero, and a few others. You have seen them. Over the years we discovered some other pictures, that my family had sent to Aunt Fanny here in the States before the war, and we made copies of them for our albums. Each picture retrieved has a story: where it was found, when it was made. Each one brings back a new memory, a moment of the past long buried, a family event long forgotten. We get excited with every picture. But I have never been able to find the picture we had at home of Father as a sergeant in World War I. What a handsome, proud young man he was, showing off the three stars on his lapel.

For a very long time, the enormous loss of life overshadowed all other losses. Yet the destruction of homes, synagogues, cemeteries, books, art and other treasures created by the hands, minds and hearts of the Jews in northern Transylvania wiped out nearly every trace of the rich culture that existed there. Among these lost treasures are Father's manuscripts.

During the war, when Father was out of work, he wrote more than ever before. Though he could no longer publish, he had drawers full of manuscripts and he continued to write even in the ghetto. He sat at a table in the backyard and wrote and wrote. When we were taken away everything was left behind.

A year later, when I returned from camp, Tzali and I went to the house in the former ghetto where my family had lived. We found none of the things that we had left behind or hidden in the attic. But in the backyard, on a pile of rotting garbage, we noticed some pages with Father's handwriting. Scattered over neighboring backyards and on other garbage heaps, there were more pages, some crumpled, some ripped, some with the writing all washed out. We gathered them with love and care and made a bundle of them. Over the following years, when we moved away from Sighet, we could find no one who could read them, to see if there was any continuity in the pages or if they contain any unpublished material. Yiddish had disappeared from those parts of the country and I myself had started to forget my native tongue.

In 1961, when we left Romania, we were not allowed to take any foreign-language material out of the country, especially Hebrew writings which the censors could not decipher. We decided the best way to save the manuscripts was for Tzali to take them to the Israeli consulate when he went to Bucharest to get transit visas for our trip. But in Bucharest he suspected that someone was following him around. As he walked towards the Israeli Embassy carrying his briefcase he saw the same person behind him. Tzali knew the risk was too great to take. Just entering a foreign embassy could be considered spying for a foreign government. Even if he wasn't arrested our passports could be revoked. He gave up the attempt.

When he returned home we wrapped up Father's writings and gave them to our friend Moskowitz for safe-keeping. But years later, when we came back for them, he had no recollection of the precious package we had left with him.

The loss of Father's manuscripts has haunted me ever since. Any Jewish museum or library would have taken those pages. Father's name, Herzl Apsan, is mentioned in the Encyclopedia Judaica and in the archives of Israel's Museum of the Diaspora in Tel Aviv. If you call for information about Sighet you get a print-out that gives the important facts about the town and its memorable people. Father is included as a writer about the Jews of Maramures, their own "Sholom Aleichem!"

I want to share with you, Miriam, a passage from Father's story about the Jews from the villages on their annual pilgrimage to their beloved Rabbi of Vizhnitz, and which the author Herman Dicker translated in his *Piety and Perseverance,* a book about the Jews from the Carpathian Mountains.

"It is already deep night, the sky is cloudy for it is

the end of the month and God's world is completely darkened in a dense cloud. Whole camps, just like the pillar of cloud in the days of our Teacher Moses, travel through distant places and strange lands, all covered by the stars in the sky; nobody knows whence they come and where they go so late in the night. The veil of the night wraps the whole world in a dream, and God, the Creator and Leader of the whole world, looks on with love just like a mother who puts her beloved children to sleep. Now all His creatures are resting. Somewhere one hears a lonely bird crying deep in the woods, complaining before the Keeper of the Forest, but no one understands his complaint. The frogs in the marshes have already finished their nightly prayers, and have stopped their croak, croak. All have moved to the side on a shore, close their eyes and go to sleep. Now the whole universe is asleep.

It is strangely quiet all around the whole horizon, on fields and roads, on mountains and valleys. One no longer hears the movement of a bird or the sound of a car. It is already midnight, simple and honest working Jews sleep throughout the journey in small wooden cubicles. Everybody sleeps and snores in his corner; everyone is worn and tired out from the never-ending labors.

Soon half the night is gone and the sky is beginning to light up on the horizon. The moon carries out God's command to shine over the entire world. He is the permanent Guardian of Israel, he never goes astray, never oversleeps or even closes an eye; he crawls out of the clouds soon after midnight, just like a thief, without any noise or movement. He wipes his eyes and mirrors his face in the great waters, and takes over his nightly duties. He rises from the south and moves northward, circling the whole world. He makes great strides, thousands of miles per minute; he pours out thousands, millions of tons of light, over valleys and mountains, across oceans and deserts. He looks into all fields and forests, overhears all secrets and is familiar with all hidden happenings of the dark night.

From nowhere a group of bees arrives strayed from foreign lands, running and humming, buzzing and searching for a place to rest, but not daring to set down in

*an unknown place. And a group of soft winds waft from the
East and travels through the forests up to the river
Sambatyon and the lands of Eternity. All wander into warm
lands, listening to every sound and every movement in the
forest, telling lovely tales in their native tongue and
language: news from one country and another; which rites
and customs are observed by these Jews in their homes,
which souls and migrants move without redemption over all
paths, lanes, walks and steps; whom they met and what they
encountered in the quiet Selichot night.*

   *And a heavily laden Special Train with Hasidim
from the whole of Maramaros chases and runs, puffs and
works with all arts; the wheels turn and the axles moan and
squeak from dryness and heat. The locomotive sweats,
makes noise and whistles, letting loose from the chimney a
dense black smoke with sparks of fire, with drops of sweat
pouring out from every particle. Chambers of metal and
walls of tin roofs race vehemently, cutting across strong
mountains through tunnels of iron, splitting and crossing
all lakes and waters, straightening out the whole world.
Everything, everyone does his work with perfection,
enthusiasm and dedication in honor of the many Hasidim
and their Rebbe and in honor of the great God of Israel."*

Isn't it beautiful? I am so grateful that Father was remembered and
commemorated in Israel.

June 5, 1984

Herbert

In the summer of 1955, one year after we moved to Hunedoara, we were very pleased to have been assigned tickets to spend our vacation in Vatra Dornei, one of the most picturesque summer resorts on the eastern slope of the Oriental Carpathian mountains. We went by train but took along our motorcycle; Tzali wanted to explore the mountain roads. One day we went for a hike up a 6,000-foot peak. We were walking around on the summit, enjoying the breathtaking view, when suddenly Tzali tripped over a rock and sprained his ankle severely.

Now we had a serious problem: he couldn't get down the mountain on his own and we were alone and without transportation. Luckily we were able to hitch a ride with a passing truck that took us down to the hospital in the city. Tzali was in severe pain. The orthopedist diagnosed a serious ligamental injury, applied a cast to the leg and ordered him to stay in bed for two days before being allowed to walk with crutches.

The next day Tzali was still in bed so I stayed with him and read. Suddenly there was a knock on the door. A policeman entered and checked our names: it was us, indeed, that he was looking for. My heart pounded. He asked if we had relatives in Timisoara. Yes, we did. Tzali's sister Zsuzsi lived there with her husband Herbert and their son Pauli. "Why? Has anything happened to them?"

"Someone had a fatal accident there."

"Who?"

He didn't know or didn't want to tell us. His job was only to notify us that an accident had happened.

Tzali couldn't leave his bed and the hotel didn't have a public telephone. I rushed to the central telephone office.

It was August 23, one of Communist Romania's major holidays. On that day in 1944 the Romanians, previously aligned with the Germans, turned against them, joined the Soviets, and helped in the final Allied effort. They call it their liberation day though they paid dearly for it, because they have ever since remained under the control of Soviet Communism. Every year the day is celebrated with great fanfare, elaborate preparations, marching, parades, music, speeches, and the chanting of patriotic slogans, and the entire population is expected to participate. It was boring and tiresome, and it was a relief to be away at that time.

Since everyone was busy with the celebrations, and offices were closed, I didn't have too much trouble getting a call through to Timisoara. Zsuzsi didn't have a telephone in her apartment, so I called the few common friends who did.

First I tried my friend Klari. Her elderly mother was at home but she was very hesitant to tell me what had happened, saying she didn't know exactly. After many insistent questions she finally admitted that she had heard about a bus accident in which an engineer had been killed. Now I knew it was Herbert.

I then called Nellu Zissu, a colleague with whom I had worked at Bega Hospital, and to my great surprise I found Zsuzsi there with Pauli. Zsuzsi was in a state of distress and bewilderment, she could hardly talk, and was not able to explain much about the accident. I didn't find out till later how it had all happened.

Herbert was a civil engineer specializing in designing bridges, and as part of his work he was frequently transferred from one part of the country to another. This was how he had come to Sighet in the first place, where he had met and married Zsuzsi. His mother, Dora, had come from Chernovitz to live with them, but she remained in Sighet when he was transferred again. Zsuzsi and Herbert moved to Timisoara just around the time we left. There they lived in a small house on the outskirts of the city, and knew very few people, mostly our old friends and colleagues.

On this day, as usual, Herbert was riding his bicycle home from the factory where he worked, carrying his dinner pail in one hand. A bus overtook and passed him, catching the bicycle. Herbert lost his balance and fell off under the wheels of the bus. The driver apparently didn't realize what was happening until some of the passengers started screaming. By the time he put on the brakes, Herbert was lying unconscious on the pavement, his head smashed, the dinner pail and the food scattered all over. He was 35.

Zsuzsi and Pauli were waiting for Herbert to come home for dinner. One hour passed, then another, and Zsuzsi became worried. By now the whole city must have known about the accident, yet no one came to tell them. Pauli, who was not quite six years old, went out to the gate to watch out for his father. Some neighborhood children came over and told him, "Your father was killed." Frightened, he ran in to tell his mother. She rushed out, and asked the neighbors gathered in front of the gate, "Is it true?" They nodded silently. Yes, it was true.

She knew of only one hospital in the city, the Bega Hospital, where I had once worked. She left Pauli with a neighbor, went out on the street, stopped a passing truck and asked the driver to take her to the hospital, explaining about the accident. Later she remembered that the driver had told his helper in Hungarian, "If she's looking for the one who was hit by a bus, he's long dead." But at that moment she didn't register.

When she got to the hospital emergency room, nobody knew about

Herbert. She became hysterical. Some of the staff felt sorry for her, started calling the other hospitals, and found out that Herbert was in the morgue of the Central Hospital.

She didn't know what to do next, where to go, whom to ask for help. She remembered that our friend, Dr. Zissu, worked there, and asked the attendants to call him. He came immediately by motorcycle and found her disheartened, sitting on the steps of the main entrance. He called the police and asked them to find and notify us at the resort, then took her home to pick up Pauli and brought them both to his home for the night.

That is how I found her there when I called the following day. She was crying, she felt completely helpless, forlorn. I told her I would come to Timisoara on the next train, and asked her to delay the funeral till I got there. There was only one train from that resort: it left in the morning and arrived late in the afternoon.

"Zsuzsi" I remembered, "did you tell Herbert's mother?"

"No, I didn't."

"You have to."

"I can't do it."

"Zsuzsi, there can't be a funeral without his mother. Herbert was her only son."

"I know, but I can't do it."

"You want me to find her?"

"Do what you want."

"Wait for us."

Herbert's mother was still in Sighet. An eccentric woman, she lived alone and did not associate with anybody. She dressed strangely, she bargained loudly in the market place, argued with everybody, talked incessantly, even to herself, and never listened. People thought she was bizarre and pathetic, and often laughed at her.

I had to find Dora, but I had no idea who in Sighet had a telephone, and there was no directory. The operator finally found a name I recognized, of a former classmate of Tzali's, and put me through to him. I told him what had happened, and asked him to find the old lady, to let her know that her son had been badly injured in an accident and was in the hospital, and to tell her to take the first train to Timisoara.

I had spent the whole afternoon making calls. I came back to the hotel where Tzali was waiting restlessly and told him the bad news. This was the first tragedy in the family after the war and we worried about how Zsuzsi would take it, what she would do, and how we could help her. He was distressed and frustrated that he could not be with his sister when she needed him most, could not even talk to her to comfort her.

The next morning I took the train to Timisoara, a very long trip to the west, almost all the way across the country. Somewhere along the way, at a junction, the cars coming from Sighet and Vatra Dornei were hooked up together and Herbert's mother and I ended up on the same train, though we didn't know it. When we arrived in Timisoara that evening I saw the old lady stepping down from another car of the train and rushing with outstretched arms to Zsuzsi, who was waiting on the platform with Nellu's wife. Zsuzsi was wearing a colorful dress so her mother-in-law would not suspect the news at once.

"Where is my son?" she cried. "I want to see him. Take me to the hospital to see him!"

We explained that he could not be seen until the next morning. We all went to the Zissu's and had a bad night's sleep. The following morning, after Nellu and I took all the precautions -- injections for her blood pressure, heart problem and her nerves -- Herbert's mother was told. She was beside herself. She insisted on seeing him and she had to be promised she could. Herbert's head had been crushed and the undertaker had had a difficult job to pad and bandage it. We rushed her to the cemetery, where the casket had been left open for her. Poor mother, she hugged him, she cried and screamed. It broke my heart to see her pain and hear her wailing.

Herbert was dressed in his white formal shirt. I had ironed it that morning for the funeral. Zsuzsi was crying. "Do you remember," she said, "that you ironed the same shirt for our wedding?" How could I forget? Herbert was tall, handsome, and fastidious. When he found a few wrinkles on his wedding shirt, I had to put the warm iron against his chest and press them out, and we all laughed.

At the funeral, while his mother wept, Zsuzsi wouldn't allow herself any expression of grief. She held herself rigid, her eyes were blank. I was afraid she would jump into the grave. I grasped her tightly by the arm, but she yelled at me, "Don't hold me so tight, leave me alone!"

It was soon over and we went home. Zsuzsi decided to return to Sighet with her mother-in-law. I helped her and Pauli get ready, then accompanied them to the station to see them off. A couple of hours later, after cleaning, closing and sealing the apartment, I took the train to Hunedoara.

Tzali had gotten home the same day. He had managed to drive his motorcycle to the railroad station using one good leg and the crutches. At home, confused rumors spread that he had been injured in a motorcycle accident in which his brother-in-law had been killed, but nobody would talk to him about it. It was futile to even try to deny it.

After a brief stay in Sighet Zsuzsi came to live with us. It was an unhappy and difficult time. Three adults, three children and a maid were crowded into two small rooms. It was a long time before she was able to get a room for herself and her son nearby. At twenty-nine, Zsuzsi had no work skills whatsoever. Tzali got her a job as a clerk at the metallurgical conglomerate where she was known as "that pretty young widow who is always dressed in black." Although only peasants still wore black for mourning, Zsuzsi followed this old tradition, as her mother had done when she become a widow. And like her mother, she mourned many years for Herbert.

I have often reflected on what happened to Zsuzsi then, on the indifference of that regime toward the individual's needs, the lack of compassion for a family in distress. A man is killed in an accident, the whole city knows about it yet no one comes to tell the widow, there is no one to take responsibility for dealing with the consequences, and there are no agencies to help in such a tragedy. There is no compensation, no reparation. The breadwinner dies, and there is no insurance, no pension, and the widow is left to fend for herself and for the orphan.

What bothers me even more is that we took such heartlessness, such cruelty with complacency, as most natural. We did not know to claim anything, we did not dare to complain. Where was our anger, our indignation? It is hard to understand today why we simply accepted that state of affairs.

That was thirty years ago. After many years Zsuzsi remarried. But this year she wants to go and visit Herbert's grave and take Pauli along.

August 22, 1985

Hunedoara

Gabriel and his parents visited us last week. Spending time with my grandchildren who all live in California is so rare and precious that it becomes an event. I would tell my friends, "Last week I was a grandmother for five days." I sometimes feel that I would like to be just that, a grandmother, to give them all my energy and attention. I was so happy, when Gabriel was here, to be with him the whole time. He reminds me so much of Vali at his age -- his curly hair, his cheerful disposition, his charm.

When he went out on the terrace and brought in the few chestnuts that Tzali had gathered for him from our chestnut tree to play with, I suddenly remembered when my baby, Vali, played with chestnuts, back in Romania. I was recovering from an illness in a hospital in Cluj, far from home. Tzali came to visit and brought Vali along. He was probably two or three years old, about like Gabriel now. We went for a walk. There were many chestnut trees in the hospital park and Vali gathered the chestnuts that had fallen on the ground and carried them around in a handkerchief as toys. Tzali took pictures of him dressed in a black velvet suit with white collar. He was so cute and beautiful, with his big brown eyes and soft blond curls. I become emotional whenever I am transported to those days, when my children were young.

In 1954 we had moved to Hunedoara. Leaving Timisoara "voluntarily" had been a big decision, as Hunedoara was known to be a backward town, an industrial center where the government had made huge investments in steel manufacturing, and which had become one of the largest metallurgic complexes of Romania, with dozens of plants and thousands of workers. What lured people there were higher salaries, with bonuses for productivity for workers and engineers, better supplies in the stores than in the rest of the country, and, most important, housing: they were building a whole "workers' town" on the hills above the industrial park in the valley, and once you moved and worked for a while, you were entitled for an apartment as soon as one became available. It was incredible to see the preferential treatment that such an industrial center got from the government.

We had been impressed by all of this a year earlier, while on a motorcycle trip in that part of the Carpathians. We had stopped to visit Hattinger, one of Tzali's colleagues from Timisoara. We were surprised by what Mrs. Hattinger served us, and by their tiny but clean apartment that they did not have to share with anyone. There seemed to be an abundance of food and clothing in the stores, no lines, and even fresh food in the market.

And as they said, there were limitless career opportunities for engineers. Even the smoke and soot that filled the valley, from the furnaces down there, did not change our favorable impression, nor the dust of the yet unpaved streets of the new town quarter. It was summer then and everything looked sunny and bright.

It was also a time when we were quite dissatisfied with our life in Timisoara. Tzali's job was dead-end and he did not see any possibility for advancement. I was passed over for promotion when an opening arose at the medical school in favor of a junior colleague of mine, less qualified, but ethnically Romanian. We were both instructors, but he was promoted to assistant professor. I felt hurt, and it strengthened my belief that discrimination had not stopped, it was just more subtle and not official. Not to mention that we saw no chance to get any other apartment in the overcrowded city than our one room at the Kaufmans', where we had stayed for three years, squeezed in with our two children and hardly any space for a crib for Yancu. As far as cultural opportunities, we worked too hard to have time for concerts and operas, we rarely even went to the movies. There was very little to keep us there.

Tzali had worked in Hunedoara for a year before the promised apartment became available. He slept in a men's dormitory, ate in the factory cafeterias, and came home every Saturday night -- there was only one non-working day -- bringing with him all the provisions that could not be found in Timisoara, butter, cheese, jams, meat, cold cuts, occasionally helping friends too. He traveled by motorcycle and the trip took 3 hours. Once I visited him there, the new town was still a construction site, with no roads and so much mud after a rain that he had to carry me from the train station to the car -- everyone wore high rubber boots.

We got an apartment in the same building as the Hattingers and I moved too. It was the first time in so many years to have a whole apartment for ourselves. It was called a two-bedroom apartment, but that actually meant just two rooms plus a kitchen, bathroom, toilet, larder, all tiny, and a little partition in the cellar for firewood. Our bedroom had a convertible couch and a table, and when friends came over it also served as a living room or dining room. On one side of the table we would sit on the couch, and on the other side we would squeeze a few chairs against the wardrobe cabinet. Yancu and Silvia shared the second room and the maid slept in the kitchen on a long wooden chest that we used as a bench for our daily meals. When Herbert died and Zsuzsi and Pauli came to live with us, it became very crowded. We had to send the boys to weekly child care centers. We stopped by to visit them often, but they were home only on the week-ends. After a while Zsuzsi was given a room in a nearby building. But I was pregnant again and the prospect of a new baby made the need for a larger apartment urgent.

Our three-story building, like all the others around, had two-room flats like ours in the front and three-room flats in the back. In one three-room flat on the main floor lived three families, sharing a common kitchen and common utilities. Two months before Vali was born, we found out that one of the families -- an elderly couple -- was moving out of town. Ordinarily that would mean that a new couple would be assigned to their room. We spoke to the other two couples in that apartment. They were more than happy to trade their apartment for ours so they wouldn't have a strange new family moving in with them. They could stay together in the smaller flat.

Getting a larger apartment was not a question of money, the rent, in general, was quite low; it was more about knowing the right people and knowing how to get preferential treatment. Tzali was sure the housing authority would neither allocate one officially nor agree to the swap, so he didn't try to arrange it through them. Instead he approached some party leaders at his company, where he was already a manager of the equipment division, a very important and well-regarded position. He explained our need and the exchange plan and got their tacit approval.

When the elderly couple left, we moved in in a hurry, at night. We didn't dare to unpack or settle in because we expected a violent reaction. And it came. Four days later policemen arrived to move us back to our old apartment. They said we were in the new one illegally. We told them we had the approval of the party officials at the mechanical department, but it took weeks of disputes and intervention through the Party, through his construction company, through City Hall. Finally the move was approved and we were allowed to stay. We were delighted with our beautiful three-room suite, and we immediately made the third room ready for the baby.

It was none too early. A few days later, on December 29, I woke up at 6:00 in pain and realized that labor was proceeding fast. We called an ambulance. At 7:00 we arrived at the hospital where I had worked, but the delivery room was full. There were four other women there in various stages of labor, some on chairs, others on stretchers, moaning and groaning. A nurse gave me a chair. Busy with other patients, she was in no hurry to take down my information. I went to complain to Tzali, who was in the corridor -- husbands were not allowed in the delivery room at the time. One of our neighbors was with him, Mrs. Akim. She was pregnant with her first baby, and this was her third false alarm, her third admission to the hospital, and still nothing happened. She walked the corridor nervously, following my progress. Tzali went out to the bar for a drink. He needed it.

At 8:00 the attending physician arrived, looked around the crowded room and recognized me.

"What are you doing here?" he asked. Some question! In a show of professional courtesy he said, "I'll examine my colleague first." He put me on the examining table, placed a screen around it and a moment later was yelling for a nurse. The baby was coming, and fast. They were shouting, I was moaning and pushing and twenty minutes later Vali was born. When Tzali returned, Mrs. Akim told him the news. "You're late," she said. "Your wife did it without you. You have a boy."

Soon I was shoved out of the room because they needed the space for the other women. Later I heard the jealous comments of the other patients. "Look at her -- she's a doctor, she knows how to do it. She comes last and leaves first."

I like to reminisce about our life in Hunedoara. It was a time when we were working hard, building careers, raising a family, making friends and enjoying simple outings in the nearby hills and an occasional vacation. We also struggled with the party requirements, the privations, and later the reprisals as we waited and hoped for our "deliverance". But what we like to remember most are those precious and heart-warming moments when our children were small. Now that we see you grandchildren growing up we treasure even more those remembrances when your parents were your age, and we try to compare your lives with theirs.

Your mother, Silvia, was a very pretty child with dark, curly hair. She was strong-willed, smart and liked to perform. I recall many occasions of her singing and dancing, but the most memorable is when she attended ballet school while still in Timisoara. The students made up the children's corps de ballet at the opera house in Tchaikovsky's *Queen of Spades*: for the entire season I was a stage mother, like all the other mothers who took their children to the opera house and dressed them in their rococo satin costumes, white curly wigs and fancy slippers. Then we went down to our free seats in the house and delighted in our children's performances. I don't know why Silvia always ended up dressed as a boy. It didn't matter. She was adorable.

Just before Vali was born Silvia became a "pioneer", which she considered the greatest event of her life in Hunedoara. The Pioneers were a children's organization dedicated to developing devotion to the regime and communist ideals. Children were supposed to be nine and have good grades to be bestowed the honor of becoming a pioneer; but in fact almost everybody ended up being accepted. Silvia was in third grade, and one of the youngest in the class. She felt overlooked as most of her schoolmates had already been promoted. But then, on her ninth birthday she was conferred the same "honor" and given the pioneers' symbol, the red scarf around the neck, and she was very happy and proud. It even eclipsed the present she got from us for her birthday, a violin -- at that time she would have rather played piano, but we couldn't afford one. Eventually she enjoyed the violin, and still does.

The person who was probably the most satisfied in the first few years in Hunedoara was Tzali. His job was challenging, he was appreciated and was promoted many times. He had a pretty good salary, bonuses for increased productivity, and the use of a company car. The chauffeur assigned to him would drive him to meetings or to plants, and even go to other towns in search of some scarce merchandise for private use. There was always something we needed that could not be found in Hunedoara. On one occasion when we could not find baby shoes, we gave him Vali's foot print, and he went scouting until he found the right size in a city 100 km away.

My job was rather routine. I missed the excitement of the academic environment at the university hospital, with its professors and students, stimulating discussions, the availability of more recent discoveries, more sophisticated diagnostic techniques and treatment methods. We had a demanding working schedule, with morning and evening rounds, and frequent night calls. There was a lot of paperwork and no clerical help. Doctors' salaries were relatively low; the high status occupations in Romania were those related to "production" -- engineering, mining, construction, qualified work.

Though both of us worked, our living standard was rather modest. But we did have a great luxury, a privately owned car, one of only six or seven in our whole town. It was a 4-cylinder FIAT 100, vintage year 1941. Tzali had bought it in bits and pieces, literally, which he had carried to a workshop in boxes. The previous owner had disassembled the car to protect it from being confiscated when he was charged with some political misdeed. We paid for it with the money we got for our motorcycle, which in turn had replaced our bicycle. Tzali worked on the car for 9 months, and had to use all his ingenuity, as well as the help of many workers, to put it back together, to fix it, patch it, and locate missing parts, or hand-craft them out of materials found in junk-yards. Finally, he painted it, and we became the proud owners of an enviable shiny green FIAT. We were now able to take small excursions to the countryside, and have enough room for all of us, including Zsuzsi. There were no gas stations, and to get fuel one had to stop truck drivers on the road, who were usually only too happy to sell it to us clandestinely. Once we ventured on a long trip to the Black Sea resort of

Constanta, and we had yet another challenge: we had to stop every 200 km to fill the leaking radiator, which could not be replaced. Nevertheless, the freedom the car gave us was wonderful. We sold it, our greatest possession, when we left Romania. Who knows how many more years it ran on the streets of Hunedoara afterwards.

We all had maids if we worked full time and were willing to spend almost half of one income on a helper. Maintaining the household was hard work and shopping was very time-consuming. There were lines at every store, and many items were very scarce -- the situation had deteriorated drastically since we had first come. Meals had to be prepared from scratch almost every day since there was no refrigeration. Chickens were bought live, killed and plucked. And washing took a full day. Even when we were able to purchase a washing machine, it offered little relief: the water had to be warmed up first and poured into the tank, the brick soap had to be grated, then the cycle started. When ready, the wringing was done by the hand roller attached to the machine, then the load was taken to the tub for rinsing. After an hour each piece had to be wrung again by hand and finally carried outside in a hamper and hung on a few long clotheslines -- hopefully the weather wouldn't turn bad. And ironing was a most valued skill in a maid, there was nothing like showing off a nicely ironed formal shirt for Sunday.

House-cleaning was another chore. On a windy day there was so much dust in the air from the steel mills in the valley, and so much dirt was brought into the house from the mud after rain. We had no vacuum cleaner, just brooms. The few carpets were swept daily, but for a thorough cleaning they were taken outside behind the building, hung on rug rod, and the dust beaten out with a long-handled rattan paddle. In the winter we laid them down on the ground, and rubbed snow into them until it became dirty.

In chilly mornings someone had to get up really early to carry the chopped wood from the cellar, and make fire in the kitchen and in the tile stove of every room. In about an hour we could get up to a warm room, hot water for washing, and a warm breakfast.

Most of the maids were girls from rather well-off peasant families, mainly ethnic Hungarians in that region. It was customary for them to work for a few years in the city, be exposed to urban ways and civilized manners, learn how to manage a household, make some money, assemble a dowry and then return home, get married and settle on their farms. We were always lucky with the girls who worked for us. Other families seemed to be forever dealing with new maids, but somehow once they came to us they seemed to stay on until they were ready to marry. Over the years we married off two such girls; we went to their weddings and Silvia even spent a summer in their villages.

We had one bad experience though, with a girl named Anush. She had one peculiarity: she never removed the kerchief from her head. Other girls wore floral kerchiefs only when it was cold or when they went out, never in the house. But since Anush was young, clean, pleasant and efficient, it never occurred to me to ask her about her kerchief. One day as I was washing Silvia's hair an entire lock fell out. I checked closely and was horrified to see several bald patches on her scalp. Her hair had become thinner, too. I checked Yancu and found similar bald spots and strands of hair that came out at the slightest pull. I knew I had to go to Timisoara to consult my former professors, the only ones I trusted for a reliable diagnosis. I took a few locks of the children's hair to the dermatology professor. He put them under the microscope, took one look and told me they had a very contagious fungus. That was when I remembered Anush and her kerchief. By the time I returned to Hunedoara, she had disappeared.

I traveled with the children to Timisoara for treatment, which was quite drastic at the time. First the hair was cut very short, then radiotherapy was administered to cause the diseased hair to fall out. Two weeks later a warm wax paste was applied to the scalp. When it hardened, it had to be pulled off quickly so all the remaining hair with the roots would come off with it. The treatment was so painful that Yancu screamed and ran out of the doctor's office. Until her hair grew back, going to school was an ordeal for Silvia, and she wore a little white bonnet to cover her baldness. Fortunately, their hair grew back normally, Silvia's dark, thick and frizzy, Yancu's a crown of golden curls. I was sorry for Anush, who didn't know that treatment was available, but nobody knew her whereabouts. She must have become completely bald.

Yancu had a more serious illness in Hunedoara a few years later. He was less than seven years old, and he had to have his adenoids out because of frequent throat infections. I don't know whether it was negligence or ignorance, but no throat cultures were taken, and no antibiotics were administered before or after the surgery. For two or three weeks after the operation he seemed fine -- but then he began to behave strangely, winking and grimacing for no reason.

A few days later he started kicking and throwing his hands about in a most peculiar manner. I didn't know what to think until one day he dropped his sandwich. I started to reprimand him, when I suddenly remembered a description of a disease in my pediatric textbook: "Involuntary movements of hands, legs, face; the children drop their food and their parents assume that they are misbehaving..." I ran to the book, found the chapter and knew instantly that Yancu had Sydenham's chorea, a very rare childhood disease related to rheumatic fever and a prior streptococcal infection.

Yancu was admitted to the hospital. He was very weak, he could hardly stand, the uncontrolled movements got worse, and he fell often. Though I was no longer working there, I spent all my free time and every night with him at the hospital. His former pediatrician, who was now an associate professor in Timisoara, sent me some cortisone, still only available at the universities in that part of Romania. (She was very fond of Yancu, and she often predicted that he would become an artist.)

Yancu left the hospital after six weeks but it took a long time for him to get rid of the disturbing symptoms and to be able to return to school. For many years we periodically maintained him on antibiotics, hoping to prevent heart disease. It still distresses me when I think that it could have been prevented. Eventually he was cured and today he has a good heart. And a warm one.

One troublesome incident concerning Vali comes to my mind. I wanted to open a private office in our home, as was permitted under some new regulations, provided one met certain conditions of hospital position and seniority. Vali's room was to serve as the office, so I prepared an examining table, a desk and a medicine cabinet. By the time I ordered the shingle, the law had changed and my permit for private office was revoked. Vali was just two, and one day he was playing in his room with a neighbor's child. They must have managed to unlock the medicine cabinet, found some bottles, opened them and probably swallowed the colorful, candy-like pills. I don't know where the maid was, but when I came home, Vali was stumbling and the other child was sleeping on the floor. The sleeping child was rushed to the hospital where we waited anxiously until he awoke the following morning. But there were no other consequences, and we felt greatly relieved. Just imagine if...

When we decided, after the war, to stay in Romania, go to school, have a family, we left our past and traditions behind, in Sighet. Life was too hectic to even notice how assimilated we had become, and our friends, too. We thought we were just like everyone else, that the "Jew" thing, like class distinctions, was a thing of the past. It took years to realize that we continued to remain strangers among the Romanians, that we were sometimes barely tolerated. Our dormant feelings of Jewish identity started to be reawakened. We felt most comfortable with our Jewish colleagues, who also came from other cities in Transylvania and felt alienated. There was no official discrimination, but after our life settled down a bit we started noticing things we had been taking for granted before. Our Romanian friends would flatter us that we "were OK, not like the other Jews." Silvia was called "dirty Jew" by a schoolmate she had had a spat with; one time Yancu was hit with rocks and made fun of. When he came home with a bleeding scalp we dismissed it as a brawl among boys, but he knew it was just because he was different, and he suffered. Things got a lot worse after we applied to leave. The children's grades were tampered with so they wouldn't get the first prize at the year-end school festivities; Silvia was denied admission to music and ballet schools, and almost didn't make it into high school. The day we got our passport Yancu was returning from a soccer game, elated, and the neighbors jeered at him, "You Jew, get out of here!" But by then he did not care at all. Getting out of there was just what we all wanted to do.

January 20, 1985

Iron Curtain

A small news item caught my attention the other day. It was a story about a long-awaited reunion between a group of North and South Korean families who had not seen each other for thirty-nine years, since North Korea had become Communist and instituted its own Iron Curtain. During the following years, with thousands of Korean families divided into two separate worlds, North Korea ignored pleas for family reunions and denied any such need.

But after years of negotiations and months of preparation, a reunion had finally come about, under the scrutiny of television, the press and the watchful eyes of the whole world. Some three dozen people -- the lucky ones -- were selected for this traumatic event. Men and women in their sixties and seventies, not even sure that they recognized each other after such a long separation, were embracing, laughing, and crying. It was a joyous occasion, and many viewers were probably touched by that emotional outpouring. I was very moved, yet I found the prying of the media into their personal feelings painful to watch. This episode also reminded me of the long years in Communist Romania, when we were all waiting and dreaming of a similar reunion.

After the war, as the years passed, Romania became increasingly insulated and hostile to the western world, and we felt more and more cut off from our family abroad. How long did it take me to realize that the separation might be forever? There seemed to be little hope to see my brothers again. Would my children ever know their cousins? The Iron Curtain, the virtual barrier that separated the Soviet Union and its satellites from the rest of the world, became also a metaphor for our heavy feeling of hopelessness.

I hadn't seen my oldest brother, Alter, since May 1944, when he was on his way to the Russian front for forced labor. Yossie had left Romania after his return from a Stalinist camp in Siberia in 1946. Now they both lived in New York. Tzali's brother Bela, after leaving Sighet in 1947, spent a few years in Israel, and also ended up in New York. Miki had been in Italy since I was a young girl. The last time I saw him was when he came home on vacation from medical school around 1935. Ezu and Ebi were in Brazil. Ezu had returned to Sighet only briefly after his liberation in 1945, but Ebi did not return home since he had left in 1942 to go to a trade school in Budapest. So many brothers, all so far away for so many years.

In 1957 we were living in Hunedoara. Visits to or from abroad were unheard of. Traveling to other Communist countries like Hungary or

Czechoslovakia was considered a "favor," to be granted only to the privileged few who "deserved" it. For a long time even travel inside Romania, to border cities, was restricted. Any communication with the West was discouraged, and receiving packages was barely tolerated. How many times were we reproached for "maintaining relations with capitalistic countries," meaning that we corresponded with our family in the West!

Then something unprecedented happened. We heard that somebody, in some other city, had been permitted to visit a family member in Paris. This was almost a miracle, if it was true. I got very excited. I felt as though a cloud was being parted, and for the first time a patch of blue sky was becoming visible. We hardly dared to hope.

But soon another rumor reached us, about a person in Bucharest who was also allowed to travel abroad to see a sister. It seemed unbelievable. Very cautiously, I started to make inquiries. Among my patients were some officers from the secret police, the *Securitate*, and when they came to the hospital I hinted in our conversation to trips abroad. Were the rumors true? Did they think that someone like me could ever get a visa? Should I apply?

Obviously I couldn't ask to go to the United States, but perhaps a trip to Rome might be granted. I wrote to my brothers. They all became very excited and assured me that if I could get to Italy, they would all meet me there. I would, of course, have to travel alone, leaving the rest of the family behind to guarantee my return. This was clearly understood -- it was inconceivable to do otherwise.

I finally decided to take the gamble. I went to the police station and filed a formal application to travel to Italy. The officials were surprised, but they didn't say "Yes" and they didn't say "No," so apparently the rumors were true. There followed a few weeks of intense activity. I was called back several times for questioning and for additional information. I had to provide all sorts of documents, including an affidavit from Italy. I had to have a passport photo made. It all filled me with hope. The dream seemed possible!

This created a sensation in our provincial town. News spread, and everyone seemed to know about it. At home and with our friends we talked about almost nothing but my impending trip. What would it be like? Would my brothers recognize me? What should I take for them? What would I bring back? My friends were eager to give advice. They envied me my chance to go abroad, find out how it was "over there," and have a taste the free world, away from the oppressive atmosphere of Communism.

Meanwhile I started to prepare. I bought a few fabrics and took them to the best dressmaker in town. She was thrilled to make dresses that would be worn in Rome, and advised me on the latest fashions. I still remember those three outfits: an off-white silk shantung dress with a loose jacket; an elegant, low-cut, shiny charcoal-gray evening dress with a jacket, and a green wool suit for cool evenings, all beautiful and expensive. I was in a state of euphoria and restlessness. I expected this trip to give me emotional nourishment for years to come. It might have to sustain me forever. I started studying Italian, which sounded so romantic after listening to Verdi and Rossini.

But months passed and nothing happened. No official response was made, and I knew it was futile to inquire. Whenever a patient from the *Securitate* was on my ward he would say, "Oh, you're the doctor who applied to go to Italy." I had become an "interesting" person, one who dared to ask permission to go abroad. I would respond by asking their opinion, did they think I would get approval? "Why not, comrade?" they would often reply, "You have a good record." That was it. It all came down to my "record."

My brothers were becoming impatient, writing more often and asking when I would come. It was by now late summer of 1958, almost a year since I had applied. My anticipation and my hopes were slowly fading, turning into doubt and disappointment. By now I was asking myself, "Will approval ever come?"

Then one day I was called for another interview at the police station. Two officers explained that they wished to speak to me in connection with my petition (as if I had any doubt about it). They were very polite and again asked me lots of questions about my family, about my brothers, why they were all abroad, how I would meet those from the United States. What about my husband? Didn't he have relatives abroad, too? Had we corresponded with them all those years? Of course they already knew all the answers.

Finally came the question I was hoping for.

"Are you, comrade, ready for the trip?" My heart started to pound.

"Sure I am," I replied eagerly.

"Suppose you get the approval soon -- are you dressed to travel to Rome?"

"Yes, I am well dressed. I could leave at any time." I understood their concern that I might wear shabby clothes abroad. I was only too happy to tell them about my new outfits.

They left it at that, saying that they would let me know soon. My hopes rose again: the trip seemed almost within reach.

But then something even more unthinkable happened. The news that Jews would be allowed to apply for emigration to Israel swept through the

Jewish population. In a few days, it was said, application forms would be available at the police stations. How this incredible change of policy came about we never found out, but it caused quite a commotion among our friends.

What were we to do? Should I keep trying for the Italian visa which seemed to be so imminent? Or should we grab the new chance for all of us to leave for good? The delay and uncertainty about my attempt to simply visit my brothers abroad for a few weeks, made us realize that we couldn't trust any promises at all. I might get a visa -- or I might never get one.

On the other hand, there was no assurance that an attempt to emigrate would be any more successful, and clearly if we applied I would lose any prospect of traveling to Italy. We might end up with neither and with all kinds of reprisals. And what of Zsuzsi and Pauli? If we left, Zsuzsi would not want to stay on alone. And the idea of all of us going together was a dream we had not even contemplated before.

We had no time to weigh all this. Everyone wanted to be among the first to file an application, for no one knew if there would be enough for all the Jews who wanted to leave, and whether, or more likely when, the Party would reverse this policy. After one long, sleepless night we made our momentous decision: we would give it all we had, take all the risks. We would apply to emigrate -- all of us.

And we did.

I will tell you another time about the long years of waiting. By the time we arrived in Rome to meet Miki I had not seen him for twenty-six years, almost as long as the North and South Koreans. Our reunion was as emotional as theirs, but fortunately it remained private and intimate.

October 30, 1985

La Forza del Destino

This morning on the radio I heard the overture to *La Forza del Destino*. I don't know how much you listen to opera, but *Forza* is considered an example of Verdi's mature, dramatic style and it is supposedly appreciated mainly by opera buffs. It is not as well known as *La Traviata* and *Rigoletto,* and few people realize how beautiful the music really is. It was the same way in those years in Romania. Music lovers listened only to familiar operas and operettas, and what people listened to had a curious effect on our income.

In 1958, after we applied to leave the country, we faced new economic and political hardships. Tzali was fired from his managerial job under a certain law, whose code number was entered in his working papers, and which meant that he was a "politically undesirable citizen." Since the only employer was the State he couldn't find any work for a long time. He applied and reapplied for any type of work, and he was finally given a job, not as a mechanical engineer but as a manual laborer in the very same department where previously he had been in charge of hundreds of engineers, designers, technicians and workers. It was an embarrassing situation. His former subordinates wanted to help him and protect him from heavy labor, and even took turns lifting the weighty beams for him.

I was luckier for a while. The hospital administration didn't know how they were supposed to deal with a "traitor" like me. Tens of thousands of Jews in Romania had done the same "regretful act" of applying for emigration, but there were few Jews in Hunedoara and only a handful of physicians who wanted to leave, so the Communist Party failed to send instructions on how to handle us. I was allowed to remain at the hospital in my position as a specialist in internal medicine for some time, but I was insecure because I knew that my turn would come.

Just like my university dean and other out of favor politicians during the earlier party purges, we were both expelled from the Party during specially called membership meetings, with public accusations and speeches. No one tried to defend me -- who would have dared, when the charge was treason, leaving the Communist paradise for a capitalistic country? It was somehow different in Tzali's case, where most of the participating members were simple workers, who were not afraid to raise objections. They could not understand why joining brothers abroad should be reason for ousting him. The discussions continued until the party secretary came up with a convincing argument. "No, comrades," he declared, "the real reason is that he cannot go abroad with the membership card, he has to hand it in." And so, they voted -- unanimously -- to expel him.

Some people were granted permission to leave within the first few weeks after applying, but they had to depart quickly. They were given just one week to resign from jobs, prepare all the documents, sell their personal belongings, pack and go. The State specified what they could take with them: how many of each item of clothing, how many towels, how many sheets, even how many socks or shoes per person. Money, jewelry, furniture, rugs, leather goods and other items of value had to be left behind.

We panicked, as did many of our friends. We all wanted to be ready in case approval came, and we started to prepare. We took down payments on our furniture, carpets, radio, appliances, record collection and other valuables. We began buying and ordering clothes, bedding, quilts and covers (I still have plenty of them after 20 years), and other items we were permitted to take with us. Since the number of suitcases was also limited, we ordered trunks made to the officially-specified dimensions.

One of our friends, a physician named Pollack, was notified that his application had been approved and that he would get the papers within a few days. He resigned his job, sold his furniture and household appliances, the refrigerator and the stove. He packed his trunks and waited for the promised passport. Then suddenly the whole emigration process came to a halt. No passports were issued any more. Pollack, like others, was left "sitting on his trunks", the expression we used for such a situation. Poor Pollack! He had nowhere to sleep and not even a cooking pot to prepare a meal. Friends came to his aid. It took him weeks to get his furniture back from the startled buyers and even more weeks to be reinstated in a temporary position at the hospital. He had to wait more than a year before he finally got his passport and left.

No one knew if the stoppage was temporary or permanent. We never understood the politics behind this new emigration policy, what were the national or international reasons or incentives for the government to suddenly allow the Romanian Jews to apply for emigration and what caused them to reverse that policy and then to change it back again. Nothing made too much sense to us, but everything added to the uncertainty.

We were not as unlucky as Pollack, but after Tzali lost his job our income shrank to one-third of what it had been. There were bills to pay, the ordered quilts and linens were ready for delivery, so were the children's outfits and dresses at the dressmaker -- and not enough money to pay for any of them. After a few months we also had to return all the down payments we had received on furniture and carpets. So, as I had done before, I turned to my brother Miki for help. Though I had five brothers living abroad, Miki in Italy was the closest and he was well-established with a dental practice. He was also the most accessible when we dared to phone him.

I wrote to him and asked him to send me a recording of *La Traviata*.

When we had sold all of our records we realized how valuable they were and what a good price we could obtain for the popular Italian operas. There was no opera house in this city of 80,000, mostly industrial workers, no concert hall or theater. Intellectuals hungry for culture were eager to obtain French and Italian operas, but good recordings were rare. No one wanted the Soviet recordings of operas like *La Traviata,* which were available; Italian operas just did not sound right in Russian. Listening to good music recorded by famous singers and conductors in someone's house had become a cultural affair, an occasion for a well attended party.

In a few weeks the requested record arrived from Miki and we sold it to one of my colleagues for the equivalent of one week's salary.

The demand for famous Italian operas saved us. Soon other acquaintances were asking if we could get another *La Traviata,* a *Rigoletto,* a *Tosca.* So we kept writing for more and more records. We started requesting specific singers. The more renowned they were, the higher price we got. Every time a notice arrived from the post-office -- we requested only one opera at a time so as not to be conspicuous -- we were wondering if the right opera had come and hoping for the best performers. Beniamino Gigli, Mario del Monaco and Renata Tebaldi were the favorites.

In his eagerness to please us, Miki always sent the records I asked for, but he couldn't understand why I was so anxious to have them, especially when I ordered the same opera two or three times. He began to wonder if we were collecting them. We didn't dare explain the real reason in our letters to him; there was always the danger that they might be read by the censors. Then one day, on his own, he sent us a recording of *La Forza del Destino.* Nobody had asked for that opera and most of our costumers had never even heard of it. I still remember how long we had to keep it, all the while continuing to ask Miki for *Il Trovatore, Le Nozze di Figaro, Carmens* and, of course, more *Traviatas.*

Eventually someone bought the unrequested *Forza* very cheaply. We never listened to it. We didn't want to break the seal. Besides, who was in the mood for music?

Now I realize how beautiful the music is. I'll have to add it to our collection. Perhaps I can ask Miki to send me another copy, this time to listen to and enjoy?

February 20, 1984

Passport

I'm sitting at the window table in the hospital cafeteria, sipping some coffee. I look out and I see the trees, the green fields and the wooded area beyond the parking lot, the countryside formerly called Grassland. In front of the large windows there are trees in full blossom, pink-and-white flowers, probably crab-apples.

For years I have been watching these trees season after season, changing from tiny, barely visible rosy buds to full-blown flowers, to dense green foliage, to autumn's earth colors, to barren dark branches, and later on, white and bent under heavy snow. Somehow, the spring outside this window always touches me. Its beauty is so ephemeral, and so many events in my life are tied to this season.

It is cold and windy today. A few snowflakes float in the air around the bright flowering branches, just as they did on April 4th, 1964, when we arrived in New York. We had left Romania three years earlier, also on the fourth of April. We have been celebrating this date ever since.

I try to recall the atmosphere of that spring of 1961 and the events just preceding our departure. We had been living in Hunedoara for many years, but never really liked it there and managed to claim our former address in Timisoara as our permanent residence. We needed this if we were to ever fulfill our hope of returning there. Zsuzsi had already moved back to Timisoara and was working in a textile factory and living with Pauli in a one-room apartment. This is why all of us had to file our papers for emigration there, and we were able to do it together.

In late February 1961, Zsuzsi had a minor operation for a longstanding problem related to childbirth. I arranged to visit her over the weekend, as soon as she was discharged from the hospital. I found her quite sick, in pain and miserable. I didn't want to leave her in that condition, but I had to be back at my job on Monday. I promised to come and spend a few days with her the following weekend.

By the time I returned Zsuzsi felt better and was ready to go back to work, but I had taken time off so I decided to stay on and see my friends. I also decided to go in for a biopsy, a simple procedure usually done with local anaesthesia, which I had needed for a while. We had all been persuaded that if any surgery was required, we had better do it in Romania, where medical care was free -- who knows how expensive it would be in the "capitalistic countries?" So I went to the Bega hospital where I had once worked, looked up the chief of surgery, made an appointment to have it performed the next morning, and started back to Zsuzsi's apartment.

It was March 4th, a pleasant spring day. As I approached the apartment building I saw a big commotion. Neighbors were gathered outside the door whispering to each other, everyone asking, "Who got it?" They told me that a policeman from the passport office had just left Zsuzsi's place. They were guessing that he had come about a visa.

This was the moment we had been dreaming of for two and a half years. Had it really come? I ran up the stairs and found Zsuzsi in shock, barely able to utter a word.

"So, who was here?" I asked.

"He... he... from the passport office."

"Did we get it?"

"I... I think so."

"What did he say?"

"That you should go there, to the passport office."

"Who got it? You? Us? All?"

"I don't know."

"To where? To Israel? To Brazil?"

"I don't know."

First we had applied to go to Israel. When emigration to Israel was halted, we were no longer willing to turn back. Ebi and Ezu were in Brazil, so we asked them to send us an affidavit, the official sponsorship, and we resubmitted our papers for Brazil. We even hoped that joining my brothers might seem a more compelling reason to the officials.

I hurried to the passport office. A long line of happy people had gathered there to find out exactly why they had been called (though they all had strong suspicions), what had actually been approved, and what were the next steps in this unknown and exciting process that would hopefully get them out of the country. This was one queue I didn't mind waiting in. When my turn finally came, I was advised that all of us, including Zsuzsi and Pauli, had been granted permission to emigrate to Brazil, and we would receive our passports as soon as we submitted the long list of required documents.

From there I went straight to the post office, where public telephones were available, to call Tzali. I was in such a state of euphoria, bursting with excitement, that I couldn't wait to tell *someone*. I remember that I ran into a former colleague, and although she was just a casual acquaintance, I spilled out the big news, "We got the passport!" It is difficult to convey today the impact of these few words, all the promise, the hope, the new vistas that they opened. Winning the lottery pales by comparison.

I went to the operator and placed a long distance call to Tzali's office in Hunedoara. As I sat and waited I tried to figure out how to tell him the great news, and how to play down my emotional turmoil. Some words were taboo over the telephone. One could never mention "Israel" or "Brazil" -- or any western country for that matter -- or "passport" or "emigration." Suppose someone was listening? Who knows what might happen? The risk was too great.

"Hunedoara on the line," I finally heard.

Tzali, at the other end, was alarmed. A long distance call? To his office?

"What happened?" he asked.

"Oh, nothing important," I said, as casually as I could." You remember the books Ebi sent us?"

"What books?"

"The ones we were waiting for from Ebi. They just arrived."

I chuckle whenever I try to imagine the scene at the other end of the line. Tzali is sitting at his desk, he has been recently "promoted" to a junior engineer position after months of working as a skilled worker at a construction site. His new colleagues know about his application and subsequent demotions, and empathize with him in his difficulties with the management. His ashtray is empty, in the last year he has given up smoking, and whenever someone offers him a cigarette he declares, "Only when I get my passport."

And now Tzali picks up the telephone, a long distance call. A brief conversation, he looks incredulous, he smiles, he stretches out his hand to a colleague's desk and grabs a cigarette. A moment of silence, then all sinks in and everyone starts yelling, "He got it! He got it! Zoltan got it!"

I took the next train home, but not before calling a friend at the hospital to cancel my appointment (the message never reached the chief and I heard later that he was annoyed with me for years). I traveled overnight and arrived in Hunedoara at sunrise. I took the only cab there was -- a horse drawn carriage. The coachman was an old Jew, the father of a friend of ours. Again I couldn't contain myself. As he drove me home, I told him the big news, asking him not to tell anyone about it, not yet. But after dropping me off the old man must have driven around to all of our friends, stopping at each one's house to tell them, for in a couple of hours they were all in our apartment to celebrate and rejoice with us. They even brought *tzuica* (Romanian brandy).

The following four weeks were full of excitement and aggravations, farewell parties and official business. Assembling all the necessary papers and paying off all the fees and taxes turned out to be such a frantic job that it left us exhausted. Some records, so important for our future -- diplomas, school transcripts, exams, -- were flatly denied and had to be obtained later through the Romanian Embassy in Brazil. We resigned our jobs, sold all our household belongings again, packed whatever we were permitted to take with us, and spent all the money we had -- those were the rules. Zsuzsi was doing the same things in Timisoara.

As if all this wasn't enough, I had been hit with a lawsuit. The problem had begun two and a half years earlier. I had been working for many years as a specialist in internal medicine and was on the verge of being promoted to director of clinical services. For a long time, no certification had been necessary for a specialist. Seniority and experience were enough. But in 1958, the Ministry of Health had issued new regulations: from then on, it would be necessary to take a specialty examination in order to qualify for the title and position. The exam would be given twice a year at university centers. Those who, like me, were currently functioning as specialists had to take the exam within two years to maintain their status.

We had no idea how the exams would be graded for the Jewish doctors who applied to emigrate but we were convinced that the authorities would think of a way to hold us back. Indeed we soon found out that there were to be two parts to the certification: we would undergo a rigorous professional examination at the university, and we would be evaluated for our "political standing," based on our political and social activities and affiliations. The maximum score for each part was 20 and a combined average of 15 was required to pass. I let the first couple of sessions go by, waiting to see what would happen to the others and hoping that in the meanwhile we would be approved to leave.

After a year we heard that one or two physicians in our situation had taken the examination and passed. This was encouraging news and since time was running out, about five or six of us in Hunedoara decided to go ahead and take the test. It was given in Cluj. I had studied very hard and was well prepared, but I was anxious as never before to make high marks to counteract a presumably low social score. There were three days of oral tests in basic sciences and in all the subspecialties of internal medicine, plus a written essay in internal medicine on which the candidate's name was sealed. After being graded, the seal was opened in public on the last day of the tests.

I did very well on the oral examinations, and I was pleased to find out I had gotten a 20 on the essay. Although I didn't know my social score, I was hopeful. On the last day, Tzali came with Silvia to pick me up. In the evening the three of us celebrated, attending a performance of *Un Ballo in Maschera* at the Hungarian Opera House. We then drove through the night home to Hunedoara.

Every week, the Health Department Bulletin published a nationwide list of those physicians who passed the specialty examination and those who failed. My Jewish colleagues from Hunedoara were all listed as failed and were soon transferred from the hospital to the clinics on the outskirts of the city, at construction sites, foundries or rolling mills. My name never appeared at all -- it was not listed as passed but it wasn't listed as failed, either. So I assumed that I had passed. Didn't I get a score of 20 on the medical part? I continued working in the hospital.

One year later, I was notified that since I had failed my specialty examination, I was not only to be demoted and transferred to a far-away clinic but that I owed the hospital the difference between the two salaries for that period. I was indignant and decided to fight it. I appealed and won my first hearing with the hospital administration. Next I had to plead my case at the Workers' Union and I prevailed again. The health department appealed; I was called to City Hall and I won a third time. They had thirty days to contest and to ask for a legal trial but they did nothing. I was transferred, my salary dropped to half of what it had been, and I assumed that the case of retroactive reimbursement had been dropped.

Six months passed. We were getting ready to leave. I went to the hospital administration, resigned my job and asked for my "liquidation papers" -- documentation that I had returned all hospital property and had no further obligations. And now the director of the hospital declared that I still owed them the few thousand *lei* and he would not give me the papers until I paid up. I refused again, and although he had missed the deadline, he asked for and was able to arrange a court hearing in record time.

Three days later, I went to court for a trial that was completely illegal even by the laws of that regime. The courtroom -- a small claims court -- was full of people. The judge asked me politely,

"And you, comrade, you are leaving the country?"

"Yes, sir."

"You have the passport?"

"Not yet. I am getting one as soon as the hospital gives me the liquidation papers."

"And where will you emigrate to?"

"To Brazil."

There was total silence in the room. I think there was not a single person there who did not envy me. The judge smiled. He listened to the arguments. It was over in ten minutes. I had won again.

I shudder to think of the risk I was taking challenging the system at that moment. Yes, it was unfair, but fighting for principles under those circumstances was certainly foolish.

There is an amusing coda to our life in Communist Romania. Two days before leaving Hunedoara we had to participate in the national elections. There was no reason to go to the polls. We had already given up our Romanian citizenship, had no papers and obviously didn't care about the outcome. But we were registered, and the Party wanted good voter turnout. Party activists went from house to house to send people to the polls. They refused to accept our explanations.

So we went to the polls and voted. I don't think that the predictable overall victory of 97% or 98% for the Party candidates -- the only candidates -- was changed by our votes. But we were only too happy to oblige, and thus show our gratitude for being allowed to leave.

April 7, 1985

Exodus

Today, April 4th, we celebrate freedom. It was on this day in 1961 that we left Romania. For years we had felt enslaved, with little ability to make our own decisions about how and where to lead our lives. We struggled to get out, we gave it all we had and took all the risks, but in the end the outcome depended not on us, but on overwhelming forces we never understood. When the passports were in our hands, our bags packed, and our tickets bought, we still feared that we could be recalled, that the "pharao would change his mind." When we crossed the border, it was our exodus, as if the Red Sea had parted and closed behind us. We had our freedom now, our chance for a fresh start. We were optimistic, though we had no idea of what lay ahead. We even 'wandered' for years before we came to *our* chosen land -- exactly 3 years later. And we celebrate this date every year as a turning point, and the event with the greatest impact on our family's future.

As we left Timisoara toward the checkpoint of Arad, we were constantly afraid something would happen. We had heard many stories of people being stopped at the frontier and taken off the trains on the pretext that their documents were incomplete. Some were arrested on charges of trying to smuggle forbidden items out of the country. Although the luggage had been painstakingly searched and sealed before boarding the trains, personal belongings and documents were checked at the border, particularly for those suspected of having hidden savings from earlier businesses or from more recent illicit deals. People nevertheless tried to take out objects of value. My friend Klari hid her only diamond in a tube of tooth paste, but the frontier guards discovered it and she was arrested. After being freed she had to wait another two years before eventually being permitted to leave. We also knew of an acquaintance from Timisoara who had hidden foreign currency inside the sole of his shoes. At the last minute he lost his nerve and exchanged shoes with his brother who had come to see him off all the way to the border. He was a former "bourgeois," who had owned a textile factory before the war, and he was carefully searched. The border guard even took apart his shoes, but luckily found nothing. With his shoes ripped, he convinced the guard to let him trade shoes with his brother. He could not have planned it better.

On April 4, toward evening, we boarded the train to the West at Arad, near the Hungarian border. We said good-bye to the few friends who had accompanied us. We were nervous and apprehensive, and the anxiety kept mounting as we approached the frontier. By the time we crossed into

Hungary a few hours later, the tension, the excitement, the anticipation, and the physical and emotional exhaustion overwhelmed us, and we broke into tears of relief and happiness.

Tzali, Zsuzsi and I felt as if a miracle had happened. The years of hardship, of hoping and waiting had come to an end. Silvia, who was old enough to understand what was happening, was crying for the friends, the school and the happy memories she was leaving behind. Yancu and Vali enjoyed the commotion, the trip and the new adventures waiting all of us "over there." Pauli was so angry at being forced to go a "capitalistic country" that he threatened to kill himself. At eleven, he was old enough to have been indoctrinated with Communist ideas, but too young to see through the lies and the propaganda.

We rode through the night across Hungary toward the Austrian border. All of us were crowded into one compartment. The children slept on blankets spread over the luggage. We adults couldn't sleep, we were too agitated. We spent the night talking in whispers about the unknown world that was waiting for us on the other side.

In the morning we arrived in Vienna. No one was waiting for us, and we had no money at all. Someone gave us a token so we could call HIAS, the Jewish relief agency, and they picked us up and took us to a hotel where we were to spend a few days. This organization helped refugees from the East with room and board and documents to travel further. Vienna was only a short transit stop, from where Jews went either to Israel, or to France or Italy to wait for visas to the United States or South America. Though we had Brazilian visas, we were still unsure as to where we should settle, and didn't want to make any decisions before discussing them first with Miki.

As soon as we arrived at the hotel we rushed to the public telephone and made collect calls to Rome, New York and Sao Paulo, to tell our brothers that we were finally "out". The great event of the next day was to wander through the city and find the Central Post Office to pick up the one hundred dollars that Miki had sent *poste restante* in anticipation of our arrival. To refugees like us this seemed like a small fortune. With this money we could savor the beautiful city. During the five days we waited in Vienna, we splurged on luxuries like taking the children to Prater, the famous amusement park, to the Zoo and the Schonbrunn Palace. We admired the imposing buildings, the tree-lined boulevards, the beautiful Opera House, the Danube boardwalks. We marveled at things we had never seen before, the beautiful stores, the window shops with mannequins dressed in shiny evening gowns and pointed high-heeled shoes, the variety of merchandise, the photographic equipment, the fantastic toys, the colorful housewares. Even plastic kitchenware came in bright, cheerful colors. In Romania the only choices were white, beige and gray. We walked everywhere to save on subway fares, and when Vali was tired, we carried him.

The abundance and selection of food was astounding. There were stores with nothing but cheeses, or chocolates, or different types of cold cuts and sausages. There were restaurants and cafes on every street corner. We were tempted by the pastry shops with their artful displays of Viennese confections and tortes. We didn't see anyone waiting in lines. We ate Swiss chocolates, we had soft, swirly ice cream in a fancy underground mall, and drank the famous Coca Cola, known to us as the epitome of decadent Capitalism. We also bought our first bananas, but they were green and didn't taste good. We had to throw them out. We were sorry for the money we had wasted on them.

We counted our money and decided on a special extravagance; we would go to see a movie entitled: *Brazil, the Land of the Future.* We wanted to see the exotic land where we were supposed to go. The film, a documentary, showed Brazil's natural beauties, its beaches and forests, its modern cities -- and also jungles and naked Indians. We saw Brazilians celebrating the carnival in brilliant, showy costumes with wild dances and pulsing music. It was exciting -- almost too exciting. Zsuzsi was so shocked and scared by what she saw that she declared she wouldn't come with us to Brazil, that it was too wild for her.

After five days our papers were ready, we had our tickets and we got on a train for the day-long trip to Rome. There were many other refugees on that train, but they were all headed toward Trieste to board a ship to Israel. They all seemed to be thrilled by the novelty of crossing more borders and by the beauty of the surroundings. I myself was too tense to admire the majestic snow-covered peaks of the Alps, the romantic castles hanging on mountainsides, the long tunnels, or the sunny landscape of Italy. All I could think of was the quickly approaching moment when I would finally see my brother. I was reviewing in my mind all the years when I had been dreaming of this encounter. The young girl he had said good-bye to last time he visited Sighet was now a 40-year old woman with her own family. In between lay a war, the Holocaust, family tragedies, shattered dreams and so many frustrated hopes. My restlessness grew with each passing hour. Miki and his family would be waiting for us at the end of this ride. As we approached the outskirts of Rome I became quiet, I could not contain myself, my eyes filled with tears of anticipation. Tzali held my hand, Silvia embraced me.

April 4, 1984

Part V: Free World

Free World

Dear Miriam,

It was April 11, 1961, when we arrived in Rome as refugees, one week after we had crossed the border out of Romania. Miki was anxiously waiting for us. He had been on edge for a month, ever since we phoned him in early March to tell him that we had gotten the passport. He called at least once a week, asking why we didn't leave immediately. I couldn't explain to him on the phone that all the delays were due to the bureaucracy. I couldn't even tell him that the phone conversations were being listened to, and that everything we talked about was spread all over Hunedoara. So I told him only part of the truth: that we weren't ready, that we were packing and shopping for our trip. He must have thought we were crazy. At one point he cried, "Just come as you are, barefoot or naked, but come right away!"

And now, at last, we had come.

Those first days and weeks in Rome were full of the thrill and excitement of being free, of being reunited with my brother, of getting to know Mantzi and the children, Claudio and Rosanna, and seeing all those places we had been dreaming of for years.

Miki more than fulfilled all my expectations as a dear brother. He was so happy to have us there, he went out of his way to please us, to guess our needs, to buy us necessities. He introduced us to his friends, most of them from Romania, and dentists like him. He showed us Rome and its surroundings. He took us to the Colosseum, the Forum, and other Roman ruins in the heart of the city. We saw Trajan's column, which impressed us the most. We knew from our history books that Trajan was the emperor who conquered Dacia and returned in triumph to Rome leaving behind colonists in what one day would become Romania. The whole story is carved on the column he built to celebrate his victory.

We visited museums, the Vatican, and many of the famous Roman churches. We walked about the modern Rome, its wide avenues, the famous Via Veneto. We stopped at espresso shops and savored Italian pastries. Miki introduced us to Hollywood movies and celebrities; we saw Ben-Hur, the latest epic, and first heard of Elizabeth Taylor and Frank Sinatra. And the Opera? My brother knew how much we longed to see a Roman Opera -- not just listen to records -- but he personally had no interest in it. One day he surprised us with two tickets to Puccini's *Manon Lescaut* with Renata Tebaldi. What an event, for us to be in the Opera House in Rome, and to see and listen to such a famous singer in person!

Another day, as we drove past a huge building on one of the main streets, Miki said, "That's the headquarters of the Italian Communist Party. Do you know that there are two million members of the Party in Italy?" Silvia was startled. "Two million?" she asked, "Do you have enough jails for all those Communists?" That was what she had learned in school -- that Communists were persecuted in the capitalist world. We all carried the baggage of the values we had acquired, willingly or not, over so many years under Communism.

Silvia, who was fourteen, was the only one of our children who had been aware of our problems, our hopes, and our struggle to get out and rejoin the rest of the family. But even with her, we had to be very cautious about trying to counteract the effects of continuous indoctrination in school -- she had been a devout Pioneer, and obviously, her view of the world had been influenced by that. I remember her concern when I received a letter saying that Yossie, now living in New York, was unemployed. "He must be starving," she said, "is there anything we can do for him?" She had followed my correspondence with my brothers and felt a strong connection to them and to her cousins. A couple of years earlier Yossie's 12-year old son had been involved in a severe car accident and had closely escaped death. Silvia cried with me as we read the letter and stared at his picture -- the once beautiful boy now with a bruised and swollen face, his father holding him in his arms and looking happy and miserable at the same time.

For our boys, who were so much younger, the relatives we were so eager to see again weren't quite real yet. Nor did they understand the magnitude of this accomplishment or the extent of the consequences. But they were excited about the travels, about going to Italy, about adventures. And they were curious about their cousins, too.

Miki took us to his office downtown, which was covered with his paintings and cartoons, and the awards he had received from the Dental Society of Rome, where he often exhibited his work. I came to understand the importance of art in my brother's life. He had drawn and painted all his life. He was so compulsive that he couldn't sit on a bus or train without finding some interesting characters around him, and sketching them. His first caricatures in Italy, about Mussolini, had earned him a scholarship to medical school. His painting style recalled the impressionists, his streets of Rome reminded me of Utrillo's Paris, and his landscapes brought to mind Cezanne, with an Italian twist: nuns, catholic priests, ruins, and churches. He never wanted to sell any paintings, for they were his cherished offsprings. But he used to say that he could not be a painter and feed his family three times a day.

He did not like being a dentist; it just seemed a convenient and profitable specialty after completing medical school. He was reticent to charge his patients, and definitely hated pulling teeth (he had made many cartoons on this topic.) The income from his second office, in the working class neighborhood of Garbatella, hardly covered the expenses, but the patients loved him. And he felt at home there.

Miki had no sense of the value of money, it just slipped through his fingers. Mantzi was the practical one. She took care of his business, his appointments, even helped organize his exhibits. She knew all his patients, talked to the technician and followed up with the orders, and did the billing. She planned their vacations and kept track of all the museums they visited throughout Europe. She kept drawers and folders with Miki's records, exhibit announcements, reviews, even scrapbooks. She was so proud of them! Mantzi knew all the painters and cartoonists Miki admired. Her life was her husband's practice, his art, the daily household, shopping and cooking, and the children. Their apartment was modest, but its walls were covered with Miki's portraits, Roman landscapes, and caricatures. Miki never wanted a fancier place. He loved the neighborhood, talked to all the neighbors, and was known by all the merchants on his street.

He was very generous with everything he had, and often helped refugees from Romania who passed through Rome and called on him, even if he did not know them. I later heard many stories about his largesse from Romanian immigrants in Israel and the States, how he treated them in his office, never charged them, offered to show them around Rome, and even took them to his home for dinner. Mantzi never complained when he brought uninvited guests.

The Jewish relief organization (HIAS) in Rome was helping refugees obtain their visas and continue toward their final destinations. They provided rent money, supplied bulk dry foods like powder milk, flour, rounds of cheese, salami, and rice, and helped with other items from their warehouse, like pots and pans that were of such good quality we use them to this day. In our case, however, Miki offered to take over many of the daily living expenses. He and Mantzi had rented an apartment for us, which was very satisfactory -- it was close to his home, had three bedrooms, and Mantzi made sure we had everything. I remember the first night as we checked the pantry and refrigerator and found all that expensive food, canned delicacies and fancily packaged cheeses. I could see with how much care they prepared for our coming. They often had us at their home for dinner, always a big affair. Mantzi took me to fancy department stores and boutiques just to admire them; but for shopping, we went to fabric stores, where I could find beautiful remnants with little money, and she helped me sew a few dresses that looked less old-fashioned than the ones we had brought. We often went to the flee market, where we bought clothes for the children and nice women's shoes, among them Silvia's first with a little heel.

Our beautiful possessions, which we had acquired for the trip at great expense, and brought to Rome with pride, turned out to be hopelessly provincial. Our custom-made trunks, particularly, always invited teasing. They had been custom-made for us to government approved dimensions but of superior wood. Why? Well, who knows what one could do with good trunks. Friends who emigrated to Israel used them as furniture for a long time. We could not take the money with us, nor could we buy objects of value, so why not good trunks? But when we arrived in Rome, Miki and Mantzi were dismayed at the sight of those enormous wooden trunks. They could not believe that we weren't allowed to carry our belongings in suitcases, that the number of pieces of luggage was limited. They were even more surprised at what was inside the trunks: clothes, bedding, ordinary linens, kitchen utensils, rather than our carpets or crystals, jewelry, leather coats, or other things of value. It took a lot of explaining to convey how things were in Romania.

After we emptied the trunks, the big problem was how to dispose of them. We would no longer use them, but no one wanted to carry them away, not even the garbage collectors. The only solution was to break them up into small pieces, then chop those into slivers and throw them in the regular garbage. That's what we did, though with regret.

The expensive outfits I had made for the boys created a similar reaction. A few years earlier I had come down with meningitis, and I was hospitalized in Cluj, far away from home. I lay in bed, feeling miserable and lonely, the shades drawn and my aching head buried under the blankets to avoid the light, fearing that I was going to die there alone, far from my family. I dreamed of the day we would emigrate, and would proudly stroll along the great avenues of Rome with the children. I envisioned the two little boys beautifully dressed in white sailor suits.

So when the time came and I had to order clothes for them -- ready made garments were of very poor quality and almost never available in the sizes one needed -- they had to be sailor suits. But in Italy they were outlandish and funny, and so were the very short shorts that were worn in Romania. The boys were embarrassed. Their cousin Claudio and all the other boys in Rome wore Bermuda shorts. We couldn't do anything about the Romanian shorts, but we cut off the trousers of the sailor suits and turned them into Bermuda shorts. Now our boys looked Italian, too, and they felt more comfortable playing with their cousins. Yancu and Pauli particularly enjoyed checking out the cars parked on the streets; they ran from one to another trying to guess the make of each and reading their maximum speeds. We went together to Roman festivals, to the beaches of Ostia, to the Zoo and to picnics.

There were also anxieties and soul-searching about how to choose realistically among the many options that seemed available. The most pressing question about our future was, where should we go? What would be best for us? What would be best for our children? We had the Brazilian entry visas Ebi and Ezu had arranged, and Ebi kept sending us all the job ads for mechanical engineers from the Sunday edition of the Sao Paulo Times. They weren't exactly what Tzali was looking for, but he did get excited about all those opportunities. And yet we were undecided. Brazil seemed so distant, so far from Europe and civilization. Zsuzsi had already resolved to go to the United States, and asked her brother Bela in New York to submit the necessary papers. We also got letters from our brothers in New York who wanted us to come to America, but Tzali and I knew we didn't have much chance to get visas because of our political background. Aunt Czili wrote from Israel, insisting that we settle there, that Israel was the only country where Jews could reside and feel at home. Miki, on the other hand, offered to bring me into his dental practice and teach me his trade if we chose to stay in Rome. We would have loved to stay in Europe, we enjoyed Italy and cherished the Italian language, and it would have given us so much assurance to have Miki's help. But we also knew that Italy would never grant us citizenship though we could live there forever. Then cousin Hedi came to visit and tried to persuade us to go to Sweden, where many Jews had settled after the war. We also got in touch with our aunts and uncles in the United States and they all wrote us and tried to advise us. The more ideas we got, the more confused we became. It was bewildering.

Our first choice would have been the United States. Not only did most of our close family already live there, but Zsuzsi was going there, and it was the place where both of us could most likely find work and build careers. We also knew more about the States than other places, as mother's sisters and brothers had settled there before the war. Miki had an acquaintance, Judy Heller, who was an important official at the Jewish relief organization. We arranged to meet her to get some advice about our plans and our options. We told her quite directly that we had been Party members in Romania and asked about our chances of getting an American entry visa. Miss Heller was very sympathetic. She told us that she didn't know enough but offered to call her counterpart in Paris, who handled more Romanian refugees and might know better. She was as good as her word, and a few days later she informed us that our chances of succeeding were very slim and in any case, if we applied it would take at least a year to get an answer.

That determined our decision: Brazil it would be. We couldn't wait a year for such an uncertain outcome, with children out of school and without work, when we could go to Brazil and start to rebuild our lives at once. After a few months we decided we had seen enough, had enjoyed all that was worthwhile, and had taken advantage too long of Miki's and Mantzi's hospitality. It was time to leave.

November 10,1985

Israel

Somehow leaving Europe for another continent seemed to have a finality about it, a sense that we would never return. I couldn't go without seeing Israel, without visiting Aunt Czili and her family, and without seeing the few friends from Hunedoara that had settled there. I also had an emotional need to experience for myself what others had told me they felt about Israel. I longed to be there, even if only for a short time.

The trip to Israel was expensive and we had very limited funds. I discussed it with Tzali and we agreed that I would go alone and by boat, the cheapest way. We made inquiries and found that there were various fleets cruising the Mediterranean. We found a Greek steamer sailing from Brindisi to Tel Aviv and back with a one-week layover in Israel for $100. That seemed acceptable. We bought the ticket and I took the day-long train ride to the south of Italy. Miki had told us about Brindisi, how Ezu and Olga went there in 1946, but returned disappointed because the ship they were hoping would take them clandestinely to Palestine had been intercepted by the British authorities.

Brindisi was a quiet provincial town with a breathtaking view of the Mediterranean. The ship, a freighter that carried a few passengers, was small and shabby. I had a berth in the cheapest four-passenger cabin on the lower deck near the boiler room. There was a tiny porthole, almost always covered by waves. The three-day trip included stops at Piraeus and some of the Greek islands.

Most of the passengers, especially on my deck, were plain folks: workers, peasants, students. As passengers boarded, I tried to figure out from their clothes, their features, their luggage and their language, where they came from. I think my own clothes -- a simple skirt, a cotton blouse, and a bulky hand-knit sweater -- probably made it quite easy to recognize my Eastern European origin. My only jewelry was the two wedding bands I wore on my left ring finger, the only valuables we had been allowed to take out of Romania. Since Tzali's ring had become too tight for him, after we crossed the border I put them both on my finger so as not to lose them, and they remained there. In Piraeus, a new passenger joined my cabin, a woman about my age who I assumed was Greek. We tried to start a conversation with a little English, a little Italian, some French; we could both talk a creditable French. We did talk a lot in the next two days but not French: when the steward brought in her suitcases I recognized them as Romanian. We both laughed at the confusion our assumptions had created. She had taken me for Italian.

She was Jewish and on her way to visit her family in Israel, but she

- 249 -

lived in Athens with her Greek husband, whom she had married in Romania. Did I know about the Greek children who were forcibly taken from their parents by the Greek Communists and sent to Communist countries to be educated and indoctrinated, and bring these teachings back home? Did I know! There were a number of them in Hunedoara, but as they grew up they invariably discarded all ideology, and many tried to find their families in Greece. Some were unsuccessful, -- nor were the Romanians too willing to let them go. What fate! Their exile produced the opposite result to the one intended: they hated the host country despite the schooling and other advantages they were given, yet they were stuck there. My cabin mate's husband had been one of the lucky ones who had found his family and was able to return to Greece and bring her along. She often visited her own family in Jerusalem and she appeared happy with this arrangement. She didn't seem to have any identity crisis.

Did I have one at that time? Yes, I think we all did. I remember the dilemma I had in answering simple personal questions like where I came from, or where I was going. "I come from Romania... not really... I boarded this ship in Italy, where I am in transit with my family. I am going now to Israel, but actually we plan to immigrate to Brazil." Was I Romanian? "Yes and no." What was my mother tongue? "Yiddish... Hungarian... Romanian." How come we stayed in Romania after the war? And why did I have American, Brazilian and Italian brothers? Was I a Communist?

Just trying to sort out the answers to these questions brought out all the ambivalence I had about myself then. No longer. I have developed a deep identification with my people, its history and culture, its suffering. My devotion has strengthened since I came to the realization that one can be an intense Jew even without a common language, a common place, religion, affiliation, or tradition. I am a Jew before anything else, and this has, and always will define me and my behavior. It is how I feel and I have no need to explain.

As we left Piraeus and moved beyond the myriad of islands that sprinkle the coast of Greece, the sea and winds became rough and I was soon overcome by sea-sickness. I had never traveled by boat, and I was not prepared for it. Everybody around me was sick too. The lower deck was full of people lying on benches, or holding on to railings and throwing up. Few went to the dining room, and most of those who did left immediately, swaying. I lay miserably on a bench, shivering. Just looking up and seeing the waves or following the bouncing of the railings made me queasy. The captain stopped beside me -- he must have seen me before, and finding me now so wretched, offered help. If I would come to the upper deck he would give me a lounge chair and a lemonade that would relieve my discomfort. I was grateful. He led me upstairs, found me a deck chair, covered me with a blanket and offered me tea. I already felt better. The sea looked calmer from above and the breeze helped me to recover.

The captain was a fine, soft-spoken, older man and his French was pleasing. He invited me up again the next day, brought me some light food, and we chatted. He told me about his travels. Then, as the shore of Israel came into view, he started telling me about his house near Athens -- suggesting that I could live comfortably there; I could practice medicine in Greece. I looked at him, startled:

"How about my children?" They could attend Greek schools or English schools.

I still didn't get it. "How about my husband?"

He was baffled. Did I have a husband? Then why did I wear two rings on my left ring finger? That is a sign of widowhood in Greece. He was terribly embarrassed, poor man. And so was I.

As we approached the port of Tel Aviv everybody ran to the decks. For all of us, people returning home, immigrants, or visitors like myself coming here for the first time, there was a shared sense of something great happening. Young people were singing and waving, others were crying. I too became emotional, and I felt a lump in my throat as I saw the Promised Land. And there, in the middle of the crowd, as the ship pulled close to the pier, I recognized my Aunt Czili, my dear Aunt Czili. How I had missed her!

The close correspondence we had maintained for the 13 years since she had left Romania had not diminished my longing for my aunt. After we filed the first application to emigrate to Israel, her letters to me in Hunedoara became occasions for special get-togethers. I would call all my friends with excitement, "Come and hear what aunt Czili says about Israel," and I would read over and over what she had written about people, customs, and fashion, and her advice on how to prepare, what to bring, how to dress. She wrote about every relative, where they were and how they were coping, about the hardships and rewards in building the new Jewish state. She was so proud of its accomplishments. How she loved that country! And Ignatz added at the end of every letter, "Just come!"

I vividly remember what I saw and felt almost day by day. Aunt Czili pampered me as always, and did everything she could to make my stay fruitful. But I didn't see too much of Ignatz, for he was working long hours, coming home late at night, perspired and exhausted. It was a very hot summer and we all suffered from the heat in her small, shack-like home with only one fan. Her three daughters and one son were all married and had small children. She wanted me to see how everyone lived, and we walked on dirt roads under the scorching sun to reach her daughters' homes. They were all poor, living under very primitive conditions, struggling to make ends meet. She also took me to my other cousins' homes. Faigi, the only relative from Borsa who had survived the war, finally had her own family, was now working as a dental technician, and was about to buy a modest house. Serena lived in a *moshav*, an agricultural farm, tending to orange groves and poultry. She had left behind all her socialist ideals and had become an ardent Zionist instead, fulfilling their dream to go back to the land of Israel, work the soil, and make things grow out of the desert. We also went to visit the two families who had recently arrived from Hunedoara. They were in temporary lodging, using their trunks for furniture, and had been promised some jobs. They were patient and optimistic.

The only cousin who was a little more prosperous was aunt Esther's younger daughter, Piri, who had come much before the war, and who lived in the center of Tel-Aviv in what seemed then a very spacious apartment, with terraces and breezes. I spent two nights there; it was such a relief from Czili's tight and hot quarters. Piri took me around and proudly showed me Israel's only modern city. She also bought me a ticket to go for one day of sightseeing to Jerusalem. I was grateful to her because tourism was not in my plans, and to have missed Jerusalem would have been such a pity. I remember how mesmerized I was at the first sight of the ancient city. Small stone houses, with arched entrances and flat roofs were clustered on the hills, with shiny cupolas, minarets and church towers reaching to the sky. Everything was white, with a golden glow in the rising sun, and only the rows of tall, deep green poplars gave a sense of renewal in this landscape of eternity. From far away it looked magical, just like a picture of biblical times in the holy books. The tour guide enlightened us as to why the terrain there is so full of stones: it is because every Jew who arrives in Jerusalem drops the stone that had pressed on his heart. Somehow I also felt as if a load had lifted from mine.

In Jerusalem we passed the building where Eichmann's trial was being held. This brought back painful memories with so much intensity, things I had not thought about for years. In Romania it was just not common to talk about that past. It was buried, it had to be forgotten, and we had to get on with our lives. It was amazing how little we knew about Eichmann and the infamous "Final solution." The idea of chasing war criminals for so many years, and bringing them to Israel for a trial was very foreign to us.

Otherwise I saw very little of Israel.

I found the country very militarized. All the years in Romania after the war we had been isolated from news from abroad, particularly about

Israel. We knew very little about what had happened in the last 15 years, and that mostly from clandestine western radio stations, like Radio Free Europe. So it took a long time for me to understand how that first generation had fought with their lives, what was at stake, what it meant to them to be citizens of this new Jewish state. The preoccupation with defending that little country was still overwhelming, and every family had someone in the army. I was distressed to think that my own three children were under the age of military service. I kept seeing my two boys, and even Silvia being drafted and in danger, and I thought to myself, "No, I have given enough, no more sacrifices!" But even though our choice to go to Brazil had been made, I felt torn about abandoning Israel, the country I considered a Jewish home. I longed to be among peers, and here everyone was family. In the far-away, strange and exotic land of our future, my brothers would be the only people I knew. Aunt Czili felt disheartened, too, for as much as she would have liked us to come there, she did not dare to insist and take me away from my brothers. She also feared she could not help us, and Israel itself was still struggling economically.

Next time I returned Aunt Czili had moved into a better apartment in the center of Bne Brak, a religious suburb of Tel Aviv. Uncle Ignatz, hard of hearing, was killed in a car accident at 83 -- he had not heard the honking. By now aunt Czili is also gone. Her last years were very sad: she became depressed after a medical tragedy that ended with her losing an arm. She was alone, and when in a nursing home she suffered terribly. With her passing away, a pillar of my family vanished.

Over the years Israel has meant more and more to me. The family grew, as cousins had children and grandchildren. Rolla, Klari and most of our Jewish friends and colleagues from Romania settled there, and as I visited them I came to see how satisfied they were. Their professional diplomas were recognized, and the physicians did not need to take exams or obtain licenses. They had great help with their integration, housing, expenses, and full-time language classes for months. By then the Romanian government also allowed them to bring out furniture, carpets, and other household items and valuables. They almost transferred their previous lifestyle to Israel. They kept their way of life, their language and culture, and continued their social life with the same friends. I often envied them and wished I could be part of that familiar crowd. I also remained with guilt feelings about not having chosen Israel as my home.

I have visited Israel many times since, and with each trip I have gained more appreciation and grown more attached to the beauty of the country and the miracle its citizens had performed. But that first trip remains the most memorable and the most emotional. I will never forget what I felt when I saw the land of Israel for the first time, and the moment when I saw my dear Aunt Czili waiting for me at the harbor in Haifa.

July 1989

Provence

We are getting ready for another vacation. This time we are going to spend a week with Zsuzsi and Pista in Hawaii, where they have lived since their marriage twenty years ago. We like to think of them as "living happily thereafter on an exotic island in paradise." (I had written you before Miriam, that when Miki was a high school student in Timisoara, Pista was his best friend, and the Taussig family accepted him as their own. This same Pista is now Zsuzsi's husband and a relative of ours.)

I remember the first time we visited, and how anxious they were to show us around the island, and to charm us with its tropical beauties. Were they disappointed with our reaction? We found it beautiful and enjoyable, but we could not help repeating, "It is so much like Brazil!" Indeed, the ocean, the secluded beaches, the palm trees, the lush vegetation, the rain forest, were all very familiar to us after our stay in that country.

The real surprise and the lasting impression came during our first encounter with a tropical country, and the trip that took us there in 1961.

The way for a large family to travel to the American continent at that time was by boat. The age of jet air travel was just beginning, and big ocean liners were still crossing the Atlantic. Except for my little freighter trip to Israel, none of us had ever traveled by ship before. For us the voyage from Italy to Brazil was a treat, like taking a luxury cruise today, even though we were traveling tourist class.

Our trip began with a happy coincidence. A year earlier, when we were still struggling to get out of Romania, we had tried to enhance our chances of obtaining exit visas by impressing the Romanian authorities with a letter from an Italian travel agent sent by my brothers. "This is to inform you," it said, "that we have reserved five tickets for your family on the trans-Atlantic carrier *Provence*, leaving from Genoa, Italy, on August 10, 1960, and arriving in Brazil, Port of Rio de Janeiro, on August 20." As it turned out we were still in Romania when the ship sailed, but when the letter arrived we read it and reread it with pleasure, almost as though it was a promise and a portent.

Many months later, in Rome, after we had finally decided on settling in Brazil, imagine our surprise and delight when our tickets arrived for passage on that same vessel, the *Provence,* leaving from the same port, on the same date, exactly one year later.

We left Rome several days early and went up to Genoa to see the city and the boat. Miki and Mantzi came up from Rome to spend our last two days together, and drove us down the Ligurian coast for sightseeing and swimming, stopping at beaches and restaurants along the way. We enjoyed it so much that he drove further and further along the winding roads, on the rocky coast overlooking the sea, all the way to Viareggio, as if postponing the time of good bye. It was indeed a wonderful way to end our stay in Italy. At night we returned to Genoa by train, while they continued towards Rome.

On August 10 we boarded the *Provence*. Tzali and I and the two boys were in one cabin, while Silvia was in a cabin down the hallway with another Romanian family that was going to Argentina and had a daughter her age. Our tiny inside cabin was on the lowest deck and had no portholes, but that didn't bother us. We immediately ran to an upper deck where hundreds of passengers were at the railings, following the maneuvers of the ship as it moved out of its berth, watching as the harbor slipped further and further into the distance, until the lighthouse disappeared and the horizon was all water. We were surprised at how smoothly we were going, and found the sea fascinating.

The following morning we stopped at Marseille, where we had a whole day for sightseeing. We were excited to be on French soil, and to hear French spoken after all those years of studying it in school. And wasn't Marseille the scene of the action in *The Count of Monte Cristo*? Silvia had read the book seventeen times; she was thrilled to visit the island and the prison from which the count escaped.

When we returned to our cabin we found a beautiful bouquet of roses from Zsuzsi, who had stayed behind in Rome. With all the commotion we had completely forgotten that it was our anniversary. Zsuzsi didn't forget. She never does. Nor did our children, who had slipped away during the day to buy for us a beautiful statuette of an African woman. And what a splendid setting for an anniversary!

The Provence turned south, and then west and through the Straits of Gibraltar. We saw the rocks of Africa narrowing the passage as we moved into the Atlantic. We stopped for a few hours in Lisbon, where we finally heard Portuguese being spoken, and it sounded very strange. We had brought a small dictionary with us, but it did not help. Although courses in foreign languages were offered at HIAS in Rome, Portuguese was not among them. We had to plead with the officials to let us disembark with the other passengers -- they had noted our Romanian passports, and were apparently afraid to let Communists in. This was our last stopover on the European continent, and ironically, the country we had tried so hard to leave behind was still haunting us, and made us objects of suspicion.

From Lisbon on it was high sea, and for the next two days, as far as we could see there was nothing but water with its ever-changing shades of blue and green. We stopped briefly at the island of Funchal, and the following day at Tenerife, one of the Canaries. There we splurged on a tour of the island, and saw dormant fishing villages, with small houses overrun by cascading bougainvilleas, and surrounded by the most colorful, exotic flowers. Beyond the villages we passed banana plantations and orange groves, and we were overcome by the intense fragrance of orange blossoms, almost inviting us to stretch out an arm and pick a ripe orange. We passed deserted beaches and dense rain forests, but did not have time to stop. The verdant landscape enchanted us and gave us a glimpse of what Brazil was going to offer. On our return to the harbor, we passed the market place with rainbow displays of fruit, flowers, and vegetables. We found the ship surrounded by natives in their small boats, peddling colorful straw hats and straw bags, crocheted tablecloths and other local handicrafts, or diving into the clear blue ocean to catch the coins thrown by the passengers.

Oh, those happy and carefree days, crossing the ocean and sailing to a new life! To leave the past behind, to depart from Europe seemed almost unreal and to be on an ocean liner enjoying all the amenities, all the luxuries of the Western world was beyond our wildest dream. Everything we saw and did was new, thrilling and unforgettable: the bountiful food, the nightly entertainment, the games and swimming pools. The boys roamed the decks all day long, followed the sailors around in their activities, ate dishes they had never seen, gorged on desserts they had never tasted. We could hardly contain them. Silvia discovered the library, which had books in many languages, and to her great delight found a copy of *The Count of Monte Cristo* in French and read it again, this time in original. She also took part in the Equator crossing festival with other youngsters dressed in native costumes made of crepe paper. We ourselves never expected so much fun and excitement. We appreciated the elegant dining rooms, savored the French and Italian cuisine, lounged by the swimming pools by day, and danced in the evenings. The color slides Tzali made -- his first -- convey our enthusiasm and confidence. We were so happy to set all worries aside, relax and enjoy ourselves just like our children, because we knew we would never have such a thrilling experience again.

But at night, when the bustle had quieted down, our anxieties and apprehensions rose to the surface. We worried about learning the language quickly, about finding work. We asked ourselves a thousand questions. How would the encounter be? How did my brothers look now? Did they still speak our language? What were their wives like and would they accept us as their "new" family? Would the new cousins get along and would our children be happy there? Would Tzali get an engineer's job? Would I be able to work as a physician? How soon would we be able to support ourselves?

We finally entered the southern hemisphere and approached Brazilian waters. Soon we would be there, and after so many years of separation, Ebi and Ezu would be waiting. I remembered my brothers as I had last seen them, Ebi as a freckled, red-haired young boy, stubborn and determined, Ezu a blond, fair-skinned, light-hearted and fun-loving young man. Would I recognize them in the crowd? Ezu and Olga lived in the city of Salvador, on the coast of Brazil, about a thousand miles north of Rio and perhaps 400 miles south of Recife. I didn't know if they would be able to make the long trip to meet us in Rio. Ebi lived much closer, in Belo Horizonte, and I expected he would come.

Our first stop in Brazil was Recife. I don't have to tell you how startled and overjoyed we were to recognize Ezu among the crowd in the port, waving to us. He had taken a bus to Recife and booked a passage to Rio on our liner just to spend the next three days with us. He brought us pineapples from Recife, the first we had ever tasted, and showed us how to cut them open. For the remainder of the trip we enjoyed the sun and the sky, the view of the endless ocean, swimming, eating, dancing -- and talking and talking about the past sixteen years, catching up on what had happened to his family and to ours and planning a bright future for us in Brazil. We discussed with Ezu our decision to settle in Belo Horizonte, a developing industrial center with many opportunities, and where Ebi's business connections appeared most promising. He agreed that Salvador, although a very beautiful city, was mostly a tourist and commercial center, with no industry to attract immigrants seeking professional employment. The weather, too, would probably be too hot and humid the year round for people accustomed to a temperate climate.

It was close to sunset when we approached Rio. In the dimming light, as our ship navigated inside the port past the many tiny islands, we could still see the beaches, the hills covered with lush greenery, the peaks overlooking the harbor. It was just breathtaking. As we marveled and waited for the ship to edge its way into its berth, I heard someone calling my name. I looked around; no, the whole family was on the deck with me. I heard my name again, as if from far away.

Then I looked down at the water and saw a little boat with two people in it frantically waving and calling something. I realized that one of them was my brother, trying to find us in the crowd at the railing. Ebi and Henry, his brother-in-law, were cruising around our huge ship trying to get a glimpse of us even before we landed. We started waving and calling too, and finally we made contact.

The rest of their families were waiting for us on the pier. We had arrived in Brazil to a glorious reception.

July 20, 1984

Belo Horizonte

Starting a new life, in a new world, was exciting and full of expectations. We arrived in Belo Horizonte at the end of August 1961. We had traveled a long day on a dusty and winding road from Rio de Janeiro in two cars, Ebi's and Henry's. Ebi had already secured an apartment for us, which was ready to move into, and very close to his. The apartment belonged to Abe Maged, Ebi's friend and one of my former pupils during the war years. When he heard that my brother was looking for a place for us, he offered this apartment on a main city street. The rent, Ebi said was only 18,000 cruzeiros. 18,000? That seemed like so much money when we didn't have an income yet. But Ebi assured Tzali that he had spoken to a few managers of companies where he sold office supplies and had promises of job offers for Tzali from them. As always Ebi was very businesslike, calm and reassuring. Actually that was one of the reasons why we decided to settle in Belo Horizonte.

But first there was the joyous meeting with Ebi's family. We met Shoshana at the entrance to the apartment house where they lived. Baby Helena was in the arms of a maid, and Bernardo ran out to meet us. When I saw the two cousins, red-haired Bernardo and blond-curled Vali, same age, same build, hugging and kissing, my heart melted. Family! Cousins! Who could have imagined this scene a year ago in Romania? I liked Shoshana immediately, and knew we would get along. In the evening we all had dinner in their small, crowded, three-bedroom apartment. What baffled me was the four Brazilian country girls moving around the kitchen and small dining room as Shoshana gave each one something to do.

"Maria, go and buy bread".

"Norma, take care of the baby, she is ready for her nap".

"Terezinha, clear the table".

"Merced, please bring in the dessert".

And so it went. I was startled.

"Shoshana", I asked, "why do you need four maids?"

"I need only two, one for the housekeeping and one as a nanny for Helena. The other two are for you! I am training them".

I tried to argue, that since I was not working yet I could do my own housekeeping, not to mention that we had no money to afford maids.

"That's all very true, but who will do your laundry, who will wash the floors?"

I compromised. I was to take only one for the first few weeks. And indeed Terezinha came over to our place immediately. I soon realized the

great advantage of having a Portuguese-speaking girl in a household whose
adult family members spoke Hungarian among themselves and Romanian
with the children. In the morning she was already teaching us how to greet
each other, and the names of the food we ate for breakfast.

Our new apartment was a three-bedroom flat with a dining area and
maid's quarters, complete with a separate bathroom and shower, in an
almost-new building in the center of the city on the busy Amazonas avenue.
It was more, much more than we had dreamed of for our first apartment.
Larger than Ebi's, it was so spacious that Silvia could finally have her own
bedroom, the smallest one off the living room. It was sparsely furnished
with cots and mattresses borrowed from Ebi, a carpet, and some dishes. It
had a built-in stove, and later Ezu, who was a partner in an electrical
appliances store in Salvador, sent us a refrigerator.

Belo Horizonte (Beautiful Horizon) was a new, modern, evenly
planned city, patterned after Washington, DC. It was deliberately built on a
plateau in the Brazilian midland, far from the coastal cities, to encourage
expansion and economic growth toward the vast and wild interior of the
country. It was the capital of the state of Minas Gerais, famous for its
numerous mines and its rich and abundant ores, gold, and precious stones.
The streets were parallel, straight and regular, crossing at right angles, with
broad, tree-lined avenues cutting them diagonally and emanating like the
spokes of a wheel from the center of the city and a few other major
intersections. These were the city's main commercial centers, with
triangular, imposing high-rise office buildings. Everywhere one could see
the unusual and creative architecture that Brazil was famous for. One block
away from us was the most important center, *Praca 7*, (September 7 was a
national holiday). Ebi's office was another block away. This was the
downtown, where all our acquaintances lived and where stores, movie
houses, offices, churches -- everything was within walking distance. At the
periphery there were sprawling older private homes.

One week after our arrival, Tzali landed a job through one of Ebi`s
acquaintances at *Magnesita*, a company that fabricated refractory bricks for
the steel industry. He was interviewed by an engineer who had studied in
Germany. They spoke German and the man was very excited about Tzali's
background and qualifications; in fact he was utterly overqualified for this
junior engineer position. But he did not need a license, and he could start
immediately with a salary of 50,000 cruzeiros. Suddenly, our rent did not
seem so much any more. We were thrilled and we began to relax.

We learned the language fast. Portuguese is a Romance language,
pretty close to Romanian, and our knowledge of French and Italian helped a
lot. Every morning, as he took the five kilometer bus ride to work, Tzali

would learn a number of new words from the dictionary and try to put them into use right away. Since some were not in the vernacular, his colleagues would smile and ask "Where did you find this one?" But they were very supportive, helped him with the grammar and pronunciation, and were quite impressed with his ambition and his progress in the language. I was learning too, and soon reading a newspaper, understanding signs, and watching T.V. became easy enough.

For the kids the adjustment seemed effortless. There was a well-organized Jewish community for the few hundred Jewish families in Belo Horizonte. They had a Temple, which ministered to all denominations, a club with swimming pools and other amenities, and their own elementary school on a secluded street. The school was subsidized by the Community and the tuition did not seem too much. We immediately enrolled Vali in kindergarten there and Yancu in fifth grade. They also started Hebrew studies, taught by a teacher couple from Israel. The school celebrated all the Jewish holidays, and it made us feel good that with our new-found family and community our children would get a Jewish education and learn the traditions that we had so neglected in Communist Romania. Before long Vali, who spent most of the day with Bernardo, spoke only Portuguese. Yancu, too, made friends with his schoolmates, and learned quickly. He was doing well in school and enjoyed the sports activities, mainly soccer.

Silvia went to Salvador and spent three months at Ezu's, auditing classes at a Catholic school, which required no entrance examination. She became very close with her cousins, Paulo, about her age, and Rita, a few years younger. When she returned to Belo Horizonte in December she enrolled in a special program geared at preparing students for the rigorous entrance examinations for the public high schools, which were free and were considered the best. By the time school started, in March, she had mastered the Portuguese grammar and complicated phonetic system, and was ready for high school level classes. But she had one disappointment that took years to heal: since we had not been able to bring transcripts with us from Romania, Silvia was assigned to a grade level based strictly on her age, one year behind her grade in Romania. Her consolation was than within a few months she became, and remained, the best student in her school. She also felt very accepted by her peers both at school and at the Jewish club, and spent a lot of her free time with them.

The Jewish colony was rather small in comparison with those in the larger cities in Brazil and most of its members were either old-timers like my brother's family or second-generation. There were no new immigrants and certainly none from our part of the world. Ebi and Shoshana were very active in the Jewish community, and participated in all the events, took us to movies, outings, and parties, and introduced us to their many friends. But Tzali and I felt shy and were unable to warm up to the Brazilians. Sometimes we did not feel like going to Ebi's friends. One day an industrialist, originally from Romania, discovered us and invited us for dinner. We felt utterly out of place in his grandiose mansion, and sensed that he and his friends treated us in a rather condescending manner.

Tzali made a few friends at work who also invited us, but I felt even more lost because at a Brazilian party the men stayed in one room, smoking, drinking, and discussing business, politics, and probably mistresses, while the women, in another room, very elegantly dressed and made up, their hair stylishly done, sipped coffee and discussed the 3 C's: *crianca, criada, cozinha* -- children, maids and kitchen. I learned more than I ever wanted to about these subjects.

On our first New Year's Eve we stayed home and felt lonely, recalling the last celebration with our friends at the fanciest restaurant in Hunedoara, dressed up and dancing to the familiar tunes of a large band. I went to the terrace and looked down on the large avenue with its noisy traffic. Suddenly I heard Hungarian music from the terrace adjoining ours, a familiar *csardas*. I called, "Tzali, come and listen to this." We heard Hungarian being spoken and became excited. We waited until someone came onto the terrace and started talking. They were also thrilled. It turned out they knew Ebi and had heard about his family who had recently arrived, and they invited us to join in their party. We enjoyed it, and made more acquaintances, but again no friends. We realized that language and common background are important but cannot be the only link in a friendship. I only had one good friend, Margot, whom I sought out often. She was a German Jew who had come to Brazil before the war. She was bright, exciting, well read, and loved music. With her I could talk about books, ideas, art, world affairs. Her son, Larry, Yancu's best friend, was a promising pianist, already performing in local concerts.

We finally got to meet Abe Maged who came to visit from Sao Paulo. By then, rents everywhere were constantly increasing, so he also raised ours to 20,000 cruzeiros, but that was still much less than the going rate. With rampant inflation and Tzali's income doubling several times, it was a very convenient amount indeed. He never raised it again, perhaps because he never forgot our relationship in Sighet, when I tutored him in math and calculus. He invited us to his home in Sao Paulo and later on to his summer home in Guaruja. He wanted very much to help us, and he even suggested we move to Sao Paulo.

On Tzali's salary we were able to start buying furniture, carpets, kitchen supplies, lamps, and slowly the house began to look lived in.

Actually the most urgent necessity had been curtains, because the brightness of the tropical sun interfered with our sleep. I even entertained on the children's birthdays and showed off my culinary skills. And before a year went by we had a car too, a brand new VW bug, a far cry from the ancient FIAT we had in Hunedoara. Tzali was elated, he could drive to work instead of taking the bus, and was all too anxious to try out the Brazilian roads and visit the famous towns and historical sites.

We saw a lot of Ebi's family. Shoshana was a strong willed, energetic, exuberant lady. Even before she became Ebi's wife we were related. Our grandmothers were sisters, and her family, the Katinas, lived in a hamlet south of Sighet. I only knew her older sister, Magda, who often visited us when she came to our town to sell the coffee surrogate they made from the chicory grown on their farm. She liked my mother very much, and the two of us were of the same age and enjoyed being together. After being liberated from the camps, Shoshana, Magda and their third sister started out together toward Palestine and spent some time in a Displaced Persons' camp close to Rome. While there they saw Miki often, and later on they met Ezu and Yossie who were on their way to Brazil.

I finally learned how Ebi got out of Budapest in the midst of persecutions and deportations. Rezso Kasztner, the president of the Jewish Community, was able to buy permission from Eichman to take a transport of children out to Switzerland, and Ebi was fortunate to be among them. But when the convoy left there were only about 300 children on that train among the 2000 or so rich people who had paid the ransom money, as well as Kasztner's own large family. The train was intercepted by the Germans and they all ended up in the Bergen Belsen camp. Having Swiss passports, however, they were spared the fate of the other inmates, stayed in separate barracks, and remained under the protection of the International Red Cross. After a few months they were allowed to go on to Switzerland, from where Ebi, still a young boy, was smuggled into Palestine at the end of the war. Kasztner himself came to Israel later, and was promptly accused of having rescued his own family under the pretext of saving children, but a trial acquitted him.

Ebi joined the Kibbutz Givath Brenner, and for some time did construction work. Later on he was drafted and fought in the War of Independence, and he earned several medals during the months he spent on the treacherous Lebanese front. When Aunt Czili emigrated, soon after the Jewish State was founded, she often wrote to me about his hard work, his struggle to get good housing, his loneliness, his frequent visits to her house to have a good meal and meet the cousins. She hoped he would marry one of them.

But his heart was engaged elsewhere. There is a story that Ebi never told me, but I read it in one of the letters he wrote to Miki that impressed me, that showed me one aspect of my brother he would not let me or anyone else know. He writes, "Last Sunday was Rifkas's wedding, the girl I courted for 3 years. That day I worked but my head was not there... In the evening I went to the Synagogue on Herzl street, in my working clothes, so I wouldn't be recognized. What a beautiful wedding it was! I watched Rifka, she looked like a doll in her wedding gown, like an angel. We had split only 3 months ago because I did not have any money and I was sorry for the girl I loved so much to keep her waiting forever. Now she got a very good man for a husband: he had enough money to buy a small house in Chulon, six kilometers from Tel-Aviv. I was sorry to let her go, but that's all right, I will make it through". It broke my heart to read this letter. Ebi, that imperturbable and cool man, had such a warm heart. He was barely twenty-one then, my youngest surviving brother.

Meanwhile his brothers had settled well in Brazil and wanted him to join them. He yearned to be with his family, and continued to struggle and hope while eagerly waiting for the documents. This took a few years, and he came to Brazil in 1953. By then he had met Shoshana, they were in love and had promised to wait for one another. He started working as a peddler, the same way Ezu and Yossie had done before, then landed a salesman's job for office supplies. Shoshana joined him one year later and they celebrated their wedding in Yossie's apartment, in Belo Horizonte. They both worked hard and managed to build a pretty good business. While they were starting their own family, Yossie decided to move to America where he saw a better future. At the same time, Shoshana, who liked Brazil and saw good opportunities for her family, brought Magda from Israel, and her brother Henry, who had been in Montreal since the end of the war.

Throughout all the years he spent in Israel doing construction work, or radio and telecommunication that he learned in the Army, Ebi always dreamed of furthering his education. Going to Brazil only strengthened his resolve. He became very interested in politics and economy and read a great deal, and patiently waited for when he would have the means and the leisure to pursue a college degree.

With us here, a great deal of his time and energy went into helping us settle and resolve our problems, and he felt great pleasure and a sense of accomplishment with our every success and achievement. And indeed, we started to integrate into Brazilian life, learning the language, doing well in school and at work, furnishing the apartment, starting to appreciate movies and television, meeting people. I knew that the next step was for me to explore the possibilities for resuming my career. Yet there was also a growing sense of unease. Though family was the most important aspect of our new life, only Ebi lived near, I saw Ezu rarely, and I longed for my brothers in New York, and for Zsuzsi. We missed cultural activities, music, theater, libraries, and museums. We weren't sure whether we could ever feel at home, overcome the difficulty we had making friends, or adjust to the tropical climate and the reversal of the seasons (it felt so strange to celebrate the New Year's in the middle of the summer.) And most importantly, the future remained nebulous, we could not envision where we wanted to be ten, twenty years hence.

Nonetheless, we never had regrets, never longed for our lives in Romania, and never questioned our decision to emigrate or to come to Brazil.

June 15, 1992

Salvador

You may be surprised, Miriam, as I was, to learn about some of the challenges foreign physicians encountered in trying to get their degrees recognized in Brazil. Not many doctors came into the country, so the Brazilians hadn't set up any system for accrediting them. Since there were no regulations to follow, each one tried his own way. It was apparently very difficult, some said almost impossible, but I knew of a few foreigners who had done it.

We had been living for a few months in Belo Horizonte and were settled by then. Tzali had a good job, we had a nice apartment in the center of the city, the children were in school and I had a housekeeper. It was time to start finding my own way to become a Brazilian physician.

One thing was certain: before I could be accepted by any medical school to obtain accreditation to practice in Brazil, I had to learn some Portuguese and take a Brazilian high school equivalency test. That was one of the few rules. The test was given once a year, in December, in Rio de Janeiro. We had arrived in Brazil in late August, and by the time I found out about the test I hardly had the time to apply. So I packed my bags and went to Rio, to stay with Magda, Shoshana's sister.

At that time Magda was living in a beautiful apartment in the Copacabana district. Her husband was a prosperous jewelry importer. They were very religious and observant. Their two boys attended yeshiva schools, they celebrated all the Jewish holidays and observed all the dietary rules. Magda was intelligent, a superb housewife and cook, and she made all the celebrations the more beautiful, rich in tradition yet with a Brazilian flavor. After Friday night synagogue services, dinner, chanting, and singing, we would go for a stroll along the famous Copacabana beach, only a few short blocks from their home.

The Brazilian bureaucracy was not rigid or ideologically motivated like in Romania, but it was as inefficient. One could usually find a way to get things done, if one had the patience to deal with the exasperating slowness and the casual attitude of the civil servants. The Brazilian coffee breaks almost sabotaged my efforts. When you went to an office for the first time, you could be sure that you wouldn't find the official you had come to see: he was at a meeting or he had just left for his *cafezinho*. If you returned half an hour later, he hadn't returned from his coffee break -- but if you returned an hour later, you were too late -- chances were that he had been back and had already gone for his next *cafezinho*. And if you ever found him, he would postpone his decision till tomorrow -- *amanha*.

One had to personally go to many offices and present hundreds of papers, each one in so many duplicates that I would have been lost without

Magda's help. Her Portuguese was very good and she was a feisty lady, and knew how to get around the never-ending roadblocks. I managed to get the necessary approvals and register for that year's high school equivalency examination with barely a few days to spare. Magda was more nervous than I was.

The test had three parts: the history of Brazil, the geography of Brazil and Portuguese. I was hoping to get through the five centuries of Brazilian history pretty easily. Not much was known before the Portuguese arrived there in 1500. Colonization, expansion, and economic development took off a century later, sustained by immigration, the enslavement of indigenous populations, and the import of African slaves. The greatest events were the declaration of independence in 1822 by the Portuguese regent, who crowned himself emperor, and the bloodless revolution that created the Republic in 1889, one year after the peaceful abolition of slavery. But still, there was a whole history book to read.

And geography? I had to read another whole book on geography. I learned the cities, rivers, falls and cataracts and ignored vast lands which were still unknown. Brazil is a huge country and there were unlimited areas of deep tropical forests where civilized men had not penetrated and various tribes of primitive Indians lived secluded. (While we were living in Brazil, it was discovered that some native tribes of the rain forest still practiced cannibalism. This was such a shock to the modern man that for months, there was no other topic but "the cannibalism of the 20th century" in the press, magazines, radio, television and even in the Brazilian Congress.)

Obviously, the Portuguese would be the hardest part. No matter how much I studied the vocabulary and rules of grammar, I wasn't going to become fluent in such a short time. In fact I failed in Portuguese but my marks in history and geography pulled me through and to my great relief I passed.

I returned to Belo Horizonte to plan my next move. I had to find a medical school willing to accept me for accreditation. I made a list of the schools nearest us. Since the deans wouldn't answer letters, I started to visit them. First I went to the medical school in Belo Horizonte. They were willing to accept me and give me credit for the first two years, but I would have to repeat the last four years of medical school. I gave up on Belo Horizonte.

I went back to Rio and to Niteroi, its twin city just across the bay. Both medical schools required me to take three years of courses before receiving a Brazilian diploma. I gave up on Rio and Niteroi too. But while I was in Rio, I met a Romanian physician who had arrived earlier, had taken the exams and was now licensed. He said that the school in Recife was more lenient and only required that an applicant pass the exams, which he did in one year. That suited me much better.

So I decided to go to Recife. It was a long way from Belo Horizonte, in the north of the country and pretty close to the Equator, and I had to fly, which was expensive. I thought this was a wonderful opportunity to stop in Salvador en route and see Ezu and Olga and meet their children, Rita and Paulo, who had not come to Rio when we arrived

Salvador is one of the most beautiful cities in Brazil, and I was quickly enchanted with it. Although it has maybe a million people, it is not as well known as Rio or Sao Paulo, nor as accessible or modern, but all this makes it more exotic and more attractive to tourists. Salvador is an ancient city in Brazilian terms -- it was founded in 1549 by the Portuguese. It was Brazil's first capital, and it remains the capital of the state of Bahia. The old section of the city has a colonial flavor, with narrow winding streets and colorful old buildings with wrought iron windows and balconies. There are beautiful baroque churches on almost every street, some of them richly decorated with gold and silver, heavy chandeliers and statues brought by the Portuguese colonists. The downtown is bustling with shops and street vendors, and the port overlooks the scenic bay with a large island, Itaparica, in its center.

On the hills there are mansions, luxuriant gardens, modern high-rise apartment buildings and exclusive clubs. There are beaches and beaches -- with white sand or dark sand, with solitary coconut trees or palm forests, with cliffs and rocks, some crowded, others deserted. Bahia was the center of the African slave trade in colonial times, and many of its people came from West Africa. Black Bahian women, beautifully dressed in lacy white blouses and colorful ruffled skirts, cook and sell spicy, juicy African dishes on street corners, parks and beaches. There never seems to be a cloudy day in Salvador.

Ezu is outgoing, good-natured, and exuberant, and everyone is his friend, from the city mayor, his business associates, his employees, to the garage man and the porters. Though he is not part of the high society, he gets invited to their exclusive clubs, and he plays cards, drinks, and parties with them. He enjoys the people around him and he enjoys life. He gets up early in the morning, jokes with the cook and praises the freshly squeezed orange juice, goes to the window and admires the breathtaking view of the Atlantic Ocean: "Isn't that beautiful? Isn't it great to have such a view, to live in such a city, to enjoy the sun and the ocean, to go swimming? I love it!"

One day Ezu and I were walking on the beach alone, admiring the glowing sunset. We sat down on a tree trunk, and talked about old times, about Sighet, and how we would both love to see it again. He wanted to know more about our parents and our last days together. I wanted to know about his year in the camps. He had never wanted to talk about that before, but now he was willing to tell me a little about what he went through.

Ezu spent twelve days in Auschwitz. He arrived there from the Hungarian detention camp of Garany, where Tzali had also spent some time, and saw Mengele during the first selection. From Auschwitz he was sent to Dornhau, another camp in occupied Poland, to work in the coal mines. He told me one story about what happened there. One day he injured his hand and developed an infection that had to be drained surgically (he showed me the scar). He could not work in the mines for a while and was assigned to the kitchen where he had to peel potatoes.

"Potatoes," I wondered, "were there potatoes in the meals?"

Very few, about a sack in a dinner for 1000 people. Anyway, when he carried away the potato peels, he stole whatever he could find in the kitchen on his way out, usually sugar, hid it in his hat and put the hat in some hiding place. One day, during a search of the barrack, the SS found a hat full with lumps of sugar and asked for the thief to step forward. Ezu was not sure it was his hat, on which he had written all the camps where he had been, including Garany. Nevertheless, the other inmates were scared, and they insisted that he turn himself in. In exchange they promised to continue helping him get food, since most probably he would be returned to the mines. He did so, and told some story about getting the sugar by shaking out the garbage sacks whenever he took them out. When the kitchen supervisor denied ever sending the garbage out with him, Ezu had to accept the punishment for the theft, 20 lashes, and an extra 5 for lying. A volunteer was called to administer the flogging, but no one responded. After a second, more threatening call came, a young fellow stepped forward. He whipped Ezu, who was stretched out undressed, and counted the numbers out loud. Ezu still shudders at the recollection of the pain and humiliation he felt, more so because the fellow was from our hometown. When he was sent back to the mines, where the work was extremely heavy and the food rations small, he survived with the help of the inmates working in the kitchen.

I saw how painful it was for him to remember, and I did not ask for more. We rather talked about the liberation and reminded ourselves of our joyous encounter in Budapest in 1945.

Ezu met Olga after the war, in a displaced persons' camp. Olga came from Budapest, and she was never deported. Her family, together with a couple thousand other Jews, had been under the protection of the Swedish Embassy, hidden in the Embassy compound and in neighboring buildings. They married and went to Brazil when their attempt to emigrate to Palestine was thwarted. Her sister, mother and grandmother ended up in California.

In Salvador Olga was a typical Brazilian housewife. Her daily activities revolved around her husband, children, household, beauty parlors, social life. Servants play a big part in a Brazilian housewife's life. Every modern apartment is built with maids in mind, with a maid's room, utilities off the kitchen, a service elevator and a service entrance, just like our apartment building in Belo Horizonte. Every middle-class family has at least one or two servants. Olga had four, counting part-time help. Two lived with the family: a full-time cook who kept busy in the kitchen all day, starting lunch as soon as breakfast was over, and dinner once lunch was finished, and a full-time cleaning woman who also ran errands and did light laundry. Once a week a woman came to iron. And once a week a laundress came by, picked up the heavy laundry and the linens and took them home, returning the following week to bring them back and pick up a fresh load. There is a whole subculture of laundresses: on the outskirts of the city, one can see miles of clotheslines and linens drying in the sun, and hordes of women carrying laundry into town in baskets on their heads or over their arm.

One day Olga and her friends were chatting over afternoon coffee. The subject was, as usual, *crianca, criada e cozinha*. "I don't understand, Olga," one of her friends said, "if your ironing lady comes only once a week, who is ironing Rita's blouses? Doesn't she need a clean one every school day?"

It was strange for me to see all this and to hear such a conversation. It is true, I also had a maid in Romania but everything was so different: I worked full-time and had three children. Keeping a maid probably used up half of my salary, mostly because the food was expensive, but I couldn't have worked otherwise. Paying for household help was the price of being a professional. And if a woman was a housewife, it was unthinkable for her to hire a domestic.

But here, running a household with servants was an important job for the lady of the house. And what a headache to handle such a household. One was always looking for new girls, either a cook or a cleaning woman or a nanny. They were very inexpensive. Most of them were illiterate and unskilled, poor country girls flocking to the city, desperate for any type of work that was available.

It was February and Carnival time when I arrived in Salvador, and Bahia is famous for its brilliant celebration. That is when I began to understand what is important in Brazilian life.

Carnaval -- the last few days before Lent and its fasting begin -- is the most celebrated event of the year, not only in Salvador but all over Brazil. The anticipation and the preparations start months before. People join clubs called "samba schools" in their neighborhoods, even in the slums, to practice singing, dancing and marching for the parade. They make fantastic costumes out of shiny satin, beads, and feathers, and compete for the best costume, the best dancers and the most accomplished clubs. When the three days and nights of *Carnaval* finally arrive, the city fills up with tourists. There is dancing, singing, music, drums and noise-making everywhere -- in the streets, parks, beaches, pool-sides, the fanciest clubs. Every year brings new hit songs that you hear everywhere. There are performances in all the theaters and music halls. Nobody works and nobody sleeps, the whole city is high with excitement and samba music and drink.

Another Brazilian obsession is soccer, and at that time Pele was soccer king, the greatest, known to sports fans the world over. I am not a fan, but all the men in my family are, and in Brazil everybody was. They build the biggest, most impressive stadiums in the world, and soccer teams abound in schools, factories, all kinds of companies, on the streets. When the soccer season is on, the excitement, the ticket buying, the cheering and the bets are all-consuming. And if your city's team wins nationally, or if the national team becomes American or World champions, in the *Copa do Mundo,* the city or the whole country goes mad with joy.

The third great national pastime is beauty contests. The preoccupation with beauty is excessive. For weeks before the Miss Brazil contest, the magazines carry pictures and stories about local contestants, their physical endowments, their height, weight, and measurements of all the "circumferences." There are features about eyes only, or smiles only, and how each girl's compares with the "perfect" one. And everyone is rooting for the local beauties to make it nationally. The Brazilian girls are indeed gorgeous, and Salvador in particular is noted for its splendid girls, some of which have become Miss Brazil, and even placed at the Miss Universe contests.

I was glad I'd stopped for a few days in Salvador on my way to Recife. I was enjoying it immensely. Then Ezu had an idea.

"Before you go to Recife to take exams, why don't we see if you can do the same thing here in Salvador?"

"Nobody told me it could be done here."

"But we have two medical schools. I know someone who is a friend of the dean of the Catholic University. And I have a business associate who knows someone... Let's try."

Why not?

What followed was so typical of Brazil. There are no rules, no absolutes -- you need influence, patience, and persistence. I went with Ezu to his connections, friends of professors, friends of the dean, priests with influence at the schools. I was not refused outright, which gave me some hope. First I heard "Come back tomorrow;" "We'll see next week;" "The faculty meeting will be after the *Carnaval*." Then I began to hear, "It is acceptable, but..." "We need more documents;" "It could be approved, but... "

Meanwhile I was studying and I was ready in some subjects. It was rather interesting to read medical manuals in so many languages. I had a few Romanian books with me and I went to the library to get more specialty books. I had learned a great deal of Portuguese since I had come to Salvador, having to use it all the time to talk with the maids and with Ezu's friends and his children. But they didn't have many Portuguese translations of the standard manuals, so I brought home some in Spanish and a few in French. I was reading in four romance languages, and if I looked up from the page, I didn't know which language I had been reading in because the medical text was so similar, and in my mind all the words had Romanian pronunciation and endings.

It took six weeks of lobbying and pulling strings to convince the faculty committee that if I passed the exams I should be awarded a Brazilian doctor's degree without having to go back to school. They agreed to let me take seventeen exams in the clinical subjects I had studied in my last four years of medical school. I took a test every three days for a few weeks, doing half of the subjects. My professors, who had never examined a foreigner before, were impressed with my medical knowledge and with my mastery of Portuguese. It was still very poor, but Brazilians are always flattered when a foreigner learns their language.

My family back in Belo Horizonte was getting restless with my absence after so many postponements and delays, and I was too. So I went home to Belo Horizonte, studied some more, and then returned to Salvador in June for the rest of the exams. It was an exhausting tour de force, but I passed.

My last examination happened to be on the very day when Salvador welcomed home its returning beauty queen, who had become Miss Brazil. The city was wild with pride. The downtown was jammed with crowds celebrating her triumph. When I started back to Ezu's from the university, my bus got stuck in the middle of the celebration. I watched the parade with the crowned beauty, bouquets and floral offerings, music, dancing and general rejoicing.

I was so happy and relieved to be through with my ordeal that I felt like they were celebrating me. I felt like I was the queen of the day.

December 12, 1984

You may wonder why and how, after all our peregrinations, we ended up in the United States. Though we would have preferred to come here straight from Italy, we had assumed that we had no chance because of our political background, and immigrated instead to Brazil.

In the late summer of 1962 we had been living in Belo Horizonte for more than a year. Tzali continued working for *Magnesita*, where he was well respected and was frequently promoted. His projects were stimulating and his career was on the upswing.

I, on the other hand, was rather unhappy. I had worked hard to get re-accredited, I had spent many weeks in Salvador, away from my family, taking exams at the Catholic University there, and I spent a good deal of money on the trips. But now that I was a Brazilian physician, I didn't know what to do next. In Romania, doctors were assigned to positions. Here I had to look for a job or go into private practice, and the only way to do either was to have connections, and, as I learned, capital.

Ebi, who lived nearby, introduced me to every important person he knew and every physician that his friends suggested. There were many promises -- but nothing materialized. I applied to insurance companies, hoping, that I would be employed to see their patients, to no avail. I tried working as a volunteer, helping a surgeon friend at the municipal hospital every morning. We had coffee with the other surgeons, we scrubbed, and I handed him the instruments like a surgical nurse. But there were no jobs there, and it took me quite a few months to realize why. Only the very poor were treated there, very haphazardly, often after being left at the door of a hospital or a church. Those who could afford anything went to private care. The public hospitals hardly had a paid staff, just a handful of overworked, junior physicians. Most of the work was done by student volunteers, decisions were made by nurses, and some physicians and surgeons donated their time a few mornings a week as a public duty or to operate and better their skills.

Private medicine was a different matter. It thrived, depending on the business skills of each physician. There were beautiful clinics -- small, elegant villas owned by groups of doctors -- but they didn't hire staff physicians. When I inquired about a job, doctors in such clinics suggested with irony that I might want to become a partner, if I could contribute a few thousand dollars and if I had connections and referrals. A physician friend of Ebi's who had a private office on the outskirts of the city offered to let me use it in the afternoons. I don't know whether it was because prospective patients found out that a foreigner -- and a woman to boot -- was there in the afternoon, but for whatever reason, nobody ever came.

In Brazil women held a traditional, dependent role. There were few women professionals. A woman doctor, especially, was not taken seriously unless she was a pediatrician or an obstetrician, expected to treat only women and children. But I had been an internist for years and a Brazilian man would never go to a female internist, even if one could overcome the communication problems until my Portuguese got better. I had no chance whatsoever.

This macho society had its aspects which seemed outright ridiculous. I attended a cardiology course in Sao Paulo, as I became more interested in cardiology after Shoshana's sickness. There were about twenty men and two women at the course. The Institute was located on the outskirts of the city and we had to take the bus. At the end of the day, the other woman and I were waiting at the bus stop to return to the city. Our male colleagues passed us in their cars; not one would stop to offer us a ride. I could not believe this lack of common courtesy, but my colleague, who was Brazilian, explained it simply for me: "Suppose someone sees the guy in the city with another woman in his car?"

I seemed to have exhausted all possibilities and I was frustrated. I realized how naive and inexperienced I was and how alien these matters were to me. Yet I couldn't just stay home and enjoy full-time leisure. And we had money problems, too. Tzali's salary was good, but with the triple-digit inflation that was besetting the country every cost-of-living raise would only help for a couple of months, then we were hard up again and he couldn't expect another raise for four months.

The most unhappy episode during our stay in Brazil was Shoshana's prolonged illness. She had not felt well for some time, was often short of breath and tired and woke up in the middle of the night coughing. One day I took her pulse and it was 120 at rest, but she was already seeing a cardiologist, and they trusted him. I spoke to him several times, and he was very evasive about what the problem was. "Some heart trouble," he kept saying, and placed her on some medication which evidently did not help. I was very worried. As an internist all these signs pointed to progressive heart failure, a disease one can expect to develop gradually in an older person, but is very disturbing in a young woman with no prior history or symptoms. When I saw her wheezing I became alarmed and I insisted on her seeing another specialist. In Romania, in the hospital where I worked such a patient would be admitted, a work-up would be done, followed by a discussion of the case at rounds by various specialists. This practice of one doctor taking charge, acting like God, not accepting his limitations and ignorance, never made sense to me. It still bothers me profoundly.

Shoshana was finally hospitalized for a couple of weeks after an acute episode of pulmonary edema, but she just got progressively worse in the next few months. By now she spent the nights sitting up, propped on pillows, coughing, no longer able to sleep. Finally her sister Magda got panicky, came from Rio and took Shoshana to see a professor there. He gave her a thorough examination, reviewed the tests and gave us the possible diagnosis, a rare "collagen disease" that relentlessly damages the muscles of the heart and eventually causes it to fail.

"Are you sure?" I asked the specialist.

"We cannot be sure... only an autopsy can confirm it." Ebi was there but he did not seem to hear it, or he just did not react to this gloomy prediction?

About a week later I was with Shoshana when she developed a stroke, became unconscious, and by the time Ebi came home she was dying. There was nothing that could be done for her. We just sat there and watched, heartbroken. She was only 33 years old. To have survived the camps and to die in the prime of life, leaving behind a young widower and two small children, was a real tragedy.

After Shoshana's death Ebi seemed to lose control. He did not know what to do next, and how to handle the children and household, where Shoshana had always been in charge. He tried to act "rationally." He decided he could not take care of the children, that Bernardo would be better off in our place with me and Vali, and Helena would be best cared for by Shoshana's best friends Jozsie and Luiska Weiss, a childless middle-aged couple from Israel who adored her and liked nothing better than to satisfy all her fancies. Ebi also felt that his career would be best served if he moved to the central office of the Company in Sao Paulo, where he would get a higher position as sales manager. He handed over the Belo Horizonte business to his brother-in-law, Henry, sealed the apartment and left.

Bernardo came to us with one of his parents' maids, Norma; the other maid went with Helena. He turned out to be a very difficult child; stubborn, resentful and unyielding, he could not be disciplined at all. Although he and Vali were like brothers, he was unfriendly to us and completely rejected any emotional overture by me. He caused me so much anguish just because I tried so hard to compensate for what he had lost. If I wanted to hug him he would run away, when I took the two boys on my knees to watch the popular show *Papai sabe tudo* -- Father Knows Best -- he would escape. Bernardo would not eat what all of us ate, but wanted special dishes which Norma was all too happy to satisfy along with all his whims. At the pool he would jump into the deepest water though he could not swim. Tzali came home one day to find him on our sixth story apartment's window sill, looking at the street below. We got so scared that

Tzali pulled him down and gave him a spanking.

Ebi came to visit often. He was very lonely in Sao Paulo, missed the children, and soon realized that he would have to get married again to make a home for them. He would take Bernardo to a restaurant, buy him any toy he wanted, spoil him and ignore all we tried to do. But Bernardo was happy with his father.

Now, so many years later I can understand much better Bernardo's behavior; a young child loses his mother, his father moves away, his home ceases to be, he is separated from his sister, he lives with a new family that don't even speak his language. He must have felt completely abandoned. Unfortunately we did not have such insight at that time.

I felt increasingly alienated. With Shoshana gone and Ebi in Sao Paulo we no longer had any close relatives in Belo Horizonte. The main reason why we had come here almost two years earlier had ceased to be. Ezu was far away and I hadn't seen him since the funeral. I wondered more and more, when was I going to see my other brothers? And Tzali his siblings in New York? Would we ever make enough money to travel? I knew then that Belo was not the place where I would like to spend the rest of my life. It was too provincial, too far from the important or interesting places in Brazil. Although constantly growing, with already one million people, it lacked cultural activities and intellectual stimulation, and there was so much poverty, ignorance, illiteracy and superstition around.

Socially we fared no better. We had no peers, there was no middle class to speak of. We did not play tennis or cards, did not swim, and could not even dream of joining any of the very expensive clubs. Brazilian society, even the Jewish community in which Ebi had been an active participant, remained aloof to us, most of its members patronizing. After all this time we still felt like outsiders, and did not feel comfortable with the customs and way of life. Finally, the heat and climate also got to me, I needed the sequence and variety offered by seasons. I longed for winter, spring and fall, for something more civilized, less exotic and alien, and professional challenges. I tried to keep myself busy with the household and with the children, with knitting, reading, even painting, but still I was not satisfied.

We had long discussions with Tzali and reviewed all our options. There was always the possibility of going to Israel, where any Jew was always welcome. There would be no waiting for a visa, no obstacles to practicing our professions. We knew from our friends how much support they got from the government as new immigrants "returning to the ancient home." We would certainly feel at home there. If we stayed in Brazil, we would have to move out of Belo Horizonte. Sao Paulo was a larger and more cosmopolitan city, probably with good opportunities for both of us. It had a sizable Jewish community, there were many new-comers, and even the Brazilian society might be more forthcoming. There was culture, music, entertainment and many places to see in the vicinity, including beaches, good schools for the children and choices of universities.

We were searching for a solution.

Then one day I opened the Sao Paulo daily and started to look at the want ads. To my surprise, there was one for a doctor. The only problem was that the job was not in Brazil, but in New York: Harlem Hospital was looking for interns. In Brazil? It seemed strange that the Americans were advertising in a Brazilian newspaper for jobs in New York. Little did I know then of the problems some hospitals faced in getting house staff.

I became intrigued by this new possibility and I wrote a letter to Bela and to my brothers, Alter and Yossie, in New York. They got very excited and immediately started making inquiries on my behalf. Sure, there were jobs in New York and not only at Harlem Hospital. They put me in touch with the Committee for Resettlement of Foreign Physicians in New York, which sent me detailed information about jobs and requirements. They assured me that they would arrange for a contract if I passed the examination required for foreign medical graduates (ECFMG) and got a certificate. Another set of exams!

We considered all the facets of staying or moving again: the family, the children's future, our careers. We knew it was a great sacrifice for Tzali, but he had reached a high career mark both in Romania and in Brazil, why not again in the United States? And his brother and sister were there. I would be sorry to leave my Brazilian brothers behind, but Ebi did not need us now, and Magda was happy to take care of Bernardo; and Ezu had the means to travel and visit us in the future. By the end of the year we had decided to give it a try. I went to the American consulate and registered. I learned that we would no longer be considered political refugees, but that if I had a contract, we might be granted preferential status. This would be faster than simply asking to join brothers. Taking a long-shot chance now made more sense than when we were in Italy, in a completely unsettled situation. We had a home, an income, the children were in school, and even if we didn't succeed, we would still be legal residents of Brazil.

Over the next year, I became a constant visitor to the consulate. I registered for an English course with Silvia. Not working and having a maid was an advantage: I had the time to deal with the never-ending process of gathering documents and filling out forms. I remember very well the first application form. It had about twenty questions. Question 19 asked if we had been members of any political party, to which I answered that we had indeed been members of the Worker's Party, the name the Communist Party took in Romania after merging with the Socialist Party.

I was sure there would be a reaction at the consulate about that statement, but I had many meetings with the consul and it was never mentioned. There was always one document or another missing, like a birth certificate or college transcripts, and the consul just talked to me about how to obtain them.

The examination for foreign physicians -- the ECFMG -- was given in Rio de Janeiro in March 1963. It was a standard exam, given simultaneously worldwide. I knew I was pretty good at taking tests and since I had just reviewed all the material for the Brazilian license, it was still fresh in my mind. My English, however, was not very good. I understood that our coming to the United States depended on my passing the exam and that made me very edgy. At least 70% of the questions had to be answered correctly in order to get even a temporary certificate, valid for one year. A 75% grade was required for a permanent certificate.

Once again I went to Rio de Janeiro and stayed with Magda. I was one of about thirty or forty candidates. There were two parts, medical knowledge and English proficiency. I had no problems with the medical portion; I thought I understood the questions and answered most of them satisfactorily. Then came the English test. A young American with a heavy southern accent read for us a long medical history that we had to summarize. I could hardly understand him. I wrote down all the words I could make out and left empty spaces for the rest. They didn't connect into a coherent whole at all. I looked around at the other candidates and saw in their perplexed looks that they had the same problem. Since the whole classroom was upset, the young man was asked to read the text again. I strained to catch more words and wrote them in the empty spaces. It was like a puzzle, with the words as pieces. Somehow I was able to put them together into a credible history.

We were told that it would take six weeks to get the results. The entire family was anxious. Every day I went downstairs to the mail room of our apartment house. Every day I came back empty-handed. After exactly six weeks, I gave up. Very disappointed, I wrote to Bela and Zsuzsi that I was sorry, but clearly I hadn't made it. I was so accustomed to the lack of consideration within the Romanian bureaucracy that it never occurred to me that I would be notified even if I had failed the test. Sure enough, the day after I wrote to them the results arrived. I had passed the examination with a high enough score to receive a permanent certificate and it would be issued to me through the consulate.

We were moving again -- to the United States!

From then on it was a matter of procedures and legal routines.

There was nothing to do but wait. Meanwhile, I continued studying English and went to the American library almost every day to browse through the beautiful magazines and catalogs. Sears was my favorite, it showed me the products one could get in America. It must be so convenient to just go to the stores and find everything you could think of, ready-made clothes in all the patterns and sizes, the enormous variety of household items, and even the reasonable prices.

I was in constant correspondence with the Committee in New York about a job. Around September I was notified that I had received a contract for an internship with Jewish Memorial Hospital in Manhattan. A couple of months later, the State Department in Washington approved my "first preference status."

It took another two more months to get passports and visas. We needed pictures, medical examinations, X-rays, more documents in connection with our income tax. I worked feverishly, but I was still very apprehensive. All along I had a vague suspicion that the nice, ingenuous American consul had not carefully read or studied my application. Suppose he discovered the answer to Question 19 at the last minute, and we were wasting time, energy and money. I kept writing to the family in New York, telling them of our progress, and plans, but always adding that I was not sure we would succeed.

Tzali had mixed feelings about the move. He had just been made head of the engineering department at *Magnesita* and his salary had taken a significant jump. He was very involved with his projects and quite content with his professional progress. And he liked Brazil. Yet we were preparing to pull up the stakes again and leave.

Everything seemed to be proceeding smoothly. By early March the consul had received visas valid for thirty days, and he told me cheerfully that in a couple of days he would hand them over. My anguish reached new heights. On March 25, I went to the consulate to pick them up. I entered his office, he got up from behind his desk and very ceremoniously came toward me to congratulate me on our successful achievement.

"Now," he said, "since you are from Romania, the only formality left is for you to sign this statement that you have never been a member of the Communist Party."

I looked at him, puzzled. "But I can't sign it. I declared a year ago that we had been members of the Party."

He was shocked, he didn't understand. He couldn't believe it. I started to explain to him the facts of life in Romania: that the Worker's Party was not something subversive, but legal and government-sponsored; that membership was almost a must for professionals, required for advancement;

doctors and engineers had to join, sometimes in school, otherwise they were looked upon with suspicion.

"Yes, yes," he said, "I understand. But what do I do now?"

He was rather embarrassed. He had accepted my explanation, but still he didn't know what to do. He considered how to minimize the damage. Since there was no time to discuss the situation with the State Department in Washington, he decided to call the ambassador in Rio de Janeiro. I was to come back the following day.

At home our anxiety was extreme. We didn't sleep all night. What if all the effort had been in vain?

Tzali and I came back together in the morning. The consul was cheerful. He announced happily that the Ambassador had agreed "that we should grant you the entrance visa to United States."

And that is how we made it here.

July 16, 1986

Dear Miriam,

April 4th marks the beginning of a new chapter in our lives. This is the day when we arrived in this country twenty years ago, three years to the day since we had left Romania in 1961. This day has become our holiday, our Exodus and our Thanksgiving. Though we will not have matzah or turkey, we will go out to a familiar Hungarian restaurant with Yancu, Vali, and Vali's wife and child, Gabriel, our second grandchild who is now one year old. We will celebrate with a festive dinner, we will eat and drink and remember all the good times we've had since we came here. I am only sorry that Silvia, who lives in California, cannot be with us, but like every other year we will call her and congratulate each other.

When our plane landed at Kennedy airport on that cold April morning it seemed almost incredible that we had actually made it there in spite of all the hurdles in our way. The last one had been just two days before we left Brazil, when a military coup attempted to topple the leftist government of Joao Goulart. Though there was no bloodshed, the outcome of the coup was not known, and the country was in a state of panic. The banks were closed, and we couldn't withdraw our money or buy American currency. We had to reach Rio for our night flight to New York, but the trains were jammed, everybody wanted to be somewhere else. It was quite hectic. We finally managed to get to Rio, but before taking us to the airport there was one more thing Magda insisted that I do: "You must come with me to my hairdresser, you have to look pretty when you meet your brothers in New York." And when I look back at the pictures I have to admit that I did, indeed, look pretty.

The pilot announced the local temperature, 32° Fahrenheit, freezing. We had boarded the plane in tropical Brazil. As we disembarked on the runway and walked to the terminal, the boys in their short pants and thin sweaters were shivering, they had long outgrown their winter clothes from Romania. We saw a crowd of people on the top level of the terminal, waving and shouting, and we heard our names being called. Our impatience grew as we made our way through the long lines at customs. When we finally emerged we were greeted with hugs, kisses and tears after almost a lifetime apart.

I won't even write about the joy and happiness of that encounter. All my brothers were there, of course, Yossie with Riva and their three children, and Alter by himself, since his wife Sara and son Howie don't travel on Sabbath. Tzali's brother Bela was there with his wife Irene and their two little girls, and Zsuzsi and Pauli, who had grown into a handsome young man since we had parted in Rome a few years back. So many brothers, so many children, such a large family, and how they had changed since I last saw them!

They all drove us to a furnished apartment in Kew Gardens, Queens, in a charming wooded area with squirrels running around. Zsuzsi and the others had filled the refrigerator so we would lack nothing for the next several days, and had prepared special foods we had not had in years. Yossie had bought us a television set, and as we flipped the dials to explore the American shows we came across a Jewish program. When we head the familiar Tumbalalaika song our pleasant surprise gave way to an immediate sense of comfort and belonging. We had arrived at the end of our wanderings, our final destination.

But what came after the excitement and happiness of the arrival was a very difficult period. The first year was the longest and the most trying. If we had known all the difficulties we would encounter, who knows whether we would have come?

Our admission to this country had been granted on the basis of my contract with Jewish Memorial Hospital, but when I signed it back in Brazil I had no idea that it was one of the worst hospitals in New York. The administration was insensitive, there was almost no teaching, the pay was low, and the house staff was so overworked that no American interns or residents would work there; that's why they had to recruit them abroad. The salary of $300 a month hadn't sounded as bad as it really was.

Two weeks after we arrived I started working -- without any preparation, any acclimatization, any familiarity with the American ways and American hospitals. I spoke such poor English that the first few days I had a constant headache from the effort of trying to understand what I was being told and the tension of being thrown into such a strange new environment and left to sink or swim. At the end of the first day I met a Romanian pharmacist in the hospital; what a relief it was to speak my own language.

We lived in Kew Gardens in a temporary furnished apartment. The hospital was in Upper Manhattan. I had to walk to the bus, ride the bus to the subway, take a fifty-minute subway trip changing trains twice, then walk another twenty minutes. Tzali wasn't working yet so he went apartment hunting. He found a one bedroom apartment in Forest Hills and with the few thousand dollars we had saved in Brazil he furnished it and bought carpets, drapes, kitchen utensils and other necessities. It was a nice neighborhood, close to Zsuzsi and Bela, and not quite so long a trip from the hospital. Yossie was very disappointed: he had just bought a two-family house in Brooklyn and was hoping that we would move in on the second floor. We declined the offer, Brooklyn was too far from everything.

The internship was grueling. I worked long hours and was on call at the hospital every second night and every other weekend from Saturday morning until Monday evening. It added up to 104 hours a week. There were only two interns assigned to one floor and we were paged constantly for new admissions, real emergencies or false alarms. Some nights I got no rest at all. If I had a few free hours while on duty, I washed and ironed shirts so that when I was home I could do other things. But it was not only the workload that overwhelmed the interns, it was the condescending attitude of the senior staff. Some were downright rude; others, even residents, offended us by assuming we needed to be taught the most basic techniques. I had practiced internal medicine for seventeen years, performing more procedures in one year than a resident here had done in all his years of training. The chief of surgery, when I rotated to his service, was particularly abrupt and insulting. I had to swallow everything and just hope to make it through this year.

After a while I learned that other Romanians physicians had a much easier time. To begin with, they never declared their former affiliation with the Party, and were admitted to the United States directly from France or Italy as refugees. Once here, with the help of relatives or relief organizations they were able to find more suitable jobs. Some friends from Bucharest did their internships in suburban hospitals that provided housing nearby, they could take night calls from home, and could eat in the hospital cafeteria with their families; they had a helpful staff and pleasant working conditions, and got much higher salaries than I did.

During my weekend shifts Tzali visited, bringing the children and friends who wanted to see me. On such an occasion I finally met Aunt Fannie and her daughter Sylvia, whom I hadn't seen since they came to Sighet in 1930. I was shocked to find my "glamorous Aunt Fannie from New York" old, short and stooped, with thick glasses, and looking not at all like my mother. Yet she sounded so much like her -- her voice, her intonation, her familiar Yiddish. She was the only one of Mother's siblings that I had stayed in touch with over the years, and through her I reconnected with the other elders of the family, Herman, Aaron and Goldie.

When I came home I was exhausted and overwhelmed by all I had to do and all the problems we had to solve. If I could spare a Sunday afternoon I would try to visit my brothers, at their homes in Brooklyn or at their work places. Yossie owned a tie workshop in an arcade off Times Square, where he worked with two friends and his uncle Aaron, who had actually introduced him to this business. Alter, too, had his own "factory," a dilapidated building in Brooklyn with four knitting machines out of which one or two were always idle, in disrepair or with missing parts. But he considered it a great accomplishment to be his own boss, and very proudly showed off the original patterns that he had designed on some special machines.

When Vali started school, he felt completely lost. He was seven years old and in the second grade, but he didn't speak any English and was put in a class for slow learners. He had a particularly difficult problem with language confusion: he spoke Portuguese but he had forgotten Romanian and now, as we switched back to Romanian at home and Hungarian with relatives he didn't understand anything. In the mornings he would cry that he didn't want to go to school, so Tzali had to take him. Sure enough, he spoke English fluently before anyone else.

We had more problems with Yancu. He was twelve and should have gone into the seventh grade, but because he didn't speak English he was put back a year. In June he was failing his tests and was denied advancement to junior high school.

We were stunned. I asked to talk to the principal. I explained to him -- in my own poor English -- that Yancu had only been in the United States for three months. I showed him his previous records and good grades and argued that he had learned several languages before and would soon be good in English too. The principal was unsympathetic but he agreed to let Yancu take a test at the end of summer and postponed the decision until then. We thought the problem was solved. At great sacrifice, we sent the boys to a camp in the Catskills to be immersed in English the whole summer. They enjoyed being there, it was a totally new experience for both of them and they felt accepted. When they returned to New York they spoke English fluently, but when Yancu took the test the principal failed him again, saying that he was still two years behind the national average and would have to repeat sixth grade.

We could not accept this decision. In our culture, and in the rigid Romanian school system, this was the worst thing that could happen to a child, to fail in school and to have to repeat a year. It was humiliating for both the child and his family and was thought to leave permanent scars. So we didn't give in so easily. We looked for a private school with a more open-minded attitude, and were able to find one in Manhattan. They took Yancu into the seventh grade and gave us a break in tuition, probably hoping that he would continue there when we could afford to pay more. We were very satisfied. Yancu liked the school and worked hard. He graduated first in his class and the following year we transferred him to the eighth grade of the public junior high without any problem.

It is painful to think how many of these problems could have been avoided if only we had received appropriate advice. But because we had not come as refugees, we were on our own and relied entirely on relatives, who had no experience in these matters. We did not even know to seek out the relief agencies whose purpose was precisely to assist new immigrants, and whose expertise could have helped us so much.

Silvia had an easier time. She had studied English in Belo Horizonte and with the credits accumulated in Brazil and even in Romania she was placed into the junior year at Richmond Hill High School. She learned that with some extra effort she could even graduate in December, and was eager to take this chance to make up the year lost with the emigrations. It wasn't easy. English was still very difficult, and would take hours to complete simple reading assignments. Everything in History or Social Studies was new and took extra effort to assimilate. In the summer she had to go to a school all the way in lower Manhattan to take some math classes she still needed. I would often wake up in the middle of the night to see the lights still on in the kitchen, where she was studying. And she also had to help out with cooking and the other household chores, especially after Tzali got a job. Studying did not leave much time for vacation, for entertainment.

Silvia did graduate in December, and in January she entered Queens college. At the suggestion of her high school calculus teacher she had also applied to some better schools, and in the spring she was accepted at the Massachusetts Institute of Technology. She realized that her ambitions as well as her abilities would be more fulfilled there, and she really wanted to go. We argued about the high tuition, but when her loans and scholarships were approved our worries were dispelled. In September 1965 she went to Boston and started again at MIT.

For a long time, Tzali was quite unhappy with our new life. It was hard to find a job, and in the meanwhile he had to carry most of the family burdens. When he finally did find one a few months later, it was as a junior engineer in a Manhattan company, poorly paid and a far cry from the prestigious position he had left in Brazil. He had great difficulty with the language. He felt frustrated, humiliated and dissatisfied with everything. On the nights when I was home, we had so many domestic problems to solve, shopping, cleaning, cooking, laundry, we hardly had time to talk about anything else. He was so discontented and unhappy in the United States that I was overcome with feelings of guilt: he had come here because I wanted it.

One weekend Tzali visited me at the hospital. I found someone to cover for me for a couple of hours and we went across the street to the park outside the Cloisters Museum. We talked about our present situation and the difficulties we all had in adjusting, and I finally agreed that if he was still unhappy with his job, with our income, and with the United States when my internship was over, then I would be willing to return to Brazil. Tzali was hoping I would say that; he had not given up our Brazilian passports.

But it never came to that. Things started to settle. One year later, Tzali had a new job that was a great improvement in position and in salary. He was able to buy a car, and was happy to chauffeur us around. After unsuccessfully trying to get a residency in Internal Medicine, I resigned myself to a new specialty that was more open to "older" foreigners like myself. I started a residency in Rehabilitation Medicine at the Bird S. Coler Memorial Hospital on Roosevelt Island, much closer to home. The work was less strenuous, the patients, with disabilities and chronic conditions, had fewer emergencies, and I was on call only every fifth night, allowing me to spend more time with the family and to take care of the household. My salary was doubled, I was feeling more secure and independent, and started taking driving lessons and preparing for the State Board Examination. Silvia was away at college and considering a major in Physics, Vali was adjusting well, and Yancu was happily settled in junior high school. They all had made friends. We found time now to do things together, we visited the famous Manhattan landmarks, the Statue of Liberty and the Empire States Building, we went to shows at Radio City Music Hall and to free concerts and operas in Central Park. Our life was enriched by our large family here. We were invited to gatherings on holidays, to weddings and Bar Mitzvahs. We found cousins we had long forgotten, and discovered more and more old friends and acquaintances from Sighet.

We felt comfortable, we felt accepted, we liked the American way of life and we realized we were here to stay.

April 4, 1984

Epilogue

Epilogue

We lived in New York for more than 30 years. We raised our children, had many friends, we worked, we traveled a great deal to see family, and we enjoyed the amenities that this great city had to offer. We thrived in exciting fields, Tzali worked as an engineer in air and water pollution control, and I specialized in rehabilitation medicine, practicing and teaching at a prestigious medical school. We resided most of this time in the suburb of New Rochelle, where our large and beautiful house became the heart of many happy family and social events. Weddings, birthdays, New Year's celebrations, the visit of a brother from Italy or Brazil, all became an occasion for a joyous reunion. At every gathering there seemed to be new cousins, spouses and babies. Our backyard, in full bloom in the spring or majestic colors in the fall, would fill with happy laughter, hugs and kisses, wonder and joy. Those were good times.

Gradually our children left for college and careers. Silvia went to school in Berkeley and stayed there, eventually marrying and starting her family. After college Vali married, started his family, and lived for a while on the East Coast, but soon he also settled in the San Francisco Bay Area. Yancu remained in New York to pursue his artistic ambitions. As the years went by many of the older relatives I have written about, uncles, aunts, and cousins, passed away. In the last 10 years I also lost my brothers Alter, Miki and Ezu to illness, and even Yossie's wife, Riva, who was so much younger. My close family shrank and only Yossie and Ebi are alive now. I grieved for those departed and I miss them all, but I am reconciled with the thought that they had a long and fulfilling life with their families, and I am happy to have been part of it, and grateful that for so many years after the Holocaust we were spared sickness and misfortune.

I retired in 1992 and for the next few years Tzali and I came quite often to the West Coast to see our grandchildren. We finally became convinced that our place should be close to them, to be around while they were growing up and maybe help their parents.

We live in California now, where we settled in the town of San Rafael. It has not been that easy to give up a lifelong commitment to medicine, and to change gears while still full of energy and ambition.

Medicine had always been an essential part of my life, fulfilling my desire to be socially productive, and to work in an intellectually stimulating environment. My particular specialty also taught me a lot about the value of life, it brought me close to old age and disability and it prepared me to accept with serenity that one day these will come to us too. But I was soon to learn that there was a lot that could fill my life beyond medicine. My first lesson came from my youngest granddaughter. Upon hearing that I was a doctor, Madeleine, barely 5, wondered "You are a doctor? I thought you are a grandmother!"

Indeed, I am not a doctor any more, and being a grandmother has taken center stage in my life. I give it all my time, my love and my energy, and I am quite happy for the trade-off. I can help my children (I remember how hard it was for us when we had to build careers and raise our kids with no family around to help), and spend time with my grandchildren and be part of their world. I did not want them to miss having grandparents, the way my children did. I love them dearly, I knew I would, but their affection and warmth gratifies me, and it gives me pleasure to hear that I am 'the greatest grandma.' I am still learning what grandparenting is and how to impart experiences, ideas, feelings and values. And I learn so much from them in return. I find this interchange stimulating – after all we are 60-70 years removed from our childhood and a world apart, values have shifted, thinking has changed and knowledge for kids has multiplied. They seem so much smarter today than we were at their age. I do hope that their generation will be able to grow up in a more harmonious world than we did, control their own future, and find the peace that eluded us.

The long ago past is now behind me, the major events that determined our fate happened over half a century ago, a lifetime. I have always wanted to return to my hometown, to try to immerse myself in the old, intimate atmosphere, to search for remnants of my family's life there, and to feel their spirits close to me. With the passing years my longing intensified, and I did go back several times. But I realized, more painfully each time, that the world I was searching for had disappeared together with our people, and the new inhabitants had no connection, or even knowledge of that world. I did not find what I was searching for, the familiar houses and streets brought me no solace, the spirit of my loved ones did not reach me.

I have returned to Auschwitz, too, on the fiftieth anniversary of our arrival there. On this pilgrimage I wanted to fulfill the sacred Jewish tradition of visiting the graves of the departed. Auschwitz is an enormous cemetery for the millions who perished there, yet it has no graves. I looked at the remnants of that inferno. I walked once more through the gate with the infamous inscription, *Arbeit Macht Frei*. I followed the road to Birkenau, and entered the brick barracks where I had spent the first few months. The built-in bunkbeds were as I had remembered them for all those years. I kept a moment of silence and I wept at the platform between tracks where the first selections took place. I reflected by the ruins of the crumbled structure that was once a crematorium. All that was left was tangled wires, chunks of concrete, heaps of rubble, and pieces of collapsed roof. I collected a fistful of pebbles and ashes from the debris – who knows, maybe one speck of the ashes belonged to my mother, my father, my brothers or my relatives. Though I did not feel comforted I had a revelation: I finally understood that what I hold in my memory is the most precious gift of all, it warms my spirit year after year. The past is in my heart, it does not need reminders and I will cherish it to the end of my life.

But the past that I have witnessed is not just mine to keep. Being a survivor is a burden, and for me it carries the responsibility to share it with others, to impart that experience to young people and acquaint them with the dangers of hatred and intolerance. I give talks in schools, temples and churches. I am aware of the impact of an eye-witness account over the reading of an event in a history book, and the response of the kids has been most rewarding. Sensitizing the new generation to discrimination and suffering has become my mission.

We like to live in California. Our small house is surrounded by lovely rolling hills that come to life in deep green shades after the winter rainfalls. I can't help admiring the picturesque Bay Area whenever I cross the Golden Gate Bridge to get to San Francisco, the wild coastline, the twisted cypresses and the scented eucalyptuses. I keep telling myself, I am so lucky, I live near the most beautiful city in the world. I visit it often and find it both accessible and stimulating. The climate is pleasant, and if I crave the familiar snow, Lake Tahoe is not far away. And the people? I feel very comfortable living among people who are so diverse, open and accepting. And to think that I will end my life by the Pacific Ocean, having started it in that small town at the foot of the Carpathians!

We are still around, still together and still healthy. I have already lived through a lifetime of losses, dislocations, accomplishments, and happy events. Many more may happen in the future. It is time to be at peace, to relax and to enjoy a happy old age.

Life has been good to me. I have been fortunate after all.

April 4, 1998

Dora Apsan Sorell was born in a small town in Northern Transylvania. She completed her high school around the time the war started. She spent the war years under Hungarian and Nazi occupation and was deported to Auschwitz in 1944. She lost parents, brothers and numerous relatives in the Holocaust. Upon returning she married and along with her husband she completed her higher education in the new Communist Romania and started to build a family.

Dora and her family were able to leave Romania in the early sixties, and came to New York in 1964 to join brothers and other members of the family. She built a successful career in medicine and recently retired as full professor from a prestigious medical school. In 1995 Dora and her husband moved to California to be closer to their grandchildren, and settled in the town of San Rafael.

Dora is active in organizations and projects that aim at educating the public and particularly children about the consequences of hatred and discrimination. She is a speaker affiliated with the Holocaust Center of Northern California, has interviewed for the Shoah Foundation, and was recently honored for her contributions by the Older Women's League of San Francisco. Dora feels that writing the book and talking to young people has become her mission and her legacy to the future generation.